# Irony
# and Consciousness

# Irony
# and Consciousness

*American Historiography
and Reinhold Niebuhr's Vision*

Richard Reinitz

*Lewisburg*
*Bucknell University Press*
*London and Toronto: Associated University Presses*

Associated University Presses, Inc.
Cranbury, New Jersey 08512

Associated University Presses
Magdalen House
136-148 Tooley Street
London SE1 2TT, England

Associated University Presses
Toronto M5E 1A7, Canada

**Library of Congress Cataloging in Publication Data**

Reinitz, Richard.
    Irony and consciousness.

    Bibliography: p.
    Includes index.
    1. United States--Historiography. 2. Irony.
3. Niebuhr, Reinhold, 1892-1971. I. Title.
E175.R44        973'.07'2        77-92574
ISBN 0-8387-2062-5

PRINTED IN THE UNITED STATES OF AMERICA

I wish to thank the following publishers for having given me permission to quote from published works:

Columbia University Press, for permission to quote from William Haller, *The Rise of Puritanism*, 1928, published by Columbia University Press.

Harcourt Brace Jovanovitch, Inc., for material excerpted from *The Liberal Tradition in America: An Interpretation of American Political Thought Since the Revolution*, copyright © 1955 by Louis Hartz. Reprinted by permission of Harcourt Brace Jovanovitch, Inc.

Harcourt Brace Jovanovitch, Inc., for material excerpted from *The Founding of New Societies: Studies in the History of the United States, Latin America, South Africa, Canada, and Australia*, © 1964 by Louis Hartz. Reprinted by permission of Harcourt Brace Jovanovitch, Inc.

Alfred A. Knopf, Inc., for permission to quote from *The American Political Tradition*. Copyright 1948 by Alfred A. Knopf, Inc. Reprinted by permission of the publisher. (Quoted by permission of Jonathan Cape Ltd. and the Estate of Richard Hoftstadter also, whom I also thank).

Charles Scribner's Sons, for permission to quote from Reinhold Neibuhr, *The Irony of American History*. Quotations from *The Irony of American History* by Reinhold Nieburh are used with the permission of Charles Scribner's Sons. Copyright 1952 Charles Scribner's Sons. (Quoted by permission of James Nisbet & Co. Limited and Mrs. Reinhold Niebuhr for the Estate of Reinhold Niebuhr also, whom I also thank).

The University of Chicago Press, for permission to quote from Daniel J. Boorstin, *The Genius of American Politics*, 1953. (Copyright © 1953 by The University of Chicago. Quoted by permission of Professor Boorstin also, whom I also thank).

For Janet, Rachel, David, and Ruth

# Contents

# Preface

Irony pervades our understanding of the history of recent decades. Any period can be perceived ironically, of course, but the contradictions of the world of the late twentieth century seem particularly to stimulate such perceptions. Paul Fussell observes that "we have become irony hounds because we have been instructed by the events of our time. We are the first generation to experience how wholesome, progressive ideas have a way of ending as motor accidents and traffic jams, stinking rivers and state trials, bureaucracies and soul shivering architecture."[1] The late war in Indochina, racism, official crime in the service of national security, environmental destruction and urban decay, corruption and Watergate, persistent poverty in the midst of plenty, deterioration of the quality of life, energy depletion, and the sense of loss of personal freedom and effectiveness even among relatively affluent Americans — all stand as ironic refutations of our values and our aspirations, all give our material success the taste of ashes.

This book demonstrates how a particular kind of ironic perception of America came to occupy a central position in the writing of American history. The irony used is a secularized version of that developed by Reinhold Niebuhr. A focus on this dramatic ironic form exposes continuities and oppositions in American historical writing that are obscured by the more common historical categories. Chapter 1 locates this type of irony in relation to other ironic forms and other related literary devices, examines the suitability of Niebuhrian irony for historical writing in general, and suggests some of the larger implications of its use as a historical form. The second chapter discusses the function of irony in the writings of some European historians. The third chapter explores the occasional appearance of Niebuhrian irony in some American histories written during the nineteenth and earlier twentieth centuries. Chapter 4 is devoted to a close reading of a selection of Niebuhr's later works,

11

particularly his *Irony of American History*, the book that deliberately applied his ironic concept to the interpretation of the history of
the United States. Finally, I examine the presence of Niebuhrian
irony, or its absence, in several important general "consensus"
histories of America.

The central argument of the book can be simply stated: the
growth in the use of Niebuhrian irony in American historical writing
is an indication of a maturation of American historical consciousness and is representative of the development of a more
critical attitude toward our past. The writing of American history,
like American culture in general, has been afflicted with exaggerated conceptions of American innocence, virtue, wisdom, and
power, and with the pretension to chosenness. The movement of the
use of Niebuhrian irony from the periphery to the center of our
perceptions of our past is an indication of the diminution of such illusions and myths.

By tracing that movement I hope to show how the literary analysis
of historical writing can reveal perspectives on the interpretive
significance of that writing, which is not visible if only traditional
historiographic categories are used. For some time David Levin has
been urging American historians to recall that written history is a
form of literature.[2] His *History as Romantic Art* remains the best
demonstration of how the literary criticism of historical writing can
illuminate the substantive meaning of the writings of American
historians.[3] More recently, Hayden White has argued powerfully for
the view that not only is history a form of literature, but that the
writing of history is an act basically shaped by the poetic tropes
chosen by the historian.[4] In contrast, Peter Gay maintains that style
is a means by which historians arrive at more realistic representa-
tions of the past as it actually was.[5] For White the poetic trope itself
governs our attitude toward what is seen as realistic. For Gay the
real is given, and the art consists of reconstructing it.

It seems clear that, as interest in history as literature grows, this
implicit debate will continue. My assumption about the relationship
between literary form and historical interpretation lies somewhere
between those of White and Gay. I agree with White that any form
can be used to shape any past event, and that the reality of that
which it shapes will be to a considerable degree determined by the
form chosen; but it also seems true to me that certain forms are
more appropriate to particular histories than to others. As White so
clearly demonstrates, poetic tropes and narrative plots have moral
and aesthetic implications. His view that we chose such tropes and
forms purely by aesthetic and moral criteria, which then determine
what counts as realistic, would be true if we started with no

knowledge of the past at all. But that is never the case. The act of writing history is always a struggle against previously existing interpretations, an attempt to impose a new ordering on old and at least partly known materials. We always live with a picture of the past in our heads and our reshaping of it is affected by what we already see. Given that condition, there are limits to what it makes sense to say about specific events in the past, and the subject matter bears some relationship to the suitability of the form. Whereas Gay's assumption that style is the servant of an external reality seems to me to be based upon the false belief that the past exists in the present, appropriate style is in fact limited by the visions we already have even as we try to change that vision. My governing assumption, therefore, is that while it would be inaccurate to say that irony is given by the actualities of the American past, it is a form particularly fitting for the interpretation of that past.

I follow the methods of Levin and Gene Wise. Since I am concerned with the history of the use of a particular form for historical writing, my literary analysis of specific works is less comprehensive than Levin's; in my critiques I focus more on the structure of interpretation than upon style as such. Wise has made an extensive examination of the "explanation forms" that historians of America have used. My study can be seen as an exploration of the development of a particular explanation form, one important set of "experiments with explaining historical experience in America."[6] Because of the subtleties sometimes involved in exposing the presence of Niebuhrian irony, I have tended toward the intensive analysis of a relatively few works rather than the extensive treatment of many. This is particularly true of my treatment of the more recent American historians.

This book is not a comprehensive study of irony in historical writing. Neither is it a general examination of how literary modes such as irony, tragedy, and pathos have been used in the writing of American history.[7] It is rather an analysis of the development of the use of a particular kind of irony in the writing of American history and an exploration of the significance of that development. Although I am convinced that in the last twenty-five years that kind of irony has become central to the interpretation of the American past offered by many historians, I do not attempt to prove that here. I rest my case for the importance of irony in recent historical writing on its presence in key works of Richard Hofstadter and Louis Hartz, scholars who produced major statements of the consensus interpretation that dominated American historical thought in the 1950s and early 60s.

# Acknowledgments

I wish to thank the many friends and colleagues, too numerous to mention, who have commented on earlier versions of parts of this book. Grant Holly, Robert Huff, Michael McGiffert and Stanley Palombo have made particularly important contributions to my understanding of various aspects of irony and American historiography. Marvin Bram, Richard Drinnon and Nancy Struever read various drafts of the book and provided much useful criticism. Gene Wise originally drew my attention to Niebuhrian irony in the writing of American history. I am deeply indebted to his important work on irony, particularly as it is found in Perry Miller's writings, and to his insightful critique of much of my manuscript, especially the chapter on Niebuhr. In addition to reading more than one version of the book, Sacvan Bercovitch, John P. Diggins and Robert Skotheim have at times displayed more faith in it than I could muster myself. I want particularly to thank them for that faith and for the numerous enlightening comments they have made. Janet Braun-Reinitz has repeatedly gone over this work with her skeptical eye, leading me to deflate some of my grander claims and tighten my prose. She has also helped with many of the details of preparing the book for publication, as has Midge Wiggins Kerlan. All of these people, and many others not mentioned, have contributed to whatever virtues this book possess, but none of them is responsible for any of its remaining flaws.

I am grateful to the Faculty Research Committee of Hobart and William Smith Colleges for several grants-in-aid and summer grants which helped me to write this book. At a late stage in its development I had the benefit of participation in a National Endowment for the Humanities Summer Seminar for College Teachers at Princeton University. I am indebted to the National Endowment,

15

the other members of the seminar, and particularly to its director John F. Wilson, for an experience which helped me to clarify my ideas about irony and American history.

Richard Reinitz

# Irony
# and Consciousness

# I.   Irony and History

## 1.   Niebuhrian Irony

We perceive a human action as ironic, in the sense in which I shall use the term, when we see the consequences of that action as contrary to the original intention of the actor and can locate a significant part of the reason for the discrepancy in the actor himself or in his intention. I shall refer to this as Niebuhrian or, somewhat arbitrarily, humane irony. This stipulated definition, which is based upon the usage of Niebuhr and Wise, must be distinguished from other meanings of irony and from related concepts such as paradox, pathos, and tragedy.[1] Paradox can refer to situations in which we behave in self-contradictory ways or perform actions that produce consequences contrary to our intentions. But paradox rises to the level of irony only when it can be shown that the contradictory outcome is at least in part a result of an unconscious weakness in ourselves, when we are seen as bearing some responsibility for the discrepancy. The crucial factor in transforming paradox or incongruity into irony is the causal relationship between the terms of the paradox or incongruity. In Niebuhr's words: "If virtue becomes vice through some hidden defect in the virtue; if strength becomes weakness because of the vanity to which strength may prompt the mighty men or nation; if security is transmuted into insecurity because too much reliance is placed upon it; if wisdom becomes folly because it does not know its own limits — in all such cases the situation is ironic."[2]

This kind of irony has significant ethical implications. Its perception requires a stance from which it is possible to see both the evil and the virtue in the actor. The power of humane irony as a device for focusing moral attention is suggested in Kenneth Burke's comment that it "provides us with a kind of 'technical equivalent for the doctrine of original sin.' Folly and villainy are integral motives,

19

necessary to wisdom or virtue."[3] When a person acts ironically he is responsible for the outcome of his actions not because that outcome is what he intended but because his actions express the vice of his virtue, the pretension and self-deception that frequently accompany innocence, power, or wisdom. The responsibility is unconscious because he does not see how his pretensions affect his action, but it is a real responsibility nonetheless insofar as his unconsciousness is in part a product of his unwillingness to face his own limitations.

It is this responsibility for the consequences of his actions that sets the ironic actor apart from the pathetic one, and it is the unconscious quality of that responsibility that differentiates him from the tragic one. Again to quote Niebuhr: "The ironic situation is distinguished from a pathetic one by the fact that the person involved bears some responsibility for it. It is differentiated from tragedy by the fact that the responsibility is related to an unconscious weakness rather than to a conscious resolution." (This is only one way of conceiving of tragedy, chosen by Niebuhr to complement his definition of irony; tragedy has as many different meanings as irony does.)[4] Pathetic people do not, in a rigorous sense of the term, act at all; they are acted upon by forces beyond their control. Tragic people act heroically; they knowingly accept the evil consequences of their action for the sake of the good they accomplish. In both pathos and tragedy the universe of possibility is more limited than it is in irony; determinism and necessity play larger roles.

A crucial distinction must be made between the attribution of irony to a situation in itself and the argument that it is most appropriate to perceive a situation ironically. Irony inheres in the human condition; so do pathos, tragedy, and comedy. The consequences of the same action can be truthfully described as the result of deliberate and fulfilled choice, fate, or unconscious flaws in the actor, depending upon the angle of vision. To transform an ironic account to a pathetic one, for example, all that is needed is to emphasize the role of external conditions rather than internal flaws in bringing about unintended consequences. The decision to describe an event ironically is a choice to see it in one way rather than another. Bert O. States generalizes the idea of irony as a mode of perception to encompass a possible vision of anything in nature: "Irony is a perspective *on* something, not a presence *in* it. Hence, there is nothing in all nature that cannot be viewed ironically, and in doing so, the ironist will emphasize nature's capacity to produce certain effects. And what the ironist will always emphasize in his eternal role as metaphysical heckler, is an unsuspected relatedness among things, the insufficiency of thinking you can have one thing without getting something not bargained for as well."[5] According to Douglas Muecke's apt comparison, "irony, like beauty, is in the eye of the beholder and is not a quality inherent in any remark, event, or situation."[6] But like beauty, irony is a term more appropriately applied to some situations than to others. It carries with it moral implications different from the perception of an event as unavoidable or as the intended product of human action. Irony is a device for focusing moral attention, for drawing certain relationships between phenomena into the center of our vision.

Niebuhrian irony may be a way of describing almost any human situation, but it is far more suited — almost as a matter of moral taste — to some than to others. It is possible to conceive of nearly any event as the unintended consequences of purposive action and to find the source of the incongruity in the actor, but such an approach would distort much of human life. Perhaps it is more appropriate to describe most people most of the time as the relatively passive victims of circumstances or of the power of other people. But since all individuals contribute in at least some small measure to their own fate, irony can be treated as universal to that degree. To present a slave as responsible for his continued bondage because he makes some accommodations to his situation might obscure more than it would clarify, even if we concede a germ of truth in such an account. Irony is an appropriate way of perceiving people to the extent that it is reasonable to say that they have some significant degree of power over their own lives. Only then are they in a position to be responsible for the consequences of their own actions. Even in dealing with such persons irony must be used discreetly. The effect produced is very different when the result of an action is seen as the intended outcome of evil motives, or the deliberate choice of a lesser evil, from what it is when perceived as the unintended outcome of a benign intention. The choice to use irony is a choice to emphasize both the role of self-deception in human action and the role of purposive action in constantly remaking the social world. It draws our attention to the human, to the dramatic, and to that complex area in life where unconsciousness and moral responsibility overlap.

Irony is an enormously rich term and has a number of forms and connotations. Even by the mid-nineteenth century it had become an extremely complex and rather ambiguous concept. Kierkegaard says of irony "that it has a problematic history, or to be more precise, no history at all." Irony is repeatedly referred to, "but if one searches for a lucid discussion one searches in vain."[7] According to Muecke even in 1969 there still was "no adequate classification of irony" and "no history of irony in European literature, or even the outline of a history."[8] He refers to the "acknowledged conceptual vagueness of the term" and "the conceptual fogginess of irony." Although he presents "something like a definition," he has "no brief and simple definition that will include all kinds of irony while excluding all that is not irony."[9] Wayne Booth begins his recent study with the comment that "there is no agreement among critics about what irony is, and many would hold to the romantic claim, faintly echoed in my final sentences, that its very spirit is violated by the effort to be clear about it."[10] In view of the confusion and uncertainty about the concept in general it is important to distinguish the Niebuhrian irony I wish to use from some of its other forms and connotations.

Rhetorical irony is the oldest and most common of these forms. The term is frequently used to describe the devices by which a writer or speaker communicates the opposite of what he states. This is the primary sense in which White uses the term. For him

> the aim of the Ironic statement is to affirm tacitly the negative of what is on the literal level affirmed positively, or the reverse. . . . Irony . . . represents a stage of consciousness in which the problematic nature of language itself has become recognized. It points to the potential foolishness of all linguistic characterizations of reality as much as to the absurdity of the beliefs it parodies. . . . In Irony, figurative language folds back upon itself and brings its own potentialities for distorting perception under question. . . . The trope of Irony . . . is, in short, a model of the linguistic protocol in which skepticism in thought and relativism in ethics are conventionally expressed.[11]

Although irony of this kind can be used in giving an account of the unintended consequences of purposive action, such an account does not require presentation in ironic language.[12]

Niebuhrian irony is different from the idea conveyed by the cliché "the irony of fate." That idea encompasses the unintended consequences of purposive actions, but it removes all responsibility from the actors and compromises the moral implications of Niebuhrian irony. It assumes that, whatever human beings intend, powers beyond them determine the results of their actions. Niebuhrian irony rests upon the recognition that people are not able to control completely the outcome of their actions, but it does not imply the degree of absence of control that the "irony of fate" suggests.

The "irony of fate" is related to another ironic form from which Niebuhr's concept must be distinguished. If irony is taken to imply extreme distance from or even contempt for the subject, it is not humane irony. This other kind is characterized clearly by

Northrop Frye: "if inferior in power or intelligence to ourselves, so that we have the sense of looking down on a scene of bondage, frustration, or absurdity, the hero belongs to the ironic mode."[13] Kenneth Burke identifies this attitude of superiority with "romantic irony," which he describes as "the kind of irony which did, as a matter of fact, arise as an aesthetic opposition to cultural philistinism, and in which the artist considered himself *outside of* and *superior to* the role he was rejecting."[14] States suggests a view of irony as encompassing a range of attitudes from contempt to empathy: "pure irony shades off on the one hand into irony of ego superiority . . . and on the other into the irony of consolation, the irony . . . which is the last refuge of the powerless against the powerful."[15]

When Frye says that "irony stresses the humanity of its heroes, minimizes the sense of ritual inevitable in tragedy, supplies social and psychological explanations for catastrophe, and makes as much as possible of human misery seem, in Thoreau's phrase, 'superfluous and evitable,' " he has in mind something very different from the irony of superiority.[16] The irony that laughs at people and says "oh, what fools they be" is very different from the irony that laughs and cries with others and says "oh, what fools we are," or, in Burke's words, "there but for the grace of God go I." Burke strongly emphasizes the relationship between humility and irony: "True irony, humble irony, is based upon a sense of fundamental kinship with the enemy, as one *needs* him, is *indebted* to him, is not merely outside him as an observer but contains him *within*, being consubstantial with him."[17] Niebuhr describes clearly the quality of critical sympathy required to perceive his kind of irony: "The knowledge of it depends upon an observer who is not so hostile to the victim of irony as to deny the element of virtue which must constitute a part of the ironic situation; nor yet so sympathetic as to discount the weakness, the vanity and pretension which constitutes another element."[18] One way to contrast this humane kind of irony with the egotistical implications of the term is to distinguish between an ironic attitude, which does imply distance and sometimes even contempt, and an ironic perception, which is based upon the empathetic recognition of our common human limitations.

Irony has been described as a middle-range concept, one that lies between grand general theories of the universe and the interpretation of particulars, an approach that is especially human and neither theistically nor naturalistically deterministic. The Niebuhrian form might be regarded as a middle-level mode of irony. It rises above rhetorical irony, which is generally comic and narrow, but does not aspire to the universality of the irony of fate because it remains rooted in human intentions, actions, and consequences. This humane irony is a middle-range concept also in the way in which it leads us to try to understand specific human actions without pretending to explain all human behavior. It preserves some mystery, an area of uncertainty, while encouraging the effort to increase the area of understanding. It is able to do this because it allows for an incomplete human freedom. As a mode of perception that focuses our attention on human beings as active agents in the drama of intention, action, and consequence, as a distinctively human approach, it is peculiarly appropriate to history, the discipline most sharply concentrated upon human action.[19]

Irony is primarily a humanistic concept, with much comment on it in literary and philosophical writings, but the Niebuhrian irony with which this book is concerned bears a close relationship to an important sociological idea. The title of an article of Robert Merton in itself suggests that relationship: "The Unanticipated Consequences of Purposive Social Action." The moral focus provided by Merton's concept is not unlike Niebuhr's. "In considering *purposive* action, we are concerned with 'conduct' as distinct from 'behavior,' that is, with action which involves motives and consequently a choice between various alternatives." Merton's account of what may lead to a disjunction between the anticipation or intention of the actor and the consequences of his action is stated in terms similar to Niebuhr's. The excess of pride in innocence, virtue, power, or wisdom that Niebuhr finds to be the source of irony is not very different from the imbalance of values that Merton describes as a reason for unanticipated consequences.[20]

One final general question about irony to be considered is the argument that it is an attitude of detachment with conservative, or at least antiradical, implications. Irony and radicalism were clear-cut opposites for Thomas Mann: "Irony and radicalism — this is an alternative and an Either-Or. An intelligent man has the choice (*if* he has it) to be either ironical or radical."[21] Nietzsche makes a similar point in regard to the irony-inducing tendencies of the study of history, irony being classed with cynicism. Because of "an excess of history . . . an age reaches a dangerous condition of irony with regard to itself, and the still more dangerous condition of cynicism." These conditions undermine hope and energy. "Close to the modern man's pride there stands his irony about himself, his consciousness that he must live in an historical, or twilight, atmosphere, the fear that he can retain none of his youthful hopes and powers." Life in such an atmosphere may lead one to "the full surrender of his per-

sonality to the world-process," for Nietzsche the debasing acceptance of the status quo resulting from Hegelian historical consciousness. He does value critical history, but for him irony is not a
tool of criticism. Rather, it is the result of the view that the men of
his time stood at the pinnacle of evolution, at the end of a long
historical process, a view that for Nietzsche destroyed the possibility
of creative action to make the future.[22] White also argues that irony
leads to passivity and defeatism: "irony tends to dissolve all belief in
the possibility of positive political actions. In its apprehension of the
essential folly or absurdity of the human condition, it tends to
engender a Mandarin-like disdain for those seeking to grasp the
nature of social reality in either science or art."[23]

But some other commentators on irony suggest that the concept
can have a radical function. States distinguishes the broad thrust of
irony from its narrower meaning, arguing that in the most general
sense irony keeps open the possibility of change:

> By irony, in its widest context, I do not refer to that negativity of
> attitude we associate with common irony, but rather to the very
> principle of negation itself. . . . Kant says that the great value of
> the negative proposition is that it prevents error. Irony is the
> dramatist's version of the negative proposition: it helps him to
> avoid error, and by this I mean that it widens his vision, allows
> him to see more circumspectly the possibilities of his 'argument':
> and in so doing it ensures his not falling into the incomplete at-
> titudes of naiveté, sentimentality, self-righteousness, or unearned
> faith.[24]

Muecke acknowledges "that for some men the habit of irony may be
a corrosive and paralysing disease of the spirit or that an ironical attitude *might* result in perpetual ennui or nihilism." But he sees the
predominant effects of irony as healthy and necessary. It offers a
mode of criticism that destroys pretensions and radically exposes
that which many would keep hidden. "The business of irony is to see
clearly and ask questions. Its victims are the blind; its enemies those
who do not wish to be pressed for answers. . . . It is not the ironist . .
. but the man who does not wish to see or enquire, who incites men
to war or establishes a totalitarian state. . . . Those who close their
eyes to the ambivalence of the human condition — the proponents
and adherents of systems, the sentimental idealists, the hard-headed
realists, the panacea-mongering technologists — will naturally find
an enemy in the ironist and accuse him of flippancy, nihilism, or sit-
ting on the fence." Though an ironist may adopt such attitudes,

they do not express his essential function. "His business is to make life unbearable for troglodytes, to keep open house for ideas, and to go on asking questions."[25]

One basic argument of this book is that Niebuhrian irony as a historical approach has the kind of critical function described by Muecke, that it can help to liberate us from the past. It is perhaps incompatible with programmatic radicalism but it is a radical tool insofar as it can expose the illusions that perpetuate the contradictions of American life. The historian as radical ought not to be committed to the construction of a new order; that is a narrowly political job. His function is to reveal the inadequacies of the old order. Irony may preclude the more simplistic of radical postures, the narrow moralism that would deny the humanity of a political opponent, but as a mode of criticism it has great radical potential, and it is not incompatible with a tentative, but real, commitment to social change.

## 2.  Irony and History

Paradox, pathos, tragedy, and various kinds of irony are all used by historians, sometimes deliberately and sometimes unconsciously, as are other forms. Many accounts of the American past fall into none of these categories but rather could best be described as success stories, or romances, with the American nation, or some part of it, as the hero. Such a vision assumes no discrepancy between intention and outcome. Virtue is rewarded, and people control their own fate. Another equally simplistic form is the Manichaean story of angels and devils. History consists of conflict between good men and bad. Such accounts sometimes have tragic or pathetic conclusions but, generally, when this approach to America is used, either the good triumphs or, if it does not, it at least remains pure; the essential core of virtue in ordinary American people may be frustrated by evil forces—usually subversive radicals or undemocratic plutocrats—but it remains intact, permitting the nation to continue to regard itself as peculiarly blessed in the long run, whatever its short-term difficulties.

There are other, less pejorative terms that can be applied to the literary form of historical writing. The overall structure of some works of history can be usefully compared to a Bildungsroman, an account of the development of a person.[26] This kind of category deals with the shape of the work as a whole and may cut across the forms of irony, tragedy, and pathos. A historical narrative may have the structure of a Bildungsroman and also fit the pattern of

Niebuhrian irony. In general almost any literary term can be applied to historical writing, although some types of modern writing—for example, stream of consciousness or the techniques of the "new" French novel—have not as yet found much application to history. Terms referring to the style of language, symbolism, imagery, metaphor, emplotment, mode of argument, the structure of narrative, the position of the narrator, and the form of exposition (among other factors) can all be applied to works of history, and, of course, more than one can be applied to the same work.[27]

Whether consciously or not, the historian does in fact choose the form in which he writes and that choice affects the interpretation of the past that he conveys. Part of the measure of a good historian is his sensitivity in choosing the most revealing and appropriate mode, or modes, for his subject and for the needs of his own time. Irony, in my opinion, is a literary form particularly suited to historical writing. It focuses attention on the specifically historical aspects of human experience. It is a form for asking questions that does not dictate the answers to those questions—as some forms do—but does indicate the direction in which answers are to be sought. It draws to the center of our perceptions aspects of phenomena that have been traditionally recognized as central to historical understanding. Because of its emphasis on limited human freedom, irony is not appropriate to all of the past, but it can profitably be applied to much of it. It is distinctively suited to a number of aspects of the history of activist America, a nation many of whose current problems can best be understood as the unintended results of past actions. The next few pages will explore some of the ways in which Niebuhrian irony is a particularly appropriate form for historical writing.

In recent years some philosophers have restated the old view that history is in itself a form of knowledge distinct from other forms. The kind of understanding it offers is based neither upon the application of theoretical general laws, as in science, nor on a process of categorization, as in philosophy, but rather on the comprehension of things, in Louis Mink's words, "as elements in a single and concrete complex of relationships."[28] Niebuhrian irony is highly compatible with that conception of historical knowledge because its own form is narrative in structure like that of the writing of history itself. It assumes that the relationships among intention, circumstance, action, and result are complex, particularized, comprehensible, and meaningful.

Historians have long been concerned with the problem of freedom and determinism in history. Irony helps to sharpen the focus on this question in regard to any particular situation. By its own assumptions it excludes simplistic, one-dimensional answers; ironically conceived, people are free to act, but not so powerful as to be able to control consistently the consequences of their actions. Niebuhrian irony is not a causal theory like many other general interpretations, but it is compatible with a variety of causal concepts as long as they are not rigidly deterministic. It can be appropriately applied to a human action only to the extent that we can perceive that action as the product of human intention and its result as inconsistent with that intention. In effect it rules out the extremes; when we see human behavior as a function of forces entirely beyond human control, or grant to humans the power regularly to anticipate the consequences of their actions, we cannot make use of irony. This belief that history should focus on people as active if limited agents, a focus sharpened by ironic perceptions, is quite widely held in the profession. Lee Benson, a leading "behavioral historian" who might be assumed to think otherwise, shares it. He cautions against the formulation of historical interpretations in terms that "assume that 'impersonal forces' determine human behavior—a metaphysical assumption that retards histographic progress by obscuring the fact that history is made by men."[29] Humane irony is a form for historical perception that directs us to examine people in all their self-contradictions and the situation in which they act in all of its complexity.

This formulation suggests how irony also leads us to bridge a gap between kinds of history. It requires us to relate intellectual history—the study of values, intentions, and human images of "reality"—to social, political, and economic history—the study of what men do, the conditions under which they do it, and the consequences of their actions.[30] Similarly, because the basic unit of historical investigation from an ironic point of view is the process of intention, action, and unanticipated result, that approach reminds us that history deals with the tension between change and continuity. Human action as a force for change in history is frequently frustrated by the inertia of continuity; the circumstances that defeat human intention are often rooted in an unexamined past that the historical actor avoids facing.[31]

Most important is the attitude toward history that Niebuhrian irony both requires and fosters. The discreet sympathy engendered by this kind of irony, involving at once an acceptance of the humanity of the historical actor and a critical stance toward the consequences of his actions allows for both the empathetic encounter with people of the past that makes historical knowledge possible and the analytic distance from them that makes it useful.

This ironic empathy is really a range of attitudes rather than a single attitude. The balance between sympathy and critical distance and the quality of the historian's feelings toward people of the past can vary considerably within limits. In specific works examined in this book historians present such diverse groups as Jesuit missionaries, young Nazis, American revolutionaries, Jacksonian democrats, entrepreneurs, and presidents of the United States as ironic actors. Although all of these historians' attitudes can be described as ones of critical sympathy, they do not treat these diverse groups, groups with very different degrees of freedom and power and very different relationships to any ethical standard, in the same way.

The distant empathy induced by an ironic perspective is closely related to its power to focus moral attention in ways appropriate to history. From that perspective "the evil in human history is regarded as the consequence of man's wrong use of his unique capacities. The wrong use is always due to some failure to recognize the limits of his capacities of power, wisdom and virtue."[32] The historian is aimed away from simplistic, Manichaean views of history while at the same time moral consciousness is encouraged. Humane irony infuses historical writing with an ethical sensibility without reducing it to partisanship. It requires us — and here may be a disadvantage as well as an advantage — to look upon all people of the past as containing within themselves both good and evil, and focuses our attention upon the ways in which the good and the evil in any particular individual are related to each other. At the same time it does not force us into the moral relativism that this formulation seems to imply. From the perception that all people contain good and evil it does not necessarily follow that they all contain equal amounts of both. Most important, irony leads us to focus on unconscious human responsibility, on the mixture of good and evil, innocence, virtue, power, wisdom, and the false pretension to these qualities in people, and makes historians serve not as judges of the past, but as clarifiers of moral issues arising out of the past.

The purpose that White finds in the great historical thinkers of the early nineteenth century remains relevant for historians today; they "interpreted the burden of the historian as the moral charge to free men from the burden of history."[33] Ironic history may help to free us from that burden by dissolving the illusions that lead us to act so as to contradict our values and our intentions. It focuses our attention on the nexus between past and present, on the ways in which illusions arising out of experience uncritically absorbed prevent us from perceiving present problems realistically. Niebuhr describes the implications of ironic history for a country that continues to suffer under exaggerated ideas of its own virtues and power: "An ironic situation must dissolve, if men or nations are made aware of their complicity in it. Such awareness involves some realization of the hidden vanity or pretension by which comedy is turned into irony. This realization either must lead to an abatement of the pretension, which means contrition; or it leads to a desperate accentuation of the vanities to the point where irony turns into pure evil." The muted optimism implied here may seem inconsistent with Niebuhr's neoorthodox pessimism about society, but he clearly did hold out some hope for the therapeutic power of ironic consciousness.[34] In any event, his concept clearly implies that ironic history offers historians the opportunity to contribute to the elimination of social evils in the present not as an effort pursued in opposition to the duty honestly to elucidate the past, but as the fulfillment of that duty. Opening up the past can be the same thing as freeing the present from the illusions that false conceptions of that past generate, illusions that sustain evil in the present.

To be sure, as Niebuhr points out, this is risky business. There is no guarantee that an ironic exposure of the illusions that underlie social problems will lead to contrition rather than deliberate evil, but to turn away from such an exposure because of that danger is to be false to the historian's obligation to explore the past truthfully as well as to his responsibility to his own time.[35] The development of the use of Niebuhrian irony by some American historians can be taken as an indication, I believe, of the maturation of American historical consciousness, the growth of the recognition of complexity and the abandonment of myths of innocence, uniqueness, and limitless power. Such myths persist, of course, in much of the contemporary writing of American history, but the increased use of irony since the Second World War has been coupled with a more sophisticated critical attitude on the part of historians.

Throughout this discussion of how irony can help historians meet their obligations I have assumed that America can best be understood in terms of pretensions and illusions, high expectations and unintended consequences, not as the embodiment of pure evil nor as a uniquely virtuous nation, "the last best hope of man." Many Americans have had unusual power over their lives individually and collectively, and even greater illusions of such power, and they have frequently used that power in ways that have produced results they did not intend, in part because of those illusions. Pretensions to virtue and innocence also have been widespread in America and sometimes have blinded Americans to the evil consequences of their actions. I would argue that irony offers a peculiarly appropriate way of distinguishing the history of the United States from that of other nations, not in any absolutely unique terms, but through the intensification of common human tendencies. This argument will be developed later,[36] but here I would like to suggest some of the specific ways in which an ironic perception of the American past serves historians in their efforts to meet their responsibilities to the American present.

Many of our recent and contemporary problems can best be understood as the unintended consequences of purposive action. Much of the turmoil of the 1960s had that character; in Vietnam in particular, we acted so as to produce results that contradicted our presumed values and stated goals. The radicals of the sixties concluded that the war and other problems were the products of evil men or of an evil and immobile system. The bitterness of our disappointment with the persistence of war and racism, pollution, poverty, corruption, environmental destruction, and political powerlessness divided us and filled us with the kind of negative passion that destroys understanding. In the 1970s passion has diminished in America, and we appear, perhaps, for the moment to have accepted the reality of the limits of our power, but the peace that we seem to have found is based upon a heightening of our illusions of innocence and virtue. There is no American war now, but most of our problems persist and grow worse even as our consciousness of them diminishes. Historical irony continues to be useful as a means of reminding ourselves that we have not overcome the problems that fade from our awareness, that we are not so innocent and virtuous as our leaders tell us we are.

The American people have recently been invited to renounce our responsibility for our own history, while we have been asked to believe that whatever evils exist are the products of government, and that the government is not so moral as the people. To be sure, much of the evil in our society is owing to the intentional and unintentional actions of American leaders, and it is important that specific responsibility be apportioned, but the historically more interesting, and therapeutically more important, question is why such a large part of the American public accepted actions that contradicted the stated — and at least in part real — values of the nation. Here, I think, we must recognize the role of illusions of national innoncence and virtue (as well as deliberate misinformation and propaganda) in preventing most Americans from recognizing the contradictions between those values and the effects of our actions. Pretensions to absolute power among those who possessed power in America led them to act without an appropriate sense of limits; illusions of national innocence led most other Americans to ignore the evil consequences of such actions. Historical irony moves these issues to the center of our vision. Although history alone cannot stop us from continuing to act ironically, such action cannot be stopped without an awareness that the problems persist and a historical consciousness that we continue to suffer from illusions about ourselves.

An ironic historical consciousness can help to free us from these illusions and patterns of contradictory behavior, from the burden of the past, on two levels. A general recognition of the ironic process in history — and its intensification in America — should make us more resistant to a repetition of that process, less susceptible to reality-distorting pretensions. The exposure of certain specific illusions that arise out of our past, and our perception in concrete ways of how they have led us to act so as to contradict our values, should free us from the particular ironies those illusions induce. To produce such transformations of consciousness history must not only be written ironically; it must be convincing. We must be able to enter empathetically into the mind of the ironic actor of the past, appreciate his intention and his responsibility for the unintended consequences of his action. We must feel enough identity with him to suffer his irony vicariously, but we must also have enough distance from him, and the account of the reasons for the discontinuity must be plausible enough, for us to accept his guilt and share in the contrition to which consciousness of irony leads. Then we may be purged of the illusions we share with the historical actor and freed to act differently in the future.[37]

The political implications of ironic history are, of course, in the abstract ambiguous. It might be seen by some scholars concerned with the history of the oppressed as a class interpretation because it focuses on people whose destinies have, in some considerable measure, been affected by their own actions. To the degree that it is illuminating to view particular groups or individuals as responsible for their own fate, irony is fitting; to the degree that it is appropriate to see them as victims, it is not. For many people who have been oppressed both views can be helpful, and irony should be a part of a full picture of their history if we are to afford them the respect of treating them as historical actors at all.

One implication of the ironic approach is clearly conservative. That approach projects an image of human beings as inwardly divided, not fully self-aware, and limited in their ability to predict the outcome of their actions. It can in this sense discourage people from acting. But irony can be radical in one context and conservative in another. In a society in which problems are clearly understood and lines clearly drawn, in a genuinely prerevolutionary situation, it would have the effect of indicating the need for caution, of reminding potential revolutionaries of their human limitations and so militating against revolution. This description certainly does not fit America today. On the other hand, in a society that still suffers from the illusions that engender ironic action, an ironic history can have a radicalizing effect, and that, I believe, is where we are.

Perhaps in the 1970s we have come to some recognition that our power is circumscribed, but that realization has been expressed in a rhetoric that reinforces our sense of our innocence even as it deflates our pretensions to control the world. One sense in which the American past is connected to the American present is in the way in which we continue to act without any clear sense of the limits of our virtue. As long as that remains true, ironic history is radical because it serves to puncture our illusions. By revealing the irony in our behavior in the past we can hope to deter the continuation of that behavior in the present. It is radical in that it provides us with a vision that can help us "to escape the seduction of a world which is nothing but the creation of our longings."[38] In our national past we have been able, as no people before, to live in such an illusory world, but if we are to survive now, we must develop an ironic solvent for our pretensions. Here, and not where a number of us were a few years ago — in government or in the streets, is the highest duty of the engaged historian. We must learn how to act without exaggerated convictions of our power and innocence, to pursue relative virtue, knowing that our actions might produce evil yet without being deterred from acting by that knowledge, but not allowing our commitment to action to blind us to the possibly evil consequences of those actions.

One problem with the recognition of the radical potential of ironic history is the identification of that concept with Niebuhr, who was widely regarded as one of the "cold war liberals." Although some question can perhaps be raised about the applicability of that label to Niebuhr throughout his long career, it is certainly correct to identify historical irony with him. I have found many other works on irony useful but it is Niebuhr's concept, as refined by Gene Wise, upon which I rely. It seems to me nearly perfectly suited to the current needs of American historical writing. Niebuhr arrived at an ironic vision of history out of his peculiar combination of an orthodox Christian sense of original sin with a modern desire for liberal reform. This combination was given a historical cast by his conception of man as defining himself dramatically through time. The religious roots of Niebuhr's irony and the pressures of the

period in which he applied it to American history have much to do
with its apparently antiradical implications.

The utility of Niebuhr's ironic theory was greatly compromised by
the specifics of his own application of that theory to the American
past. That it was Niebuhr's neoorthodox Christianity that led him to
the idea of ironic history and also in part interfered with his ability
to write such history effectively is in itself a nice illustration of
Niebuhrian irony. Niebuhr failed to gain sufficient critical distance
from America; his treatment was too blind to the active evil in
American history for it to be effective irony. This violation of his
own ironic theory stemmed from the fact that the book was written
in an intense phase of the Cold War, as well as from his Christian
commitment. Niebuhr addressed himself primarily to the ironic
dilemmas that arose out of that conflict, particularly to what he felt
was the need for the United States to live with the evil risk of nuclear
war in order to secure a greater good, the peaceful containment of
communism. He identified the communists with the demonic, particularly with extreme pretensions to wisdom, which induced an exaggerated activism, hence he came to see the United States in contrast as relatively passive and innocent, a responding victim of Soviet
pressure, not an ironically active participant in the Cold War. This
tendency to gloss over the evil of America may have been compounded by an overconfidence in Christian virtue. Although
Niebuhr did not set up the conflict in terms of atheism versus
religion, it is hard to avoid the impression that at some level such a
perception played a part in his Manichaean vision of the world at
that time. The equation of the cause of the United States with that
of Christianity — an identification that Niebuhr warns against, but
one that he may implicitly have made — could easily have interfered
with his ability to achieve a truly ironic stance in regard to America.
This ironic failure of Niebuhr's probably contributed to the tendency of American historians to identify the idea of irony with a Cold
War posture and may have blocked the explicit acceptance of his
own extremely promising idea within the profession, particularly
among those younger historians who otherwise were receptive to an
ironic perspective.[39] The problem was compounded by the confusion of ironic with consensus history in the writings of Richard
Hofstadter and Louis Hartz.

I cannot conclude this general discussion of irony and history
without mentioning what I believe is the greatest danger of irony in
our present circumstances. A consciousness of the role of irony in
American history can itself become a source of irony if we assume
that because we are aware of some of these past ironies we are now

free of all illusions that engender self-contradictory actions. Many of the young radicals of the late 1960s who perceived the irony of America very well assumed their own innocence and thus constructed illusions that led to more irony. In a review of a work of Niebuhr's, Perry Miller warned of the danger of the pretensions to which irony itself could lead. He asked: "by what further and extraordinary convulsions of the human spirit shall paradox itself be saved from becoming merely a conventional way of explaining — and thus to some degree of rationalizing and justifying — the unrighteousness of the righteous?"[40]

# II
# Irony in European History

European historians have utilized irony of one type or another for as long as they have been writing history.[1] In the pages that follow I shall try to demonstrate the presence of Niebuhrian or closely related forms of irony in works on different periods and problems in European history to suggest how widely it has been applied and to make a tentative determination of the kinds of situations to which historians have found it particularly appropriate. I do not deal with enough scholars to draw any firm overall conclusions about irony in European historiography. There is no general book in English on the use of irony by historians of Europe, although Hayden White's study of historical rhetoric in the nineteenth century gives much attention to that form. This chapter is intended not only to illustrate selectively the uses to which historians of Europe have put Niebuhrian irony.

## 1. Through the Eighteenth Century

Among ancient historians humane irony was most clearly used by Thucydides.[2] In a rare commentary on his own narrative he himself hints at how his account of the Sicilian expedition could be interpreted ironically. After their defeat in a crucial naval battle the Athenians in Sicily were miserable, "especially when they remembered the splendor and the pride of their setting out and how mean and abject was the conclusion. No Hellenic army had ever suffered such a reverse. They had come to enslave others, and now they were going away frightened of being enslaved themselves." Although there is no causal connection stated between their desire to enslave others and the contradictory result of their invasion, there

does appear to be an implication to that effect. Thucydides also
hints at irony in his description of the attitude of one of the generals,
Nicias, to the expedition. "Nicias had not wanted to be chosen for
the command; his view was that the city was making a mistake and,
on a slight pretext which looked reasonable, was in fact aiming at
conquering the whole of Sicily—a very considerable undertaking indeed." While it is hard to nail Thucydides down on such issues, his
account of how the Athenians decided to undertake the expedition
is compatible with the point of view that he attributes to Nicias.[3]

Nicias is not only a vehicle for Thucydides' ironic hints about the
expedition; his own role in it can also be seen ironically. After the
final defeat of the expedition Nicias was put to death by his captors,
a fate that Thucydides regrets, because he was "a man who, of all
the Hellenes in my time, least deserved to come to so miserable an
end, since the whole of his life had been devoted to the study and the
practice of virtue."[4] Rex Warner, Thucydides' translator, offers a
reading of his treatment of Nicias that strongly suggests Niebuhrian
irony: "Had Nicias never gone to Sicily he would have died with the
reputation of a good general. As it was, his conduct in Sicily may
well have been the decisive factor which caused Athens to lose the
war. Thucydides sees both points and shows us a general who is
respectable as well as pathetic. He treats him tenderly, making
much of the great qualities which he showed in a desperate situation
for which he was largely to blame."[5]

The distinguished classicist John H. Finley reveals the way in
which Thucydides' overall perspective on the war as a whole fits the
Niebuhrian pattern. He was deeply attached to Athenian
democracy at the same time that he saw its flaws. "Athens,"
Thucydides thought, "failed through the excess of democracy itself,
the source of her strength" and her distinctive virtue.[6]

Irony was used by Roman as well as Greek historians. Nancy
Struever compares Sallust and Tacitus to Thucydides in terms that
suggest a parallel between the irony in their works and that in
Niebuhr's. She also observes that historical irony like that used by
Sallust can be found in the works of the Renaissance humanist
Leonardo Bruni. Her description of how irony functions in Bruni's
history reveals its similarity to the Niebuhrian form in some of its
broader implications. "Bruni self-consciously uses irony . . . to make
demands upon the reader, to invite him to participate in discovery.
Humanist irony does not simply point to the continuous victories of
cosmic fate over the human will, but attempts to involve the reader
in the imaginative re-creation of difficult choice."[7]

Irony was a very common literary device in the eighteenth century

and it can be found in many historical works of the period, particularly those of Hume and Gibbon.[8] Much of this is rhetorical
irony, although other kinds are also present. Gibbon's treatment of
the early development of Christianity is especially ironic.[9] Another
eighteenth-century writer who used a formulation very similar to
irony was Adam Smith. Although the *Wealth of Nations* is not a
work of history, Smith's concept of the "invisible hand" has had important historical consequences. Smith argues that every person in
his economic activity "intends only his own security and . . . only his
own gain," but by pursuing those selfish purposes "every individual
necessarily labours to render the annual revenue of the society as
great as he can . . . he is in this, as in many other cases, led by an invisible hand to promote an end which was no part of his intention.
By pursuing his own interest he frequently promotes that of the
society more effectually than when he intends to promote it."[10] This
benign irony, assuming as it does that natural law provides for the
congruence of private and public interest, is central to Smith's
thought. It has been found by many recent historians to have had
important pernicious and unintended consequences in the United
States, where it has been a fundamental article of faith. In the conclusion to this book I shall try to suggest how this idea has been
perceived by some of these historians as a key ironic flaw in
American culture.

## 2.  Historical Theorists: Hegel, Marx, and Weber

In considering the use of Niebuhrian irony in nineteenth- and
twentieth-century European historiography, I shall begin with a
brief examination of several key thinkers whose ideas have deeply affected our understanding of history: Hegel, Marx (and Engels), and
Weber.

The unanticipated consequences of purposive action are taken account of in Hegel's philosophy of history. He observes that "in
history an additional result is commonly produced by human actions beyond that which they aim at and obtain—that which they
immediately recognize and desire. They gratify their own interest;
but something further is thereby accomplished, latent in the actions
in question, though not present to their consciousness, and not included in their design." Those additional results are in accordance

with "the will of the World-Spirit." In explaining the mechanism by
which that universal reason utilizes the conflicting intentions of particular men for its purposes, Hegel introduces one of his best-known
concepts, a concept with a significant relationship to irony:

> It is not the general idea that is implicated in opposition and com-
> bat, and that is exposed to danger. It remains in the background,
> untouched and uninjured. This may be called the *cunning of
> reason* — that it sets the passion to work for itself, while that which
> develops its existence through such impulsion pays the penalty,
> and suffers loss. . . . The particular is for the most part of too
> trifling value compared with the general: individuals are
> sacrificed and abandoned. The idea pays the penalty of deter-
> minate existence and of corruptibility, not from itself, but from
> the passions of individuals.[11]

While this cunning of reason has more in common with the irony
of fate than with Niebuhrian irony, Hegel's Spirit or reason does
work through the desires of individual men, and is to that degree
more firmly connected to human intention and responsibility than
are blind determinism or the will of the gods. Walter Kaufmann explicitly applies the term *irony* to Hegel in a way that suggests this
connection. In Hegel's work, he writes, "we find a vision of the
of man, and of history which emphasizes development through conflict, the moving power of human passions, which produce wholly
unintended results, and the irony of sudden reversals."[12]

The irony in the Marxist conception of history is similar to that in
the Hegelian. It can be seen in Friedrich Engels, *Ludwig Feuerbach
and the Outcome of Classical German Philosophy*. Both history and
nature are governed by blind laws, but in the former human intention plays a role: "In the history of society . . . nothing happens
without a conscious purpose, without an intended aim. But this
distinction, important as it is for historical investigation, particularly of single epochs and events, cannot alter the fact that the course
of history is governed by inner general laws." The unintended consequences of human action seem on the surface to make up a mean-
ingless pattern as the wills of individuals conflict and interfere with
each other, but those consequences are organized by obscured
governing laws. Engels presents a summary statement of the role
and limits of volition in the Marxist view of history, one that makes it
clear that those laws of history work through human intention.
"Men make their own history whatever its outcome may be, in that

each person follows his own consciously desired end, and it is precisely the resultant of these many wills operating in different directions and of their manifold effects upon the outer world that constitutes history . . . the many individual wills active in history for the most part produce results quite other than those they intended — often quite the opposite." Behind these individual motives lie the larger forces of class conflict and changes in "the mode of production."[13]

In a letter written toward the end of his life, after Marx's death, Engels emphasizes even more strongly the idea that although history is governed by laws, those laws operate through human intentionality and action. "We make our own history, but . . . under very definite presuppositions and conditions." Among these conditions Engels emphasizes economic ones, but he also mentions politics and "even the traditions which haunt human minds." What eventuates from the actions of individuals undertaken under these circumstances is not what any of them intended:

> history makes itself in such a way that the final result always arises from conflicts between many individual wills, of which each again has been made what it is by a host of particular conditions of life. Thus there are innumerable intersecting forces which give rise to one resultant — the historical event. This again may itself be viewed as the product of a power which, taken as a whole, works *unconsciously* and without volition. . . . Thus past history proceeds in the manner of a natural process and is also essentially subject to the same laws of movement.

Engels is careful to warn that human beings are real factors in history even though human action produces unintended consequences: "But from the fact that individual wills — of which each desires what he is impelled to by his physical constitution and external, in the last resort economic, circumstances (either his own personal circumstances or those of society in general) — do not attain what they want, but are merged into a collective mean, a common resultant, it must not be concluded that their value = 0. On the contrary, each contributes to the resultant and is to this degree involved in it."[14]

The assumption that history in the large moves according to natural laws that individual intentions unconsciously serve differentiates this Marxist irony from my version of Niebuhr's, if not entirely from his own ultimately providential view of history. (The Marxist's implicit assumption that it is possible for men to know in which direction history is moving is entirely alien to Niebuhr.) But the

Marxist law, like Hegel's World-Spirit and Idea and unlike some other general theories of history, works through human intention and action, recognizing their historical reality if not their efficacy. The reasons for the discrepancy between human intention and the consequences of action are to be found in the laws of history, not in the pretensions of the actors, but to the extent that a lack of consciousness of those laws on the part of those who seek to act in history can be regarded as a source of discrepancy, Marxist irony moves closer to Niebuhrian. Marxists and scholars interested in Marxism are currently involved in arguments about the degree of determinism explicit and implicit in that system of thought. Marxist emphasis in general is balanced between the role of human beings in history and the role of intractable law; to the extent that the latter is accentuated, Marxist irony becomes like the irony of fate, but in the version of Marxism that stresses human decision and uncertainty, the irony becomes Niebuhrian. In both Marxist and Hegelian thought the impulse toward a total explanation of history, the desire to comprehend all human experience under one general causal theory, compromises the humane irony that can also be found there.[15]

Max Weber comes closer to Niebuhrian irony than either Hegel or Marx. For him the spirit of capitalism was to a very considerable degree an unintended consequence of the Reformation. The reformers did not seek to foster the attitudes appropriate to capitalism: "it is not to be understood that we expect to find any of the founders or representatives of these religious movements considering the promotion of what we have called the spirit of capitalism as in any sense the end of his life-work." In contrast to what some of his critics have charged, Weber was perfectly aware that the essential goals of the reformers were religious. They did not aim simply at moral improvement, let alone economic accumulation:

> We cannot well maintain that the pursuit of worldly goods, conceived as an end in itself, was to any of them of positive ethical value. Once and for all it must be remembered that programmes of ethical reform never were at the centre of interest for any of the religious reformers. . . . They were not the founders of societies for ethical culture nor the proponents of humanitarian projects for social reform of cultural ideals. The salvation of the soul and that alone was the center of their life and work. Their ethical ideals and the practical results of their doctrines were all based on that alone, and were the consequences of purely religious motives.

He is absolutely explicit about the unintended character of the Reformation's contribution to the spirit of capitalism and the development of modernity. "We shall thus have to admit that the cultural consequences of the Reformation were to a great extent, perhaps in the particular aspects with which we are dealing predominantly, unforeseen and even unwished for results of the labours of the reformers. They were often far removed from or even in contradiction to all that they themselves thought to attain."[16]

Although the reformers did not seek to promote capitalism or to modernize society, Weber definitely holds that their activities and thought were of substantial influence in bringing about those developments. His purpose was "to clarify the part which religious forces have played in forming the developing web of our specifically worldly modern culture, in the complex interaction of innumerable different historical factors." Weber disclaimed any attempt to prove that the Reformation independently "caused" the development of the spirit of capitalism. "On the contrary, we only wish to ascertain whether and to what extent religious forces have taken part in the qualitative formation and the quantitative expansion of that spirit over the world."[17] The development of capitalism and modernity was the result of a complex set of events of which the religious movements were only a part, but a real part nonetheless.

The limited but important causal role that Weber unquestionably sees human intention and action playing in history differentiates his approach from the more deterministic side of Hegel and Marx, and makes it clear how much closer he is to Niebuhrian irony. The unintended consequences of human action tend to be seen by Hegel and Marx as products of forces beyond human control, results of the disjunction between the direction in which history inextricably moves and the direction in which particular men want to go. In Weber, although history is the product of a web of forces, it is not so clearly governed by law as it is in Hegelianism and Marxism. The actions of people can have real consequences, unintended or otherwise, in the sense that they can affect, although by no means totally control, the direction in which history moves. Human beings are responsible to a greater degree. Their universe is more open. To a considerable extent people make their own history, although it may not be the history they set out to make.[18]

Although Weber's universe reamins open, so that it is possible for the actions of human beings to have consequences, consequences that genuinely "belong" to the action and not to an overriding, determining law, there still remains the distinct question of what it is that is responsible for the disparity between intention and consequence. A comment of Weber's wife on his treatment of the development of Puritanism suggests that for Weber that responsibility lay in part in the ways in which the movement went about trying to actualize its intentions: "The remarkable religious structuring of life gets destroyed in virtue of its own consequences."[19] Merton's reading of Weber also indicates that some of the reasons for the disparity lay in the historical actors themselves, in their goals, or in their methods of realizing them. The situation in which Protestant reformers unintentionally contributed to the development of capitalism is one "where there is no consideration of future consequences because of the felt necessity of certain actions enjoined by certain fundamental values." Merton interprets Weber as having "properly generalized this case, saying that active asceticism paradoxically leads to its own decline through the accumulation of wealth and possessions entailed by decreased consumption and intense productive activity," and offers a further generalization of how processes of this kind serve the "dynamics of social and cultural change," a generalization that reads very much like an account of Niebuhrian irony: "activities oriented toward certain values release processes which so react as to change the very scale of values which precipitated them. This process may in part be due to the fact that when a system of basic values enjoins certain *specific* actions, adherents are not concerned with the objective consequences of these actions but only with the subjective satisfaction of duty well performed. Or, action in accordance with a dominant set of values tends to be focussed upon that particular value-area."[20]

Weber's theses can be stated in terms of human responsibility: In seeking "subjective satisfactions" in practicing the Protestant ethic, the reformers ignored the way in which their "worldly asceticism" was contributing to the development of capitalism and the secularization of society, consequences that conflicted with their religious goals. Insofar as they allowed themselves to be blinded to those consequences by those satisfactions, they were themselves responsible for the disparity between the result and the intention of their actions. However, Merton points out that Weber also saw objective factors in the process whereby ideas and actions produce unanticipated results.[21] Still, to the extent that people themselves act out of an imbalance in values, to the extent that they accept short-run gratifications and ignore long-run effects, they also contribute to the unsought consequences of their own actions. The degree of human responsibility implicit in Weber's irony may be less than that implied by Niebuhr's, but it is of essentially the same kind and order.

With Weber, then, we come very close to the humane historical
irony that is the concern of this book. Social and cultural change
over time are complex processes involving both objective factors and
human actions, actions that have real, if frequently unintended consequences. Because of their limited vision and their tendencies to
focus on the realization of short-run values, people frequently act so
as to bring about consequences at variance with their larger intentions. Although the complexity of society contributes to this disparity, individuals do also, as they actively create a future they did not
seek.[22]

Irony requires an approach to history in which the human image
is a creative one, even if human actions do not always fulfill human
intentions. Such an image can be found in the work of some
historians of modern Europe — as opposed to historical theorists
— historians who focus on important movements of change or
revolution. In this brief examination of a few of them, I shall first
consider an important nineteenth-century French historical writer's
treatment of the French Revolution and then turn to several
twentieth-century English and American historians who offer ironic
interpretations of major turning points in the histories of Great Britain, Germany, and Russia.


## 3.   Tocqueville on the French Revolution

Alexis de Tocqueville had a complex attitude toward the French
Revolution. He was sympathetic with many of its goals, particularly
those of its earlier stages, but highly critical of its methods. His
historical perception of it was fundamentally ironic in the
Niebuhrian sense. He saw the French upper classes as inadvertently
preparing the way for the Revolution, and he saw the revolutionaries contributing to the destruction of the values for which they
themselves were fighting.

The irony of his treatment of the pre-Revolutionary elite is in-
dicated by a chapter title: "How the spirit of revolt was prompted by
well-intentioned efforts to improve the people's lot."[23] Tocqueville
noted that during the eighteenth century the French upper classes
became concerned about the condition of the poor. They did not
hesitate to discuss openly the poverty and inequity that they had
newly discovered. In "championing the cause of the under-
privileged they made them acutely conscious of their wrongs." Tocqueville cites numerous statements by aristocrats and officials
criticizing the conditions under which the lower classes lived and

calling for reform. He quotes the king's condemnation of forced labor and the monopolistic guild system, and observes that "it was indiscreet enough to utter such words, but positively dangerous to utter them in vain. For some months later the guild system and forced labor were reinstated."[24]

This is the basic pattern of irony. The French upper classes, as they developed a social conscience, expressed their concern for the poor and publicly attacked the injustices under which the masses suffered, but did very little about those conditions and injustices, so that they had the effect not of improving the lot of the people but of arousing their consciousness and hostility. The long-run, unintended consequence of this was the Revolution, which Tocqueville sees as largely a result of the elite's own behavior. He observes that "it almost seemed as though the authorities were aiming less at providing relief for the poor than fuel for their passions."[25]

Although the upper classes might be willing to give up some of the specific material benefits of their privileged position, they would not surrender that privileged position itself, a position that was very offensive to the lower classes. Tocqueville does not doubt the sincerity of the aristocrats, but the way in which they went about expressing their interest in improving the condition of the poor led to results they certainly had not sought. "In the eighteenth century . . . disinterested beliefs and human fellow feeling led the French elite to sponsor the revolutionary cause, while the masses were moved to action by the hardships of their lot and passionate desire to better it. Thus the generous enthusiasm of the former took part in activating the rancour and cupidity of the populace and, indeed, touched off revolution." Tocqueville suggests that there was a direct connection between expressions of aristocratic concern for the lower classes and the development of the movement for a revolution.[26]

Conflicts occurred between various gonvernmental agencies "in which each party blamed the other for the sufferings of the laboring classes." In these disputes "on one point it will be noticed, both parties concurred: on giving the public to understand that their superiors were to blame for the evils that befell them." Tocqueville emphasizes the open character of statements of this kind. The intention behind them was to stimulate the upper class to support reform, not the lower orders to revolt, but their public character constituted the mechanism by which the French establishment unintentionally prepared the way for its own destruction. Tocqueville comments on the way in which the aristocrats simply ignored the effects of their comments on the masses. "So inert did the working class appear that it was assumed to be not only dumb but hard of hearing, with the

result that when at long last the authorities began to take an interest
in the masses they talked about them in their presence, as if they
were not there." But the lower clases did hear and understand what
the elite said, and reacted to it in ways that hardly served the interests of the upper classes. "The effect of all this on the peasant can
be easily imagined. Now that his grievances were ventilated, now
that the men responsible for them were pointed out to him and he
realized how small was their number, he was emboldened to take
arms against them, while in his heart were kindled the primitive
emotions of envy, malice, and cupidity."[27]

Because of their continuing contempt for them, the aristocrats ignored the fact that the lower classes could hear what they said. Tocqueville observes that "despite a genuine desire to better the condition of the poorer classes, the feelings of the elite towards them were
strongly tinctured with contempt. We are reminded of the conduct
of Mme. Duchatelet, as reported by Voltaire's secretary; this good
lady, it seems, had no scruples about undressing in the presence of
her manservants, being unable to convince herself that these lackeys
were real flesh-and-blood men!" Not only did the upper classes express their contempt for the lower by ignoring the effect of their
statements about social injustice on the poor. Tocqueville remarks
on how they also directly voiced their contempt itself. He notes
derogatory terms by which the aristocrats referred to the masses and
observes with amazement that "expressions of this kind figured in
reports to which the utmost publicity was given and which were intended to be read by the peasants themselves."[28]

In this chapter Tocqueville uses what I have called Niebuhrian
irony to expose contradictions in the actions of the pre-
Revolutionary French upper classes, showing that as they became
sensitized to the injustice under which the mass of Frenchmen suffered, they gave expression to their discovery of that injustice in such
a way as to stimulate a revolution against themselves. The key ironic
flaw in the aristocracy that led them to act this way was their deep
contempt for the lower classes, a contempt that was not reduced by
their benevolent concern for them. Although the upper classes were
willing to give up some of the particularly material benefits of their
superior position in society, they were not willing to surrender their
sense of superiority itself. This exaggerated sense of their own
relative worth led them unconsciously to give expression to that contempt by discussing the injustice under which the masses suffered in
their hearing, as if the lower classes were incapable of understanding, even by openly using disparaging language in referring to

them. In acting in this way the aristocracy brought the revolution down on their own heads.

Tocqueville goes on to show how specific actions of the government, in addition to public statements by members of the governing class, contributed to the growth of a revolutionary consciousness among the masses in the next chapter, which also has an ironic title: "How certain practices of the central power completed the revolutionary education of the masses." Before the Revolution "the government itself had been busily instilling into the minds of the populace at large what were later to be known as revolutionary ideas; ideas, that is to say, which taking no account of individuals or private rights, encouraged acts of violence." The traditional institutions that might restrain such violent injustice were undermined by the last two kings before the Revolution. Some of Louis XVI's reforms in particular "violated vested rights. They prepared the ground for the Revolution not so much because they removed obstacles in its way but far more because they taught the nation how to set about it. Paradoxically enough, what made things worse was that the King and his ministers were inspired by purely altruistic ideals; for by showing that methods of violence can be employed with good intentions by people of good will, they set a dangerous precedent."[29]

Tocqueville comments on the disrespect for the rights of private property that the monarchs from Louis XIV to the Revolution encouraged in the people by their claim to ultimate title to all lands, by the slow and unfair process of compensating small landowners for property expropriated for roads and other public works, and by the way in which the provisions of charitable bequests were disregarded.[30] But the most crucial area in which the government habituated the people to the violation of basic rights was in the administration of criminal justice: "A stable, well-intentioned government gradually accustomed the nation to a system of criminal procedure better suited to a revolutionary age or despotic rule, and, indeed, prepared men's minds for both. For the people were quick to learn the lessons taught them by their rulers."[31] Tocqueville's ironic perspective leads him not only to see the injustices of the Old Regime as causes of the Revolution, in the sense that they were sources of popular resentment, but also to perceive them as models of behavior, precedents for revolutionary justice. The French ruling class itself trained the people in how most effectively to destroy it.

The way in which the French elite prepared the people for revolution by their contemptuous statements and unjust actions is not the only Niebuhrian irony in *The Old Regime and the French Revolu-tion*. Tocqueville also saw the overall consequences of the Revolu-tion as inconsistent with the objectives of the revolutionaries. They wished to do away entirely with the Old Regime, but the order they created unintentionally incorporated much of what it was designed to replace. Tocqueville argues that in spite of their desire to get away as far as possible from the past, they perpetuated it. "I am con-vinced that though they had no inkling of this, they took over from the old regime not only most of its customs, conventions, and modes of thought, but even those very ideas which prompted our revolu-tionaries to destory it; that, in fact, though nothing was further from their intentions, they used the debris of the old order for building up the new." He maintains that "many of the laws and ad-ministrative methods which were suppressed in 1789 reappeared a few years later, much as some rivers after going underground re-emerge at another point, in new surroundings."[32]

Although Tocqueville was quite critical of the Revolution, the sympathetic side of his attitude can be seen in his comments on its original purposes and early development. The revolutionaries sought both liberty and democracy "in the hey-day of the Revolu-tion; when the love of equality and the urge to freedom went hand in hand; when they wished to set up not merely a truly democratic government but free institutions, not only to do away with privileges but also to make good and stabilize the rights of man, the in-dividual." But the Revolution turned away from these laudable pur-poses. The reasons for the discrepancy between those goals and the actual consequences lay in the revolutionaries themselves. Toc-queville wants to "draw attention to the events, mistakes, mis-judgements which led these selfsame Frenchmen to abandon their original ideal and, turning their backs on freedom, to acquiesce in an equality of servitude under the master of all Europe."[33]

Tocqueville's historical vision in this book is comprehensively ironic in the Niebuhrian mode. Because of their contemptuous at-titude of superiority to the common people, the upper classes of the Old Regime unintentionally prepared the way for their own destruc-tion. Because of their own mistakes the revolutionaries, who began by seeking freedom and a total transformation of society, ended by instituting tyranny and incorporating many features of pre-Revolutionary France in their new order. Both of these groups were involved in kinds of behavior frequently productive of Niebuhrian irony when they created these unintended effects—the upper classes in attempts to reform society, and the revolutionaries in an effort to transform it.[34]

## 4. William Haller on English Puritanism

Let us turn now to some more recent historians. Niebuhrian irony colors the major themes of William Haller's sensitive and sweeping studies of the development of English Puritanism and its role in the English Civil War.[35] Early in the first of these, *The Rise of Puritanism*, Haller indicates the general line of his ironic argument. This book deals with "the setting forth of Puritanism in pulpit and press up to the moment when the Puritan clergy were called upon to devise the kind of church they had so long desired—the kind of church, it turned out, which could not be brought to being in the kind of world they had helped to create." Haller demonstrates how basic Puritan doctrines and methods functioned so as to make it impossible for them to achieve the reformation they sought; instead, without at all wishing to, they contributed to the development of a more secularized society. "They were, perhaps, dreaming of such a theocracy as indeed they achieved for a time in New England, but they were also, certainly without intention, preparing for a society in which popular education and the free play of public opinion would become the conditions under and by which government must operate."[36] Rather than uniform reformation, they created sectarian diversity; beginning as the enemies of permissiveness in church and state, they led to the growth of heterodoxy and its increased toleration by their actions. Also behaving ironically, the Anglican bishops aided the growth of Puritanism by their efforts to suppress it. Finally, in his second volume, *Liberty and Reformation in the Puritan Revolution*, Haller shows how the very instruments that the Puritans in power used to try to establish their reformed order served instead to further the transformation of English society into something quite different from that sought by either Puritan or Anglican.

The Puritan clergy—the "Spiritual Brotherhood"—had two intimately related goals: they hoped to make the Church of England into a truly Protestant church (for most of them that meant a church organized in Presbyterian form), one that would actively oversee the moral life of the community, and they wished to be the instruments through which God would bring salvation to as many Englishmen as possible. Among the methods they most relied upon to advance these objectives were the preaching of the Word, the publication of religious tracts and devotional books, and the advocacy of Bible reading by individuals in the expectation that the Holy Word would bring them to personal salvation and the true church: "The theory was that truth in scripture when brought to bear upon conscience by the force of reason would lead men to early agreement unless they chose wilfully and maliciously to resist the light. The fact was, as experience was to demonstrate, that scripture, which had more poetry in its pages than law, worked upon men of uncritical minds, lively imaginations, differing temperaments and conflicting interests not as a unifying but as a divisive force."[37]

There is great coherence in Haller's ironic vision here. Preaching, writing, and the advocacy of Bible reading were all predicated upon the assumption that, when rightly informed, individual consciences would bring the English people to a common desire for a uniform transformation of the church. Instead, this appeal to conscience set in motion a process of sectarian diversification that was quite the opposite of the ordered reformation Puritans sought. Haller shows how these methods — particularly preaching — worked so as to prevent them from reaching their goals. Since they lacked the power to set up the church government they sought, they had to

> begin by trying to convert the people and trust in God to bring about presbyterian reform in his own time. The immediate result was that, in the hope of establishing ultimately their cherished scheme of uniformity, they spent two generations preaching a doctrine and a way of life which promoted active religious experience and expression, promoted it much faster than means could be found to control or direct it. What the preachers as a whole believed was that heresy and schism should be firmly suppressed. But what they taught was that any man might be a saint and that the mark of the saint was that he obeyed his own conscience at any cost.

The outcome of their appeal to conscience, making impossible the uniformity they wanted, was compounded by the example of their own lives. "They themselves practiced conscientious objection, in whatever degree they dared and in whatever direction they chose, to the form of religion established by law. The ultimate effect, as later reformers learned to their sorrow, was to encourage in their followers the habit of going each his own way toward heaven and the notion that it was every man's native right to save himself or not in his own way without interference from anybody."[38] Sectarian confusion and religious toleration were the results of the Puritan clergy's efforts to achieve an ordered reformation, a reformation intended to decrease rather than increase the toleration of diversity in England.

Haller nicely points out how these developments were unintended consequences of the very effectiveness of the Puritan clergy. By the 1640s a dissonant collection of radical sects had appeared, awakened by the preaching of the more orthodox reformers. The same qualities that had made Puritanism appealing and powerful also stimulated the growths of these groups. The proliferation of sects, a great evil in orthodox Puritan eyes, was a product of the great virtues of Puritan teaching, and the sectarian preachers exhibited those very same virtues in pursuit of goals opposed by the orthodox. Haller argues that the cause of the disintegrating tendencies in Puritanism was the same emotional power that was one of its major strengths.[39]

The accelerated growth of heretical varieties of Puritanism during the Civil War led finally to the creation of a considerable degree of religious toleration by the Puritans when they came to power. Haller concludes this book with some comments on the irony of the Puritans' establishing such toleration in England at the moment when they had arrived at the position for which they had struggled with the original intention of imposing a purer uniformity than had existed before. Under the bishops an atmosphere of "semitolerance" had prevailed in England.

> The Puritan preachers as a body did not approve such freedom. They had, however, taken advantage of it in order to preach sermons and produce a literature which enormously stimulated individual activity in thought and expression and in other forms of enterprise as well. Moreover, by their own activities and by their use of patronage, they had promoted the new outlet for individualism of all sorts offered to the Bible-reading public by the vernacular press. This, though they did not realize it at the time, was to prove the undoing of the scheme they now embarked upon for subjecting the new society arising in England to a presbyterian type of theocracy.[40]

The long-range consequence of the manner in which they spread their influence and achieved power was the impossibility of their using that influence and power for the goal they had originally sought, a uniform and rigorously enforced reformation of English religious life.

As counterpoint to his major theme, the ironic development of Puritanism, Haller offers an account of the response of the Anglican establishment to that movement. One aspect of that response was the persecution of intransigent Puritans like William Prynne. Haller shows how the nature of Anglicanism made that persecution self-defeating. Prynne's extremism "made him a most dangerous enemy to [Archbishop] Laud and all that Laud stood for. Anglicanism, ideally conceived, proposed a humane and rational view of religion and, within certain broad limits, a tolerant church. The difficulty was that, in order to make reason and charity prevail, the bishops could in practice hit upon no way but the use of their legal authority to prosecute those who intemperately attacked the church." By trying to repress such men they inadvertently stimulated more opposition to their own authority.[41]

The selective religious persecution practiced by the early Stuarts was from the beginning counterproductive mostly because of "their failure to realize the inexpediency of intolerance ineffectively applied." James I had halted the Puritans' effort to gain control of the church, but he had not stopped much of their preaching. "What he chiefly accomplished against them was to persecute their preachers just enough to make enemies of them and to heighten their personal prestige. . . . no persecutors probably ever won so evil a reputation by doing so little harm to the cause of the persecuted and so much to their own."[42] The repression by the Stuarts led the Puritans away from efforts to take over the existing church structure and into the more productive path of stimulating a popular movement. James thus ironically fostered the growth of that which he most wished to oppose, the influence of the Puritan clergy.

In his *Liberty and Reformation in the Puritan Revolution* Haller deals with the Puritan leaders under the conditions of civil war as they struggled for and took power in England. To summarize the irony of the success of the Puritans in this book I shall quote only from its conclusion, in which Haller describes the consequences of their effort to impose an ordered reformation on England by appealing to individual consciences:

> The outcome of all their striving in pulpit and press was to be the triumph of their teaching and the disappointment of their expectation. . . . They had taught men to think that if they wished to be counted among the elect, they must feel in their hearts a command to put every ability and every occasion to the service of the Lord, assured that he would not let that service come to nothing. . . . Thus they aroused not in the humble and poor in spirit only but in men of many conditions in an expanding world and a changing society a quickened consciousness of life and power within themselves, a sense of participating in the designs of providence, and expectancy of great things to come.
> The result was not reformation but the emergence of an articulate public, free from many of the inhibitions and impediments of customary attitudes and sanctions.[43]

Taken together these two books of Haller's provide a marvelously detailed and perceptively ironic account of the development and consequences of the largest revolutionary movement in English history. The irony is applied to both the Puritans and their enemies in a rich and complex pattern. The Anglican leadership, because of their very policy of limited, informal toleration, had to persecute those who sought to impose a rigorous and intolerant order upon church and state, but in persecuting their enemies they strengthened their appeal and fostered the development of the more radical among them. The Anglican virtue of toleration led in this sense to intolerant and self-defeating behavior. To the extent that the Bishops had no choice, or were consciously making a choice between clearly perceived undesirable alternatives in the inconsistent persecution of the Puritans, they were acting tragically, not ironically, but Haller's treatment suggests irony much more than tragedy. His attitude toward the leaders of the Anglican Church is precisely that combination of empathetic understanding of their situation and goals and critical detachment from their methods which irony fosters.

It is one of the great virtues of these books that the same can be said of his attitude toward the Puritans. While he may be more interested in them, since their story is his central focus, it would be difficult to claim that he is more sympathetic to them than to their opponents. He perceives the Puritans, like the Bishops, as unconsciously undermining their own goals by the methods they used in trying to achieve them. The Spiritual Brotherhood felt themselves called to fulfill two primary objectives, which they saw as coherently related to each other: to save the souls of Englishmen and to impose upon England a divinely ordained reformation. When prevented from achieving institutional power they sought popular influence through their preaching and writing. They had considerable success in bringing large numbers of people to a conviction of their own salvation and in spreading the desire for reformation. Their preaching was their great virtue, but it also produced consequences that prevented them from achieving the ordered transformation of English religious life that they sought. Both the content of their message and the manner in which it was delivered led people to doubt the authority not only of the Bishops but of the preachers as well. Their preaching led to a reliance upon individual conscience and generated a great variety of sectarian movements, which made it impossible for the orthodox Puritans to impose their reformation when their moment of power came during the Civil War.

Haller is not explicit about the flaws in the Spiritual Brotherhood that led them to act so as to contradict their own intentions. Perhaps one might say that there was an element of pretense and self-deception in their assumption that they could control the great spiritual forces they unleashed when they asked each man to follow his own conscience. There does seem to be an illusion of their own virtue and wisdom in their assumption that all rightly informed consciences would follow their path, an assumption that not only were they on God's side but He was on theirs. But one need not make this inference to see how well Haller's treatment fits the Niebuhrian pattern. The crucial point is not only that it be possible to identify as flaws in modern terms those aspects of the character of historical actors which led them to produce unintended consequences. Equally important is the demonstration that the traits that produced those results were in their own eyes virtues, sources of strength. In this case we can see those traits as the fervor and energy of the Puritan preachers and their ability to appeal effectively to individual consciences. These characteristics were at once the main instruments through which they fulfilled their dual mission of saving souls and building a popular reform movement and the sources of that dissent and sectarianism which made it impossible for them to achieve the reformation they sought. This is true Niebuhrian irony, for the unintended outcome of their actions is integrally related to their peculiar virtues.[44]

## 5.   Germany and Russia

The Nazi seizure of power was the most dramatic moment in modern German history. Understandably, irony has not been the controlling perspective in most histories of Nazism. There was too much of the demonic in that movement for scholars to muster the sympathy needed to see the humanity of the Nazis,[45] but some of those who played a role in bringing them to power, and others who supported them, can be understood in ironic terms.

John Wheeler-Bennett's account of the way in which the German army facilitated Hitler's rise is certainly open to an ironic reading. Under the leadership of the aged Field Marshall von Hindenburg as president and the conniving General Kurt von Schleicher as chancellor in the months before the Nazi take-over, the army dominated the government. Von Schleicher was not a Nazi; his goal all along was to restore "the conservative military caste in Germany," and he expected to use the Nazis to that end.[46] He and other army leaders underestimated Hitler and overestimated their own wisdom and power.

The von Schleicher government had begun with the intention of keeping the Nazis out of office, but it ended by considering "a military *putsch* in order to ensure the appointment of Hitler as Chancellor, in order to protect Germany from the danger of National Socialism." This paradox arose out of the government's fear that other generals were planning a revolt to keep the Nazis out. In Wheeler-Bennett's view — and Hitler's — such a revolt could have succeeded. The Army leaders could have done what they wanted to do, prevented Hitler from coming to power, had they acted resolutely. Instead they plotted to bring him into power, because they "suffered from the delusion that Hitler could be made a captive."[47]

The result of their connivance was, of course, disastrous from the army's point of view as well as from that of the Jews, Germany, Europe, and most of the rest of the world. The reasons for their acting so as to bring about such unintended consequences extended beyond their illusions of power over Hitler. They were infected with their own version of the Nazi dream. Because they allowed themselves to be tempted by the bait of the advantages that Hitler could bestow on the army, its leaders deluded themselves into thinking that they could control him, make him the servant of the military. But by giving their much-needed support to Hitler they placed the German army in a debased condition.[48] The suffering that resulted from their action for millions of people passes into a realm beyond irony, whatever the motive.

In a recent article Peter Loewenberg suggests an ironic interpretation of the behavior of another group that played an important role in the rise of Nazism. Hitler received a disproportionate share of his support from younger men and women. Using sophisticated psychoanalytic and sociological techniques, Loewenberg argues that the "cohort" of people who had experienced the extreme deprivation and emotional dislocation of the First World War as children were psychologically prepared as young adults to turn to a movement such as Nazism when similar conditions recurred during the Great Depression. In childhood they had responded to the deprived conditions under which they grew up with feelings of "rage, sadism, and the defensive idealization of their absent parents, especially the father." When similar conditions recurred in Germany, people of this age group tended to regress to those infantile responses, which

made them "particularly susceptible to the appeal of a mass movement utilizing the crudest devices of projection and displacement in
its ideology. Above all" their regression "prepared the young voters
of Germany for submission to a total, charismatic leader."[49]

In concluding this essay Loewenberg adopts language suggesting
that the support of the Nazis by these young people was a choice of
fantasy over reality, a choice conditioned by the psychological effects of their childhood experiences, but not necessarily determined
by those effects. This becomes the language of irony: "fantasy is
always in the end less satisfying than mundane reality. Ironically, instead of finding the idealized father they, with Hitler as their leader,
plunged Germany and Europe headlong into a series of deprivations
many times worse than those of World War I. Thus the repetition
was to seek the glory of identification with the absent soldier-father,
but like all quests for a fantasied past, it had to fail." The young
Nazis did not get what they were seeking. Instead they unintentionally reproduced the conditions of their past from which they
most wished to escape. "What the youth cohort wanted was a fantasy of warmth, closeness, security, power, and love. What they re-
created was a repetition of their own childhoods. They gave to their
children and to Europe in greater measure precisely the traumas
they had suffered as children and adolescents a quarter of a century
earlier."[50]

What we have here is a demonstration of the power of a
psychoanalytic perspective for ironic history. By focusing on the
relationship between the physically and psychically damaging conditions under which the young Nazis grew up and their attraction to
Nazism, we are enabled to see the evil consequences of that movement from an angle other than the demonic. It becomes possible
from this point of view to sympathize with some of those who did
such evil because we can see their need to do evil as in part the product of their suffering as children. At the same time, because
Loewenberg describes the psychic damage as a predisposing factor
in the behavior of this group and not a determining one, to understand and even to sympathize are not to excuse. The young Germans
who chose Nazism were trying to undo present realities through
regression to fantasies that had been used to fend off unpleasant
realities in the past. Loewenberg's treatment of this reminds us how
the past weighs upon the present and suggests that psychoanalysis
and history have the common purpose of seeking to free the present
from the weight of the past.

The most obviously active moment of Russian history was the Revolution of 1917. In an interesting article on the historiography of the Revolution, James Billington advocates the use of an ironic interpretation explicitly derived from Niebuhr, an interpretation "that properly requires a larger measure of identification with the hopes of the Revolution and the destiny of Russia than most contemporary Western observers can honestly hold." This ironic vision increases the moral significance of the actions of the revolutionaries both during and after the Revolution. It "permits one to take seriously the hopes and fears that are so deeply felt in the revolutionary period. . . . At the same time this view enjoins the historian to brood in detail over the historical record. . . . Finally, the ironic view enables the historian to recognize the existence of 'incongruities which are more than mere chance,' without invoking supernatural forces or tragic predestination."[51]

Billington finds elements of such an ironic interpretation in a few Russian works published soon after the Revolution and in several recent Western monographs, and suggests that a particularly deep ironic view is to be found in Pasternak's *Doctor Zhivago*. He concludes with an expression of the hope that a willingness "to discard pretense" among both Russian and Western historians will lead to more use of irony in understanding the Revolution in the future.[52]

Billington's own lengthy book, *The Icon and the Axe: An Interpretive History of Russian Culture*, offers an ironic perspective on modern Russia. He quotes Niebuhr in defining irony, pointing out its utility as a humanistic historical concept. Although Billington does not focus on the way in which irony draws our attention to human responsibility, he is aware that the concept does relate to the problem of human freedom. But when we turn to his specific comments on the irony of Russian history we observe the same problem that is to be found in Niebuhr's treatment of American history; his own definition is not consistently used. Some of the developments he describes as ironic are more paradoxical than ironical.[53]

Even in regard to the Revolution, the main focus of his ironic interpretation, the ironies are not consistently Niebuhrian. He points out the paradoxical relationship between the March and October revolutions but does not present it from the point of view of historical actors who produced consequences they did not intend. Perhaps closer to Niebuhrian irony is a comment on how the Bolshevik Revolution destroyed its own supporters, but even here his focus does not quite fit the pattern.[54]

One development that does fit better involves the appearance of generational opposition within the Soviet Union. "It is high irony that the post-war generation of Russians — the most privileged and indoctrinated of all Soviet generations, which was not even given the passing exposure to the outside world of those who fought in the war — should prove the most alienated of all from the official ethos of communist ideology." This irony, the possible future consequences of which interest Billington very much, could easily be related to the pretensions and illusions of the communist leaders. It makes sense to suggest that perhaps the very belief on the part of those leaders that they could shape the minds of the young has been one of the factors responsible for their failure to do so. A similar, and related, implied Niebuhrian irony can be found in Billington's treatment of Russia's relationship with Eastern Europe.[55]

Billington suggests a general process in Russian culture and relates it to recent events in an overall ironic pattern that might be seen in Niebuhrian terms: "Repeatedly, Russians have sought to acquire the end products of other civilizations without the intervening process of slow growth and inner understanding. Russia took the Byzantine heritage en bloc without absorbing its traditions of orderly philosophic discourse. . . . High Stalinism provided a kind of retribution. Russia suddenly found itself ruled by Byzantine ritualism without Byzantine reverence or beauty, and by Western scientism without Western freedom of inquiry." If it could be said that in some way Russians brought Stalin's purges upon themselves, perhaps by adopting Marxism in the same impatient and incomplete way that they adopted so much else, then this terrible evil could be seen ironically. This is not, however, the point that Billington wishes to make here. Like Niebuhr, he is more interested in irony as a way of understanding the future than as a means of freeing the present from the past. The key to such freedom, Billington suggests, may lie in a new kind of pragmatism in Russia. "Stalin may have cured Russian thinkers of their passion for abstract speculation and their thirst for earthly utopias." He concludes with a poetic evocation of the ironic openness — even openness to a spiritual revival — of the Russian future in spite of the closed character of recent Russian society.[56]

In his focus on the potentiality in present ironic tensions for future changes Billington resembles Niebuhr, although his attitude toward those changes is different. Since Niebuhr's view of America was basically affirmative, his potential future involved ironic contradictions to be avoided, whereas Billington's relatively more critical stance toward the Russian present leads him to see positive ironic reversals as a future possibility. If, like Niebuhr, Billington fails to utilize his own concept consistently, his book nonetheless suggests how that concept might serve to open up the study of Russian history, particularly the origins and consequences of the Revolution. If, like Niebuhr's, his failure to focus on history as the story of human action and consequences compromises the moral-analytic power of irony, still the ironic tensions he describes are interesting in themselves and, unlike *The Irony of American History, The Icon and the Axe* is rich in historical detail. In spite of some shortcomings in his application of Niebuhr's irony, Billington does demonstrate that it can be used to understand the Russian past, which seems so different from the American experience, that part of the history of both countries can be perceived as the unintended consequences of purposive human action.[57]

Niebuhrian and closely related forms of irony have been used by a wide variety of European historians from ancient times until the present.[58] Among historical theorists such as Hegel and Marx, irony can be found in the nexus between determinism and freedom. In the case of Weber that irony is more clearly Niebuhrian because the structure of necessity is looser, allowing human action more autonomy and bringing human responsibility to the center of our attention. Among the historians proper, the examples here suggest that it has most commonly been applied to active moments of the past, moments when people consciously sought to bring about public changes of one kind or another. Athenians seeking to expand dramatically their imperialist democracy, French aristocratic reformers and nonaristocratic revolutionaries attempting to dismantle the Old Regime, English Puritans trying to save souls and impose a great reformation, German generals intending to use Hitler to re-create their own power and young Nazis hoping to find in him a leader to undo the horrors of their childhood, and Russian Bolsheviks carrying out the most thorough of all European revolutions — all acted so as to bring about unintended consequences, and all have been seen by some historians as responsible, to varying degrees, for the discrepancy between their intentions and the consequences of their behavior.

All of these ironic actions have been broad in scope, national or at least public in character, and led by established figures or a revolutionary elite. In American history Niebuhrian irony has been an important way of understanding the private actions of common people as well as public movements. Examples of ironic descriptions of the actions of ordinary European people, particularly in private actions, seem to be rare.[59] This may be in part a result of a bias toward public affairs on the part of historians of Europe or of a tendency on their part to perceive the masses as passive. The failure of historians to present those masses as ironically creating their own lives may also reflect the relatively little hope on the part of most Europeans that they could affect their own fate. If this is in fact an indication that European middle- and lower-class people have had less of a sense that it lay within their power to attempt, individually to change the circumstances under which they live, it constitutes one explanation for why Niebuhrian irony is a particularly appropriate way of perceiving the human dimension of the American past, in which heightened expectations seem to have engendered more such private efforts.

If historians of Europe have tended not to see the common people as active agents of history, when they have turned to the elites whom they did regard as active they have frequently perceived them ironically. Those historians discussed here seem to have achieved to different degrees that combination of empathy with and critical distance from their subjects which Niebuhrian irony requires. This may reflect the complex image of human beings as inwardly divided that has long been growing in European culture. The ironic perception of history is implicit in that image, an image that only recently has begun to be a major factor in American historical culture.

# III. Irony and American History

It is at once true that irony is particularly appropriate to American history and that American historians in general have been slow to adopt it as a way of perceiving our past. In this chapter I shall first try to suggest some of the ways in which American culture and American conditions foster ironic behavior in order to indicate why irony is an especially suitable concept for the study of the history of the United States. This will be followed by a discussion of several American historians — scholars who wrote in the nineteenth and early twentieth centuries — who made use of irony. The chapter will conclude with a brief consideration of some of the changes in the climate of opinion in recent decades that have fostered ironic visions of America.

## 1. Ironic America

Americans have been especially given to high aspirations and great activism; American culture has been reluctant to accept the realities of individual human limitation and failure. As a result, although much of our past invites ironic interpretation, only recently, since we have come to taste failure and feel the limitations of our power, and only since we have come to integrate some of the complexities of European culture, have many of our historians begun to see that past ironically. If the current form of that ironic perception originated in America among scholars newly impressed with the potential for evil among human beings in general, it has persisted among others, who have come to see particular evils in an America in which poverty and injustice continue to exist in the midst of great

61

national wealth and power. Before the first of these groups of historians appeared after the Second World War, the very optimism and activism that induced ironic behavior tended to obscure ironic perceptions, which require at least some distance from the turmoils of activism and at the most a very tempered optimism. To be sure, some of our best novelists and poets have long seen the American experience ironically, but the study of history lags behind the literary cutting edge of our culture.[1]

Because Americans have had more power individually and collectively over their destiny, and even greater illusions of such power, than other peoples, irony is a peculiarly appropriate way of distinguishing the general character of American history from that of other nations, not in terms of any absolute uniqueness, but through the intensification of certain common human tendencies. The American experience has been marked by a high level of expectation and an intense purposefulness in public and private life. Heightened expectations and increased purposefulness have been extremely energizing and productive in America, but what they have produced has often not been what was intended. The actuality of fulfillment, collective as well as individual, for many Americans has not kept up with the expectations that actuality encouraged.[2] These contradictions foster irony. The ironic sources of the unintended outcome of much purposeful action in America have frequently lain in the very illusions of power and freedom that have stimulated action, and in the false picture of social reality that has encouraged attempts to change that reality with insufficient regard for the difficulties involved. Until recently, however, there has been enough success to sustain these irony-inducing illusions that led Americans to continue to act so as to produce unintended consequences while at the same time blocking the emergence of an ironic consciousness of the process.

A comment by Roger L. Shinn suggests the unusual degree to which purposive action was involved in the origins of the United States. He relates the purposefulness of the founding of America to the persistence of an "American dream" in terms that suggest how appropriate irony may be to our collective life.

> Never in history, we may guess, did a nation get underway more deliberately, more self-consciously, than did the American nation. Despite diversity, despite ethnic variety, despite a wide range of social and personal habits, a people of this continent became a nation with a fervent sense of destiny. From 1620 until today they have sought vast purposes, aware that much of the world was watching, aware that great processes of history

centered in them. From the beginning there has been an American dream. Call it a glorious vision or call it foolish hokum, surely it is there.[3]

A nation that was deliberately founded and that persistently believed in its special destiny and universal significance was bound to suffer exaggerated expectations and illusions of "chosenness" that foster ironic behavior.

Niebuhr himself describes some of the American characteristics that lead us to act so as to contradict our own intentions. Many of these are simply exaggerations of pretensions common to modern European societies. Belief in the inevitable growth of human knowledge and progress, and in America as the exemplar of that progress, is one of those pretensions. Like all modern liberal cultures, America's culture has for the most part rejected the doctrine of original sin in favor of the irony-inducing pretense to "objectivity," the belief that we can keep selfish interests from affecting our understanding. Another major source of irony "lies in the tremendous preoccupation of our own technical culture with the problem of gaining physical security against the hazards of nature. Since our nation has carried this preoccupation to a higher degree of consistency than any other we are naturally more deeply involved in the irony."[4] Since Niebuhr wrote this it has become clear how deep this irony is; our technological efforts to protect ourselves from the hazards of nature have themselves become greater threats to human survival than nature itself.

From the beginning of our history we have tended to think of ourselves as a covenanted people, a people with a peculiar relationship to God, specially selected to fulfill a divine purpose. We have conceived of ourselves as "called out by God to create a new humanity."[5] That new humanity was originally to be organized in a specifically religious community; later it was to be the new democratic man; but in either form America was ordained to carry out God's intentions for the future of the human race.

Related to our pretense of having been specially chosen by God is our conviction of our own peculiar freedom from sin. Niebuhr notes that "the illusions of a unique innocence were not confined to our earliest years," and he nicely summarizes how our pretensions to innocence differ from the pretensions of some other nations. "Every nation has its own form of spiritual pride. . . . American self-appreciation could be matched by similar sentiments in other nations. But every nation has its own peculiar version. Our version is that our nation turned its back upon the vices of Europe and made a new beginning."[6]

Among the European vices that we thought we had avoided were social conflict and the guilt-inducing conscious use of power. "Our own culture is schizophrenic upon the subject of power. Sometimes it pretends that a liberal society is a purely rational harmony of interests." This pretense has induced ironic behavior because it is an expression of an illusion of innocence that blinds us to inequities of power in our society. The refusal in America to acknowledge significant conflict between social groups "creates a culture in which nothing is officially known about power, however desperate may be the power struggles within it." As a result we distrust the overt power of government that is the only kind we recognize, while we largely ignore the covert power of interest groups and corporations that influence our society enormously and produce much actual conflict.[7]

Power has been a source of ironic American behavior in another sense. D. W. Brogan describes our "illusion of omnipotence . . . the illusion that the world must go the American way if the Americans want it strongly enough and give firm orders to their agents to see that it is done." Richard Hofstadter points out that we had "a long history that encouraged our belief that we have an almost magical capacity to have our way in the world, that the national will can be made entirely effective, as against other peoples, at a relatively small price. . . . From the beginning of our national life, our power to attain national goals on which we were determined was in effect irresistible — *within* our chosen, limited continental theater of action." Until recently our history fostered pretensions to limitless power. "Free security, easy expansion, inexpensive victories, decisive triumphs — such was almost our whole experience with the rest of the world down to the twentieth century." Only since the Second World War has America "experienced the full reality of what all the other great nations have long known — the situation of limited power. The illusion of American omnipotence remained, but the reality of American preponderance was gone."[8] This belief in the invincibility of our power had been an illusion even in the nineteenth century, when we were the dominant nation within a limited arena. Even then it was a source of ironic behavior. Since America has come to act on a world stage in the twentieth century, the ironies that flow from our pretensions to invincibility have become ever more painful.

Niebuhr points out how our irony-inducing inability to recognize the realities of social enmity within our society has been fostered by two other tendencies in addition to our illusions of innocence in regard to power. One of these is the extreme individualism of our values that tends to blind us to the ways in which individuals are dependent upon communities and to obscure the ways in which class and group conflict shape individual lives.[9] But even greater sources of our failure to face the realities of power conflict within our society are our productivity and prosperity.

For Niebuhr this economic success is one of the most important roots of the irony of American history. Our national wealth has been in part responsible for the rigidity of many of our attitudes, rigidities that can lead to ironic blindness. Because of our sense of being a chosen people we tend to see our prosperity as earned and deserved rather than "to recognize the fortuitous and the providential element in our good fortune." Our wealth reinforces our pretensions to a special virtue. The confusion of virtue and prosperity "created a preoccupation with the material circumstances of life which expressed a more consistent bourgeois ethos than that of even the most advanced nation of Europe." Wealth, combined with our bourgeois ethos, has created a situation in which it seems as if "every ethical and social problem of a just distribution of the privileges of life is solved by so enlarging the privileges that either an equitable distribution is made easier, or a lack of equity is rendered less noticeable." Niebuhr points out that although this approach has led to an "amelioration of social tensions" it also "has created moral illusions about the ease with which the adjustment of interests to interests can be made in human society. This has imparted a quality of sentimentality to both our religious and our secular, social and political theories." Insofar as these theories have incorporated such illusions they have been sources of irony whenever they have been applied in efforts to reform social and political relationships, because those illusions obscured the perception of the reality of conflict and seemed to confirm our pretensions to innocence: "we have thus far sought to solve all our problems by the expansion of our economy. This expansion cannot go on forever and ultimately we must face some vexatious issues of social justice in terms which will not differ too greatly from those which the wisest nations of Europe have been forced to use."[10]

The sources of irony, then, in Niebuhr's account of the American situation are many. The conviction that we are a specially chosen people, rooted in both our religious origins and Enlightenment foundations, induces great national expectations and makes even failure a sign of a special covenant, a most potent illusion for inducing ironic behavior.[11] Pretenses to both power and virtue have been fostered by our sense of being a peculiarly blessed people. Because, first, of our distance from Europe and, in this century, our great power, we have been able to indulge until very recently in the illusion that we can overcome any external obstacle. Our prosperity has enabled us to retain the pretense that social harmony and justice have been achieved in America. Because our marketplace ideology, involving as it does an illusion of equal, voluntary, "innocent" participation by all individuals, has fostered great national wealth and much private prosperity, it has obscured the realities of poverty, exploitation, and social conflict in America, allowing us to persist in the pretense that we have transcended the social problems that plague other nations. Such pretensions work ironically to prevent us from dealing effectively with the social realities they obscure. Beliefs in progress and perfectibility induce exaggerated expectations and a high degree of purposive action, but such energizing illusions blind us to the real difficulties of making accomplishment meet aspirations and lead to unintended consequences.

Other historians present evidence that these irony-inducing factors affect not only our behavior as a nation but also the private lives of middle- and working-class Americans. For the most part irony is a concept relevant to the actions of men of power and wealth or intellectuals. As we have seen, in European historiography irony has been used mostly in dealing with large national or group activities led by such men. One sense in which irony may be more applicable to America than to Europe is in the way in which American productivity, economic fluidity, and prosperity have provided many common people with more choices and more possibility of control over their own lives — along with illusions of greater freedom than they really have had — and many inducements to pretensions that foster ironic behavior.

In a perceptive essay Page Smith has called attention to the widespread evidence of unhappiness in the midst of opportunity in American history, a situation that suggests the presence of irony. He urges us to face the fact that "anxiety and despair, as much as confidence and optimism, have characterized our history from the beginning. The anxiety quotient has always been abnormally high in American history. Indeed this higher level of anxiety and larger admixture of despair may well distinguish Americans from all other people in history." In America optimism and energy were related to anxiety and despair. In the nineteenth century, "beneath the strident optimism, the boastings, the frantic expansion, were endless defeats and disappointments, pinched and marginal lives, desperate and perpetually defeated dreams." America has been proud of its flexible and democratic structure, but the virtues of such a structure have produced much unhappiness: "the mobility and the classlessness which characterized American life were productive of

the cruelest anxieties." Anxiety and despair are products of the same
characteristics of American culture that have so often been
celebrated. The openness, the opportunity, the competition that
stimulated so much energetic activity have also produced much
misery. Americans sought to quiet their anxiety by accomplishment,
but frequently, since no accomplishment can live up to the fantasy
of success engendered by American dreams, much real accomplishment appeared subjectively inadequate and failed to still the anxiety. American culture offered little to relieve either the universal anxieties of people or those that the culture itself provoked.
There was "virtually nothing. The family, the community, and
the Will; the naked and fearful Will which said we shall inhabit this
inhospitable earth; we shall make it flower and bear fruit."[12] The
reliance upon the individual will was no comfort; in the context of
American competition it was more of a source of anxiety than an
answer to it. There was, indeed, no explanation for failure, a situation that may have energized people and contributed to American
economic growth, but also one that led to much wretchedness. The
ironic implications of this are that Americans have suffered from
their ambitions and expectations; they have been led to believe that
anything was possible to the individual will — an illusion of power
that has induced them repeatedly to seek unattainable goals and to
be dissatisfied with those which they achieved. Surely these are
unintended consequences of American values and assumptions.

David Potter also suggests that competition and mobility, which
he finds at the root of the American national character, have produced unsought outcomes. He observes that the behavioral scientists, whose work he integrates with that of historians, agree "that
the American character is in large measure a group of responses to
an unusually competitive situation." The mobility that marks that
situation may produce results similar to the anxiety and despair that
Smith finds in Americans.

The individual, driven by the belief that he should never rest content in his existing station and knowing that society demands advancement from him as proof of his merit, often feels stress and
insecurity and is left with no sense of belonging either in the station to which he advances or in the one from which he set out. . . .
there is a dawning realization that both our insistence upon
mobility and our denial of status have been carried to excess. The
fierceness of the mobility race generates tensions too severe for

some people to bear, and fear of failure in this race generates a
sense of insecurity which is highly injurious.[13]

It is important to recognize that both Smith and Potter assume a
basically benign image of American society. Their attention is not
focused on those who have been the worst off: blacks and other
racial minorities, women and the poor, people situated so that they
could not take advantage of those opportunities which America offered. They find anxiety and despair, tensions and insecurity among
those Americans who have been fortunate enough to be able to participate in upward mobility (although, of course, the disadvantaged
have also been subject to those feelings), those whose circumstances
have allowed them to share and act on the heightened expectations
of American life. Competitive mobility up the social scale was made
a normative expectation for many people in the society. The hope of
that mobility energized Americans and may have been a factor in
our great economic growth in the nineteenth century. But from the
point of view of many individual participants, that mobility was
ironic. If faith in the possibility of improving one's condition was
sustained by a degree of actual upward mobility, it was never possible for everyone to move up. If many experienced at least some advance, only a very few could move up as dramatically as the dream
suggested. Yet all were expected to try, and the governing ideology
of mobility allowed for no other explanation for failure than personal inadequacy. Under these circumstances many Americans suffered from culturally induced illusions of their capacity for individual advancement and in pursuing that advancement acted
ironically in that their own behavior led them to anxiety, despair,
tension, and insecurity.
    If the human condition induces illusions and ironic behavior, the
conditions of American life do so with a particular force. The conviction that we are a nation especially chosen by God to carry out a
mission — of changing content — for all humanity, makes it difficult
for us realistically to assess our strengths and weaknesses; it leads us
to act beyond our capacity while frequently denying the evil consequences that sometimes flow from those actions. For over three-and-
a-half centuries we have managed to think of ourselves as a young,
innocent people; illusions of innocence allow us to pursue the goals
of power and wealth by the same means as those used by other nations while believing that we are somehow above the guilt that those
means generate in others. Our international activities for most of
our history were largely confined to conflicts with the original in-
habitants and weaker nations of this hemisphere, convincing us that

our power was invincible until, when we emerged on the world
scene, it turned out that it nearly was — but only nearly, as our recent experiences have been teaching us. Illusions of power have also
infected our domestic life. Political liberty in our history has frequently been defined in terms of limiting the overt power of government; this has left us vulnerable to the covert power of economic
interest groups and corporations, a kind of social power that our
sense of national innocence has made us reluctant to face. Our inability to confront the inequities of power and wealth in our social
system has been in part sustained by the very prosperity that that
system produced and by the relatively widespread enjoyment of at
least some of its fruits. That prosperity has also fostered the illusion
of many individual Americans that it was possible for them to greatly improve their condition through hard work and frugality. This illusion may have been a pretense built upon a reality, but the expectation far outran the real possibility of advancement, and the many
Americans who have acted on that expectation have frequently
twisted their lives in unintended ways.[14]

What I have tried to indicate in this section in an impressionistic
way are some of the conditions of American life that induce ironic
behavior. Most of these conditions have been present from the
beginning of our history, but only recently have many historians
begun to write of our past in ironic terms. This is because most
historians have themselves been caught up in our national pretensions, illusions, and exaggerated expectations. In the last few
decades, because events have made our national limitations more
visible and European influences have made our consciousness more
complex, many historians have come to reach a greater critical
distance, a distance that, combined with the empathy for America
that most of them retain, has made irony possible. Still, some earlier
Americans were able to rise above our endemic optimism and look
with an ironic eye on our national experience. This has been
preeminently true of writers such as Melville, but a few nineteenth-
and early twentieth-century historians were also able to achieve an
ironic vision.

## 2. Nineteenth-Century Historians: Francis Parkman, Richard Hildreth, and Henry Adams

Most of the major American historians of the mid-nineteenth century, before the study of history became professionalized in the
universities, were wealthy literary men. Their approach to history

has aptly been characterized as romantic. David Levin, the leading modern student of these scholars, finds something similar to Niebuhrian irony in the way in which they dealt with the role of human intentionality in the advancement of civilization and liberty. Such historians as George Bancroft and Francis Parkman held a fundamental belief in the certainty of progress, but progress did not move in a simple straight line. It advanced rather by indirection. Providence made use of evil agents in furthering its own ends in a process that sometimes seems to resemble the Niebuhrian pattern. When Parkman writes of the aid to the development of liberty unintentionally provided by Louis XV, or Bancroft of that of George III, their histories appear to fit that pattern, and Levin specifically refers to the device they use as irony. But what we have here is a form of irony close to the Niebuhrian, in the sense that the Hegelian cunning of reason is close to it; the evil characters' actions produce good in spite of their contrary intentions because they are unconscious agents of a beneficent providence, an agency that Levin takes care to point out does not remove from them their moral responsibility for the evil of their actions.[15]

Levin especially emphasizes Parkman's use of this kind of irony, particularly in regard to his treatment of the relationship between French Catholics and Indians, referring to his *The Jesuits in North America* as a book containing "an elaborate ironic scheme." This work is filled with episodes showing the Indians' misunderstanding of Catholic doctrine in ways that reveal the weaknesses that Parkman sees, from a Protestant perspective, in that doctrine itself. An example of such irony is the way in which "the Jesuits find that their zeal in baptizing the dying naturally convinces many Indians that baptism *causes* death." Levin cites a number of passages in which Parkman demonstrates "how the priests best objects of wonder . . . and the highest truths they have brought with them are turned against them." He praises the skill and subtlety of Parkman's use of this kind of irony. Its effect in part is to expose the similarities between the Indians' "desire for good 'medicine'" and the Jesuits' belief "that saints and angels were always at hand with temporal succors for the faithful."[16] This, of course, is like Niebuhrian irony. The Jesuits' failure is presented in terms of their own intentions, and that failure is caused in part by their own faults—faults from a Protestant point of view—as the instruments they try to use to convert the Indians are turned against them. Of course, all of this takes place within a providential framework that compromises the ultimate responsibility of the ironic actor (which might be said of Niebuhr's own use of his irony), but Levin seems to be arguing here that Parkman's irony helps him transcend that framework aesthetically if not morally.

If we turn to *The Jesuits in North America* itself, Parkman's larger irony is particularly clear when he concludes that "the cause of the failure of the Jesuits is obvious. The guns and tomahawks of the Iroquois were the ruin of their hopes." Had the Iroquois not stopped the Jesuits, New France would have become very powerful. She would not have been able to halt the inevitable victory of the agent of liberty and progress, England, when the ultimate conflict came, but she would have been strong enough to make the victory more difficult and compromise the outcome. Unintentionally, then, the Iroquois served the purpose of libertarian progress: "Liberty may thank the Iroquois, that, by their insensate fury, the plans of her adversay were put to nought, and a peril and a woe averted from her future." But the Iroquois were agents of an inevitable progress, one that would have triumphed without their unintended aid. "The contest on this continent between Liberty and Absolutism was never doubtful; but the triumph of the one would have been dearly brought, and the downfall of the other incomplete."[17]

As noted above, Parkman's irony is very similar to the Niebuhrian pattern. This is particularly true of his treatment of the Jesuits themselves where he shows how the very instruments they tried to use to convert the Indians worked against them. His presentation of the Iroquois victory over the French is also ironic in that it is seen from the perspective of the English, the agents of liberty and progress, but in this case especially, Parkman's irony is compromised by his belief in the providential triumph that makes the actions of his human characters ultimately peripheral. For present purposes there is something else missing; the irony is not applied to Americans or their English forebears. They are the carriers of progress, favored by Providence. Parkman's irony is turned only upon the enemies of liberty and those who contribute unintentionally to its development. The moral function of his irony is limited; it does serve to humanize characters he sees as ultimately evil, or at least antiprogressive, but it is not used to gain critical distance from his heroes, those in the main line of progressive growth. Although Parkman's irony comes close to the Niebuhrian form, it is not used to present American history critically.

That irony can be found in the work of Richard Hildreth, the most critical of the early American historians, is not surprising. His peculiar combination of liberal, democratic principles with a tendency to favor conservative, Federalist policies was conducive to the use of various ironic forms.[18]

Hildreth uses much rhetorical irony, particularly in his first volume. One theme to which he repeatedly applies it is the Puritans' treatment of the Indians. He quotes John Robinson's reaction to an early conflict in Plymouth: "'Oh, how happy a thing it would have been,' he wrote in a letter to the colonists, 'that you had converted some before you killed any.'" King Phillip's War, in which the Indians suffered a great defeat, paradoxically led some of them to accept the religion of their Puritan enemies. "The work of conversion was now again renewed, and, after such overwhelming proofs of Christian superiority, with somewhat greater success." In a comment upon the conflict in the 1680s between Massachusetts and the Crown, which resulted in the loss of the Massachusetts Bay Colony Charter, Hildreth implies a more substantial ironic interpretation, one close to the Niebuhrian form: "all the zeal and obstinancy of the theocratic party had been aroused by the present crises — a zeal resulting, as hot zeal often does, in the ultimate loss of what it was so anxious to save."[19]

There is little irony in Hildreth's treatment of such later events as the Revolution, but his interpretation of the War of 1812 easily lends itself to an ironic reading. He remarks on how inauspicious the circumstances under which the war began were from an American point of view, although it was the United States that chose to go to war. There was a general lack of preparation for the conflict and it was unpopular. The war was the result of the Republican policy toward the British that failed to recognize that peace requires compromise. Jefferson had refused to make any of the needed concessions to Britain because of his hatred of that country. He pursued a very rigid policy that had consequences he never intended. "In adopting this stringent course, Jefferson did not expect nor intend to bring on war; for with war must come armies, navies, and public debts, the objects of his wholesome though somewhat excessive dread. Yet that such a stickling for the extreme of right, such an irritation constantly kept up, must lead inevitably to war, the Federalists had foreseen and foretold from the beginning." In addition, "under Madison's feeble and vacillating rule" a real "war party had suddenly crystalized, a natural and necessary deposit from the waters of bitterness so long mingled and stirred by Jefferson's hand." The congressional leaders of the war party produced a profound transformation of power in American politics. "A political revolution, quite as complete in its results, as the downfall of the Federalists, producing, in fact, the entire re-establishment of the Federal policy, and that by men who would have shuddered at the imputation of Federalism, was brought about so quietly and silently,

that not only the public at large, but many of the parties more immediately concerned, were quite unaware what a change was going
on." The consequences of these actions were not intended by the actors:

> The ultimate results of the new policy, few or none of which
> were foreseen by those who made it; the navy and army on their
> present footing; our costly system of harbor defense; above all,
> the extension of domestic manufactures, with a corresponding ex-
> tension of tariff protection, served with many to gild this revolu-
> tion with a reflected luster not its own. Founded as it was on a war
> with Great Britain, begun without forethought, and carried on
> without either energy or success, it imposed, at the time an im-
> mense cost on the country in money, blood, anxiety, and alarm;
> temporary indeed, and now forgotten, but terrible enough to
> those who suffered.[20]

This is an interpretation in terms of Niebuhrian irony. Because of
self-righteousness and prejudice against Britain, Jefferson and other
senior Republicans refused to make the concessions that their policy
of seeking peacefully to protect American rights required. Instead,
they contributed to the creation of an atmosphere in which younger
men came to desire war and older statesmen were unable to prevent
them from driving the country into hostilities. But the war was
ironic from the point of view of the goals of young as well as older
Republicans; its long-run effect was to turn the country toward
Federalist policies. In addition, the immediate consequences were
certainly not those sought by the war party. The Treaty of Ghent
did not resolve the issues that had led to conflict.[21] The war that the
senior statesmen of the Republican party unintentionally created
because of their own weaknesses produced results sought neither by
them nor by their more warlike younger colleagues. Certainly, insofar as these Republican leaders were very much in the mainstream
of American history, Hildreth's irony comes closer to the critical
perspective on the vitals of that history than does Parkman's irony
that is applied to Indians and French Jesuits, but the War of 1812
was something of an anomaly in the American experience, hence
Hildreth's irony does not cut so deeply as it might.

Among nineteenth-century American historians none made more
use of irony than did the greatest of them, Henry Adams. Irony appeared as a rhetorical device and as a basic structural element in
Adams's writings; it was fundamental to his way of seeing the world.
Irony was central to his perception of American history, to his
response to modern civilization, and ultimately to his conception of

the human condition. Although his philosophic predispositions led
Adams toward the use of an irony of fate, the richness and diversity
of his irony was such that the Niebuhrian as well as other forms of it
can be found in his work. A number of Adams scholars — particularly Henry B. Rule — have previously discussed his irony, so that in
spite of his importance my consideration of him here will be brief.[22]

Adams's use of irony in his earlier, journalistic writings tended to
be satiric and rhetorical. In his novels, and in his hostile biography
of John Randolph, it became more closely integrated with the narrative and the development of character. Toward the end of his life,
particularly in the *Education*, Adams turned a severe, biting irony
on the world around him and, to some extent, on himself. At this
stage his irony became a general critique of the degeneration of
American values and the morally inappropriate system of rewards in
American society. Finally, Adams came to a vision of how the expansion of human power over nature, so well developed in our
civilization, was leading that civilization to ruin. This insight, which
is so familiar to us today, is described by Rule in terms suggestive of
a Niebuhrian dilemma on a grand scale. "What Adams saw was
perhaps the greatest irony in the history of man: science, created by
man as his servant, had become the master; the creature was gather-
ing strength to destroy the creator."[23]

However, for present purposes, the most interesting of Adams's
use of irony are those to be found in his monumental *History of the
United States of America During the Administrations of Thomas
Jefferson and James Madison.*[24] There are three overlapping ironic
patterns in this work. The first of these is a kind of propitious fate,
more like a deterministic irony than a Niebuhrian one. In spite of
all the divisive actions of men in this early period of our history, the
country moved toward greater national unity.[25] Much closer to the
Niebuhrian form is Adams's treatment of Jefferson. His attitude
toward Jefferson was one appropriate to irony: he had great respect
for him as the symbol and leader of American democracy, but he
was at the same time highly critical of Jefferson's actual perfor-
mance as chief executive. His summary of Jefferson's presidency
reveals a clear Niebuhrian irony.

> He had undertaken to create a government which should in-
> terfere in no way with private action, and he had created one
> which interfered directly in the concerns of every private citizen
> in the land. He had come into power as the champion of State-
> rights, and had driven States to the verge of armed resistance. He
> had begun by claiming credit for stern economy, and ended by
> exceeding the expenditure of his precedessors. He had invented a

policy of peace, and his invention resulted in the necessity of fighting at once the two greatest powers in the world.

Adams denies that these unintended consequences were wholly Jefferson's fault, but the implication is clear that he was to some degree responsible for them. "That the blame for this failure rested wholly upon Jefferson might be doubted; but no one felt more keenly than he the disappointment under which his old hopes and ambitions were crushed."[26] The qualities in Jefferson that led him to act so as to produce unintended consequences involved the kinds of pretensions that generally underlie Niebuhrian ironies. In Rule's words: "Jefferson's disasters were not due to the jealousy of the Gods, but to the pressure of events which he could not control because his pride and dogmatism prevented him from understanding them."[27]

There seems to be a contradiction here between the irony of fate, which controls the first pattern in which America develops national unity in spite of human actions that would tear it apart, and the account of Jefferson as a responsible agent producing by his own actions unintended consequences. The third, and largest, ironic pattern accounts for this apparent discrepancy. Natural forces, not the will of men, fundamentally control the world. Wise men — Adams's ideal "practical statesmen" like Gallatin — have the humility to understand their powerlessness and accommodate themselves to those forces. That accommodation gives them a marginal ability to affect events, to move with the forces of history rather than against them. Ironic men, because of pride and illusions of power, try to impose their will upon the world without understanding the pressures that govern it. As a result their actions produce consequences they did not intend.[28] Thus Adams's irony in *The History* is similar to that of other historical thinkers who see human development as largely governed by forces beyond human control, but allow people some ability to affect their fate to the extent that they can understand and accommodate themselves to those factors.

Henry Adams made more use of irony than any American historian before the twentieth century. Some of that irony was close to the Niebuhrian form and some of it was applied to developments in the mainstream of American history. Adams's attitude toward his country was ambivalent in a way appropriate to irony. He basically accepted democratic values and shared the hope that America would prove to be a land uniquely suited to the flowering of those values. But he also had the feeling, as did some of his forefathers, that he had not been dealt with fairly by his country. More important, he was in a position to be profoundly skeptical about the direc-

tion in which American society was moving in the late nineteenth
century. He was deeply sensitive to the contradiction between the
early promise of American democracy and the realities of the Gilded
Age. Behind the developments of that period he could see the threat
that civilization itself was beginning to pose to human survival as
men gained greater and greater mastery over nature without increasing their moral ability to use that power wisely.

But Adams was unique among historians of America. The grand-
son and great-grandson of presidents, he was an aristocrat even
among the other gentleman historians of Boston. His personality,
ability, and polish, combined with his unique heritage, gave him a
moral distance from the America of his day that no other historian
could match. The democratic money-making and exploitation of
the Gilded Age could only disgust him, particularly since he had the
courage to contrast that democracy with the expectations of earlier
American democrats. Above all, Adams was a man whose cultural
sophistication came naturally; as American as he was, he was more
like a European in that respect. His sense of complexity and contradiction, his freedom from optimism, set him apart as much as did
his descent. The events of the twentieth century have led a number
of historians to an ironic vision of America; Henry Adams came to
his ironic vision much earlier, by an interior route all his own.[29]

## 3.   Early Twentieth-Century Historians:
## Carl Becker and Others

Irony did not often appear in the works of early twentieth-century
American historians, and when it did Henry May has suggested that
its presence was frequently unintentional.[30] Among the historians of
that period only Carl Becker could characteristically have written
that "history is profoundly ironical."[31] Becker is widely regarded as
having had one of the finest historical minds of his generation;[32] a
biographer has compared his use of irony to Henry Adams's. There
was also a connection between Becker and Reinhold Niebuhr in that
the Christian ironist admired the very secular and rationalistic
historian.[33]

Becker wrote European as well as American history and used
various kinds of irony in both fields. His important article "The
Dilemma of Diderot" has been described as marked by "gentle
irony," and his masterpiece, *The Heavenly City of the 18th Century
Philosophers* also used that device.[34] The irony in these works involves a contradiction between the purposes of Enlightenment

philosophy and the conclusions to which it led. The philosophes, "who with so much assurance and complacent wit have set out with the rule of reason to rebuild an unlovely universe to nature's design," encountered as a result of their premises a profound paradox. They assumed "that men and nature were one. But if man was only a part of nature, if all his action and all his thinking were determined by forces beyond his control, then 'society' must be 'natural' too; superstition was in that case as natural as enlightenment, the ancient regime in France no less a state of nature than primitive Gaul or second century Rome."[35] Even if the consequences here are only in the realm of ideas, this is still an ironic pattern similar to Niebuhr's. Since the philosophes had a strong ethical impulse to change society through the use of reason, this conclusion was hardly where they had intended reason to lead them.

The heart of Becker's contribution to American history lies in his work on the period of the Revolution, and a form of irony similar to the Niebuhrian can be found in some of his accounts of how colonists seeking to protect their rights as Englishmen unintentionally produced a War for Independence from England. This irony can clearly be seen in his delightful historical fantasy, "The Spirit of '76."[36] The style of the piece is light and humorous. Even its title has the ring of irony in that *The Spirit of '76* is a phrase that conjures up great patriotic enthusiasm, but Becker's story emphasizes the caution and hesitancy of many revolutionaries. Although it is a fantasy, Becker's obviously serious interpretive intention and the general factual accuracy of the piece, in spite of the fictitious nature of the particular characters, justify treating it as a substantial historical commentary.

"The Spirit of '76" contains three central figures, each representing a different response to the events that preceded the Revolution: Jeremiah Wynkoop, a rich Dutch-American merchant who becomes increasingly, if reluctantly, involved in the resistance to Britain; his father-in-law, a loyalist; and the narrator, a friend with fairly advanced rebel attitudes. Becker presents each of these men sympathetically and uses their differing points of view to set off the ironies in the other positions.

The central irony is the unintentional contribution that Wynkoop made to the movement for revolution and independence. The fantasy begins with the end of the French and Indian War, when Wynkoop believed that Britain and America were closely and properly wedded to each other. When the troubles over the Stamp and Sugar Acts began, Wynkoop was distressed by the intrusion of Parliament into American affairs. In a comment on the anti-Stamp

Act rioting Becker puts some ironically prophetic words in the mouth of Old Nicholas, the father-in-law. "I warn you that liberty is a sword that cuts two ways, and if you can't defend your rights against ministerial oppression without stirring the 'people' you will soon be confronted with the necessity of defending your privileges against the encroachment of the mob on the Bowling Green." When the Stamp Act was repealed, Wynkoop felt that he had got the better of the argument with his father-in-law and bragged of the success of American resistance. The passage and subsequent revocation of the Townshend duties produced much the same kind of exchange.[37]

In regard to Mr. Wynkoop's position in relation to the final crisis over the Boston Tea Party, Becker offers a comment that indicates an ironic view of the development of the situation up to that point. The narrator suggests that Mr. Wynkoop, who had just returned from the first Continental Congress, was in "low spirits . . . due to the uncomfortable feeling that he had been elbowed by circumstances into a position which he never intended to occupy." The narrator is anxious to bring Mr. Wynkoop along to a more advanced Whig position and so encourages the merchant's tendency to believe that he is not responsible for what had already happened and that the consequences of future action would be moderate: "What I counted on was a certain capacity in the man, I won't say for deceiving himself, but for convincing himself that what he strongly desired would somehow come to pass. I therefore did what I could to convince him, or rather to help him convince himself, that his past and present conduct was that of a wise and prudent man."[38]

Even after the battle of Lexington Mr. Wynkoop refused to face the reality of conflict with Britain. He agreed to serve in the Revolutionary provincial congress while still maintaining the moderate view and hoping that peace and unity between England and America might yet be restored.[39]

Wynkoop spent the winter of 1776 going over the events that had led to revolution in order to convince himself of the justice and necessity of independence and the propriety of his own role in what had happened. He "was only engaged in convincing himself that it had been from the first inevitable, that the situation that now confronted him was not of his making. His one aim from the first, he said, and he said it many times, was to prevent the calamity now impending. . . . Short of tamely submitting to the domination of Parliament, he was forever asking, what other course could America have followed but the one she had followed? What other course could he have followed?" He was now captive to his past; his previous actions committed him to further action: "this I think was the consideration of greatest weight with him; he could not deny his words and renounce his friends without losing his self respect."[40]

Becker's reluctant rebel finally brought himself to accept the idea of independence by developing the belief that "the Britain of his dreams was an illusion." In that case independence became acceptable. But Becker is too subtle to suggest that this amounted to the substitution of "reality" for dreams: "in the long winter of '76 Mr. Wynkoop repaired the illusions by which he lived, reconciling himself to the inevitable step."[41] The implication here is that, in moving from loyalty to Britain to support of American independence, Wynkoop exchanged one illusion for another.

Throughout Wynkoop argued, supported by the revolutionary narrator, that all he had done was what any honorable man would do in order to protect American rights while restraining the radicals. Becker offers another perspective on Wynkoop's actions in the person of Old Nicholas, who implied that perhaps his son-in-law bore more responsibility for what happened than he acknowledged. He saw the relationship of moderate Whigs like Wynkoop to the radicals rather differently from Wynkoop, suggesting that the radicals pulled the moderates along to independence rather than that the moderates had restrained the radicals. "'What I can't see,'" said Old Nicholas to Wynkoop, "'is why you have allowed the fanatics to run away with the cart.'"[42]

"The Spirit of '76" is a complex historical commentary in spite of its apparent simplicity. Becker offers more than one view of his Dutch merchant's role in the Revolutionary movement. In all of them it is clear that Wynkoop did not intend that his pre-Revolutionary activities lead to war and independence. Where the views differ, however, is over whether or not those activities unintentionally contributed to the development of the revolution Wynkoop did not want. He sought to avoid such responsibility and claimed that he only responded to the actions of the British ministers. The narrator supported that view, but from the beginning of the story Becker subtly discounts his objectivity by saying that he sought to lead Wynkoop into a more and more revolutionary posture, a project that would be furthered by encouraging Wynkoop's tendency to deny his responsibility for radical action. Similarly, Becker seems to undermine Mr. Wynkoop's account of his own actions by his comments on how he tried always to look at things in the best possible light, how he lived by illusions. But in the person of Old Nicholas he offers us a different perspective on the son-in-law's behavior. From the beginning Old Nicholas argues that protest will lead to treason,

that rather than Wynkoop's restraining the radicals, he was helping
them bring on the Revolution. The outcome would appear to provide considerable support for that view of the matter; always putting
the best face upon things and clinging to illusions about Britain as
long as possible, Mr. Wynkoop can be seen as playing an unconscious but active role in the development of the revolutionary
crises he wished to avoid. I am not suggesting that this is the only
reading that Becker intended, but it is clear that this is one of the
views implicit in his subtle and multifaceted story.

The interpretation I have found in Old Nicholas's perspective certainly seems to fit the pattern of Niebuhrian irony, but something is
missing. The pattern is there, but the tone is off. The style of the
fantasy can certainly be called ironical, but it is a light, playful
irony, one that lacks the moral bite of a Niebuhr. Surely, one could
say of this story that it suggests some very critical things about the
American Revolution and thus about American history. A moderate
revolutionary such as Wynkoop was able to come to the Revolution
only through self-deception and inadvertence, seeking to
manipulate the populace and their radical leaders, but being in the
end manipulated by them. Since he represents in a sense a kind of
middle-of-the-road mainstream, this could then be read as a critical
comment on the role of illusion and self-deception in American
history, one that could be seen as both sympathetic and critical. But
that is not at all what Becker's tone suggests. Although it is a bit
patronizing to Mr. Wynkoop, it does not indicate any deep criticism
of him. The implications of Becker's fantasy seem to have more to
do with the complexity of history and the self-delusion of people in
general than with the kind of moral critique of the American past
offered by Niebuhrian irony. The gentleness of Becker's irony was
certainly in part owing to his own personality, but it may also have
been a result of the limited nature of the Progressive critique of
America. In general, rather than criticizing America as such, the
Progressive historians attacked certain forces in America that they
saw as corrupting, compromising, or frustrating an American
dream that remained in its essence sound. If this reading of Becker's
tone is accurate, he is similar to most other earlier ironic historians
of America—except Adams and Vernon Parrington. Although his
irony was applied to events in the mainstream of American history,
it was usually not presented in such a way as to imply an ironic and
critical view of the American past in general.

As Becker lived through the complex and changing America of
the first half of the twentieth century, he moved back and forth between a cautious optimism and a moderately disillusioned pessimism

in response to passing events.[43] Occasionally, in his more pessimistic mood his ironic sense of what had happened to American democracy could become more cutting.than it generally was. When he looked at the late nineteenth century in this mood he could suggest, with more recent and more critical historians, that the inclusion of laissez faire in the democratic-liberal canon, in combination with industrialization, had led to consequences profoundly contradictory to the intentions of liberal, democratic Americans:

> Before the end of the nineteenth century it was obvious to the discerning that democracy had belied the hopes of its prophets. Instead of bringing in peace and good will, enlightenment and justice, an equitable distribution of wealth, and the spirit of fraternity, it had brought in, or at least had failed to keep out, political corruption, industrial brigandage, social oppression for the masses, and moral and intellectual hypocrisy on a scale rarely equalled and perhaps never surpassed. In short, liberty, for which liberals had so valiantly fought, had ironically given birth to a brood of mean-faced tyrants, and so far from walking hand in hand with equality, was to be found consorting chiefly, and secretly, with puffed and bedizened privilege.[44]

The spectacle of late nineteenth-century America also stimulated an ironic response from Parrington, a more narrowly "Progressive" historian than Becker. In general Parrington's work was marked by sharp contrasts between virtuous democrats and evil or reactionary representatives of wealth and privilege, but when he came to deal with the Gilded Age, during which the triumph of industrialization destroyed the agrarian, Jeffersonian republic he wished the United States to be, his disillusionment opened up for him a perspective on the ways in which the social evil he saw resulted in part from the development of the American democracy he loved. Parrington's account of the late nineteenth century is ironic precisely because he recognizes how the "capitalist buccaneers" who were characteristic of the period arose "out of the drab mass of plebian life." The exploitive energy that marked the Gilded Age was a legitimate product of the egalitarian spirit of the American past: "It was the ripe fruit of Jacksonian leveling."[45]

Parrington's recognition that the corruption and venality of the late nineteenth century were the results of some widely held earlier values and that the exploited majority as well as the exploiting minority shared in those values underlay a complex and multifaceted ironic vision. On one level irony could be found in the deterioration of the values themselves. The Gilded Age represented "an abundant harvest of those freedoms that America had long been struggling to achieve, and it was making ready the ground for later harvests that would be less to its liking. Freedom had become individualism, and individualism had become the inalienable right to preempt, to exploit, to squander. Gone were the old ideals along with the old restraints. . .with no social conscience, no concern for civilization, no heed for the future of the democracy it talked so much about, the Gilded Age threw itself into the business of money-getting." On another level was the development of an exploitive attitude toward government itself, "the expression in politics of the acquisitive instinct," which "assumes as the greatest good the shaping of public policy to promote private interests." Significantly, Parrington did not see this conception of government as the peculiar possession of the big capitalists. The small-time, middle-class promoter, "with his genial optimism and easy political ethics, was an epitome of the political hopes of the Gilded Age." Through such hopes "millions" were indirectly involved in the corruption of the period, although only for a few were those hopes to be fulfilled. The aspirations (and greed) of vast numbers of Americans had led to the acceptance of an exploitive attitude toward government as a part of the democratic ideal and to the destruction of communal restraints, but in contrast to the widespread expectations of the many only a limited number benefited substantially from governmental largess.[46]

Parrington describes this era as "The Great Barbecue," a feast intended by the American people for themselves. However, it was big-business, capitalist buccaneers who grew fat. Parrington carefully refrains from placing all the blame for these unwanted results of American democracy on them. "We may call them buccaneers if we choose, and speak of the great barbecue as a democratic debauch. But why single out a few when all were drunk? Whiskey was plentiful at barbecues. . . . To create a social civilization requires sober heads, and in this carousal of economic romanticism sober heads were few."[47]

The ironic pattern in this seems clear and deliberate. Americans, many Americans, but not all, allowed themselves to be caught up in "economic romanticism," indulged in the fantasy of hitting it rich and were willing to use the government to further that fantasy. Parrington makes it evident that he regards this not as an aberration in American culture, but rather as a direct outgrowth of the unrestrained, democratic individualism of such central developments as Jacksonianism and the frontier. He is sympathetic with the egalitarian opportunism of this romantic individualism but is at the same time critical of the lack of social ideals and communal sense that would have prevented the state from being turned into a kind of natural resource for general exploitation. That in the end only a relatively few drew large benefits from that exploitation was, in his eyes, an unintended outcome of the fantasy of the many and the unrestrained and irresponsible way in which they went about trying to realize that fantasy. The failure of that attempt, and the perversion of democracy that resulted from it, were not merely a product of the efforts of the privileged but a consequence of the drunken expectations of large numbers of Americans who allowed their greed and their exaggerated sense of their power as individuals to obscure older communal and restraining values.

But this inequality of benefit from the exploitation of government in the late nineteenth century was not the final level in Parrington's ironic account of the period. The ultimate outcome was to be the destruction of American individualism, the initial source of the whole process. The capitalistic ambitions of the American farmer that had led to the Great Barbecue were also in part responsible for this latter development.

> He had long been half middle-class, accounting unearned incre-
> ment the most profitable crop, and buying and selling land as if it
> were calico. And in consequence the vigorous individualism that
> had sprung from frontier conditions decayed with the passing of
> the frontier, and those who had lost in the gamble of preemption
> and exploitation were added to the growing multitude of the pro-
> letariat. It was from such materials supplemented by a vast influx
> of immigrants, that was fashioned the America we know today
> with its standardized life, its machine culture, its mass
> psychology — an America to which Jefferson and Jackson and Lin-
> coln would be strangers.[48]

This profoundly ironic vision transcends Parrington's own Progressive categories by recognizing that the unexpected and undesired outcome of the exploitive individualism of the Gilded Age was not the product merely of a capitalist conspiracy, but also of the capitalist in most Americans. He came to see the destruction of the Jeffersonian-agrarian ideal of democratic community, the America he revered, as in great measure the result of characteristics of the American farmer upon whom that ideal community was to be based. The individualistic, exploitive component of the American democratic ethos that was one major source of the strength of that ideology was also a cause of its degeneration and ultimately even of the deterioration of American individualism itself.[49] More than in any other earlier historian considered here save Henry Adams, this ironic vision lies close to the center of Parrington's conception of the American past as presented in this last, incomplete volume of his *Main Currents in American Thought*.


   Becker and Parrington can both be classified, more or less accurately, as Progressive historians, the major historiographic school of the earlier twentieth century. Although I have argued that irony is to be found in aspects of the work of both of them, irony is not in general a characteristic of Progressive history. This is true in part because of the dualistic nature of much of that history; the Progressives tended to see the American past as sharply divided between the forces of good and the forces of evil, inhibiting, if not entirely blocking, the perception of how evil can result from good intentions. In addition, I would argue that in general most of the Progressive historians shared too much of the American dream, were themselves too caught up in ideas of progress and American perfectiblity, to achieve the critical distance from the main thrust of our national history required for irony. To be sure, they were critical of many specific aspects of the American present and past, but they tended to see that which they opposed as uncharacteristic of America. They retained a basic faith in the peculiar virtues of the American people, in a special democratic destiny for America, and in at least some American institutions, which obscured ironic perceptions of the core of the American experience.[50] In this they were less critical, perhaps, than some of the consensus historians who followed them, whose political commitments were combined with a fundamentally more complex and contradictory view of the nature of man, a view that left them more open to irony.
   Later I shall examine irony in the writing of some consensus historians. Overlapping in time with these major historical categories are smaller groups of historians who share interpretations of particular important events. Certain major historical occurrences such as the Revolution and the Civil War have a historiographic development independent to a considerable degree of shifts in overall views of the American past.[51]
   Historians of the imperial school, such as Herbert Levi Osgood, George Lewis Beer, and Charles M. Andrews, reacted against the patriotic bias of many earlier accounts of the Revolution and wrote about the break with England in terms sympathetic to the mother country. There are in their works elements of irony. Andrews, for example, saw the very creation of the British Empire in North America as to a great degree unintended. England, "having ac-

quired colonies by action rather than intention," stumbled into losing them precisely as she tried to bind them more closely to herself
by shifting from the politically laissez faire doctrine of merchan-
tilism to the tighter controls of imperialism. Andrews describes the
final British step that provoked the Boston Tea Party and led to the
Revolution in terms appropriate to an ironic vision of the mother
country's behavior. "At this critical juncture, probably with the best
of intentions and with no realization of the ultimate outcome, Lord
North and his cabinet committed an irretrievable blunder."[52]

Interpretations that emphasize the role of human blunders in
historical events frequently have ironic implications. The revisionist
school of historians of the American Civil War, scholars such as
Avery O. Craven and James G. Randall, saw that great conflict as
largely the result of political blundering. For them that war was
"repressible" and "needless," but they also took account of the actions of "extremist" leadership, in their eyes evil men deliberately
doing evil, in bringing on the conflict, so that their interpretation is
not exclusively ironic, although it does include a recognition of
unintended consequences.[53]

## 4. Irony and Disillusionment in American Historical Consciousness

Irony was used by earlier historians of America, especially in
regard to parts of our past that did not fit well into their essentially
optimistic preconceptions. Parkman applied irony to the history of
the Jesuits in North America, men whose courage he admired, and
who represented a higher form of progress than the Indians they
sought to convert, but who were, in contrast to the English, a reactionary force. Hildreth, deeply sympathetic to the development of
American democracy, if less romantically so than other historians of
his time, applied it to the War of 1812, an event that appeared to be
something of a failure in the great success story of American history.
Henry Adams, a man whose family and life had complex relationships to the main drift of American history, had an ironic vision
closer to the center of his perceptions of the core of that history than
did any other historian considered in this chapter. Carl Becker, the
most subtle of Progressive historians, used a lighter irony to clarify
the ambiguities of the American Revolution. Irony enabled Vernon
Parrington to transcend his own Progressive categories when he confronted what happened to the Jeffersonian dream of an agrarian
republic in the industrial world of the late nineteenth century.

Other historians writing in the twentieth century on particular major issues saw new ambiguities in the Revolution and the Civil War, ambiguities that opened up the possibilities of ironic perceptions.

For the most part these ironic historical insights were largely individual visions; they did not in general represent the growth of an overall ironic consciousness of the American past. Parkman's ironic interpretation of the Jesuits, Hildreth's of the War of 1812, and Parrington's of the Gilded Age—all stand in contrast to the generally nonironic character of most of the history they wrote, and of their overall vision of the American past. If Adams's irony is considerably more central to his work, it is so to the extent that Adams stands apart from other historians of his time. The same can be said less forcefully of Becker. Still, there are three patterns in the historical writings of these men worth observing. One is a more or less direct connection between particularly sensitive individual historians. Carl Becker was deeply influenced by Henry Adams, an influence against which he struggled for much of his career. And, as pointed out earlier, Niebuhr much admired Becker, although here specific influence might be hard to demonstrate.[54] This suggests the possible existence of a minor line of continuity in American historiography; two of the most refined historical sensibilities in the development of the discipline seem to lead to Niebuhr, the man who made irony an explicit tool for understanding the American past.

The other two tentative patterns involve the interpretation of particular historical periods. Both Adams and Hildreth found irony in the behavior of Jefferson and the Jeffersonians in power. They had ambivalent feelings about the early democratic-republicans. Although both shared Jefferson's basic democratic convictions, for somewhat different reasons they disliked his particular policies. For them Jefferson at once symbolized the hopes of American democracy and its potential failings. It does in fact seem difficult not to see the presidencies of Jefferson and Madison in at least partly ironic terms; the consequences of their administrations were clearly at variance in important ways with their intentions, and to hold them responsible for those differences, if less obviously justified, is nonetheless plausible.

The late nineteenth century is the other period that provides a point of contact among some of these earlier ironic historians. Living through the Gilded Age certainly was one factor that sharpened Adams's sense of historical irony. Writing on the history of that period gave Becker's irony an uncharacteristic moral bite and opened up an entirely new ironic vision for Parrington. It might be suggested that in the course of the twentieth century, as the late nineteenth became increasingly a subject for historical inquiry, an ironic perception in general was awakened by the evident contrasts between the expectations of earlier America and the consequences of American democracy as manifested in the period following the Civil War.

But the development of a historical vision is at least as much affected by developments in the historian's present as it is by the characer of his past subject. If, as seems the case, Niebuhrian irony has come to be widely used to interpret the American past only in the last few decades, it is not primarily because that past has changed; the reasons are to be found mostly in the experience of those decades. As argued in the first section of this chapter, until the recent period the very circumstances that fostered ironic behavior among Americans at the same time discouraged the development of an ironic consciousness. American culture has been extremely optimistic,[55] generating high expectations and great activity to fulfill those expectations. If throughout much of our history the reality of the lives of most Americans has not in fact lived up to those high expectations, the private disappointments have not generally amounted to public disillusionment. There has been enough disappointment and unintended consequence to describe American history as ironic, but until recently there was also enough success and feeling of "progress" to sustain the illusions that both induce ironic behavior and block consciousness of the ironic process.

Since the beginning of the twentieth century this situation has been gradually changing. It would not be too gross an exaggeration to describe American intellectual history in this century as a process of continuous, or at least episodic, disillusionment resulting from developments in our domestic and international situation as well as from European cultural influences.[56] The Progressive historians, linked as they were to the past through their faith in science, progress, and American uniqueness, experienced considerable disappointment, particularly after the First World War, disappointment that contributed to such occasional biting irony as Parrington's account of the Gilded Age. The political and social hopes of American intellectuals — in this century overwhelmingly liberal or radical — have been repeatedly disappointed by the failure of radicalism and the shallow success of reform movements. The succession of war, disheartening peace, depression, more war, and cold war repeatedly reminded Americans of the realities of human evil while recurringly encouraging and disappointing illusions as to the limitlessness of American power. At the same time, ideas largely European in origin undermined simpler progressive and pragmatic concepts of human nature and furthered the belief that people are inwardly divided against themselves, making our culture more sensitive to contradictions than it had been at any time since the seventeenth century. By the 1930s among the vanguard, and by the post-World War II period among many intellectuals, ideas such as neoorthodox theology, represented by Niebuhr among others, and psychoanalysis, which contains a modern equivalent of the idea of original sin, became powerful influences. Historians were affected by these developments, and within the discipline of history itself methodological and philosophic issues raised by the Progressives worked themselves out into increasingly complex ideas of how to understand the past.

As events disappointed our hopes, as scholarship discredited simple ideas of progress, as our culture became more complex and more sensitive to inner conflicts, the ground was prepared for ironic history. In the 1930s Reinhold Niebuhr began to integrate liberal politics with a conservative theology, emphasizing original sin in an ironic and tragic vision of history, a vision that he did not apply to the American past until somewhat later. At about the same time Perry Miller began to examine the American Puritans with a unique intensity and depth leading to a profoundly ironic interpretation of that formative movement in American culture. But the larger impact of that interpretation did not come until after World War II. By the middle of the twentieth century, at the peak of American power and success, the limitations of that power and success became paradoxically more evident than ever before. Evil and even original sin took on a new reality in a world that had been devastated by one totalitarianism and that seemed to confront the possiblities of universal destruction in fighting another. A sense of contradiction and complexity took hold of the American imagination, and irony came to color much of our vision of our past.

The predominant view that emerged from that discovery of evil and contradiction was ironic rather than tragic, pathetic, or demonic, in part because of the nature of that past itself and in part because some irony-inducing factors continued to operate in America. If little of the old basis for optimism remained, much of the desire to believe in human potentiality continued to be strong. Initially, at least, what intellectuals were struck with was not so much the evil in America in itself as the contradictions between the nation's virtues and its faults. This resulted in the development of a new critical spirit, an ironic vision that recognized that the promise of America had been deeply compromised by the way in which

Americans had sought to realize it, one that saw the evil in our past mixed in complex ways with the good.[57]

In a perceptive comparison of the history of the South with that of the nation as a whole, C. Vann Woodward points out some of the reasons why irony is a particularly suitable approach to the understanding of American history, as well as some of the factors that have made its use by historians rare until recently. Vann Woodward delivered a paper in 1952, partly inspired by Niebuhr's book, in which he suggested that the experience of the South was different from that of the rest of the nation in ways that might be useful to the country as a whole in the complexities of the post-World War II situation. The history of the South had made Southerners far more conscious of defeat and disillusionment than are Americans in general. The national understanding of our past is adequate because "the tragic aspects and ironic implications of that history have been obscured by the national legend of success and victory and by the perpetuation of infant illusions of innocence and virtue." Vann Woodward argues that America "desperately needs criticism from historians of her own who can penetrate the legend without destroying the ideal, who can dispel the illusion of pretended virtue without denying the genuine virtues." He suggests that the experience of defeat by Southerners has equipped them with a greater potential for "the rare combination of detachment and sympathy" that the writing of American history required in the postwar period.[58]

The conditions of our national history that induced ironic behavior but also prevented us from perceiving it have come recently to produce a situation in which irony is increasingly obvious and an ironic perspective increasingly necessary. In the next chapter we shall see how Niebuhr contributed to the illumination of that perspective without, for a long time, quite freeing himself from those conditions. The emergence of an ironic vision of the American past coincided with the Cold War, a conjunction that tended to obscure perceptions of the critical implications of that vision. This was true in Niebuhr's work, and in the work of some of the consensus historians to be examined in the fifth chapter.

# IV.  Reinhold Niebuhr's Ironic History

Reinhold Niebuhr's *The Irony of American History* argues directly and forcefully that the United States can best be understood in
ironic terms. As we have seen, Niebuhr's concept of irony can be a
powerful historical tool but his own specific applications of it in this
book are weak, largely because when he wrote it his attitude toward
the United States was not sufficiently critical for him to make effective use of his own ironic vision. The very source of that vision — his
Christian faith — under the conditions of the Cold War frustrated his
efforts to apply it, but before the end of his life subsequent historical
events made it possible for him to regain his critical distance on
America. In several articles on race relations and the war in Vietnam, Niebuhr suggested how irony might become a cutting instrument for historical analysis.

## 1.  *The Irony of American History* in the Atmosphere of the Cold War

In this section I shall try to determine how true Niebuhr's use of
his own theory in *The Irony of American History* was to the
historical and critical implications of that theory. His humane
irony — the conceptual framework of his book and the source of that
of mine — is clearly presented in the introductory and concluding
chapters of the work. Rooted in a Christian conception of sin, it is a
vision that both requires and fosters a sense of the interrelationships
between virtue and vice, strength and weakness, wisdom and folly in
all people, a vision of the human being as both active and acted
upon, responsible, even if unconsciously, for his or her own fate, a

dramatic conception of history as a process moving through time, and a stance at once critical and sympathetic toward the historical subject. Finally, in spite of Niebuhr's Christian pessimism, it offers the hope that historical consciousness can free us, not from irony in general, which is the human condition, but from the specific ironies in which we are trapped.[1]

The exposition of this framework in the theoretical parts of Niebuhr's book is powerful and persuasive, but many of its applications to the specifics of American history are deeply flawed, untrue to the implications of the framework. The reasons for this are perhaps in part ironic. In his failure to expose American evils Niebuhr was hardly alone. Most liberal intellectuals in the late forties and early fifties tended to see American virtues more clearly than American faults in the atmosphere of intensive Cold War, but Niebuhr's irony by its own logic should have been a device for exposing the pretensions involved in those virtues. Niebuhr himself used it in that way later in his life and, as we shall see, at about the same time Richard Hofstadter was able to perceive the American past with a critical and ironic eye. It may have been his Christianity that prevented Niebuhr from using his own ironic concept critically at that time. His great perceptiveness about human beings in history was owing in large measure to his ability to comprehend history in terms of the Christian doctrine of original sin articulated in ways that made sense in the modern secular world.[2] If his great strength as a historical thinker was derived from his faith, so too was his failure; as a Christian during the Cold War Niebuhr seemed to be incapable of maintaining enough distance on the United States — he had certainly been more critical earlier in his career[3] — to concretize his ironic vision, to see, as that vision demanded, how the dilemmas we confronted in the 1950s were in part unintended results of our own past actions, the products of unconscious flaws in ourselves, as well as of outside forces over which we had no control. Much of *The Irony of American History* is too generalized and ahistorical, above all too uncritical, to be effective Niebuhrian irony. The book fails to connect the ironic dilemmas that it exposes to the active American past, and so tends to exonerate the United States of responsibility for its own problems.[4] It might well be reasonable to argue, as some would, that our problems in that period were largely forced upon us by external pressures, but however plausible such a view might be, it is not compatible with Niebuhrian irony, which is supposed to focus on a nation's own responsibility for its difficulties. My criticism of Niebuhr's book throughout this chapter on this point is not based upon any particular assumption about the "objective" causes of the

Cold War, but rather on the implications of his own theory and the contrast between those implications and Niebuhr's application of his theory to the problem of Cold War origins.[5]

Niebuhr does make some effective use of his concept of irony in this book, and a number of specific ironies that he sees in American history are critical and penetrating. His Christian perspective helps him expose the unanticipated results of the shallowness and pretentiousness of American ideas of happiness and success:

> The irony of America's quest for happiness lies in the fact that she succeeded more obviously than any other nation in making life 'comfortable,' only finally to run into larger incongruities of human destiny by the same achievements by which it escaped the smaller ones. Thus we tried too simply to make sense out of life, striving for harmonies between man and nature and man and society and man and his ultimate destiny, which have provisional but no ultimate validity. Our very success in this enterprise has hastened the exposure of its final limits. Over these exertions we discern by faith the ironical laughter of the divine source and end of all things.[6]

Niebuhr finds a potential irony in our failure to perceive the arbitrary character of much of our national success: "it has remained one of the most difficult achievements for our nation to recognize the fortuitous and providential elements in our good fortune." In a comment remarkably prescient in light of events in the 1970s he notes that if we take credit for our undeserved property we shall have only ourselves to blame when that prosperity ceases: "We have . . . complicated our spiritual problem for the days of adversity which we are bound to experience."[7]

Niebuhr is particularly effective in pointing out the unintended virtues of American vices. Our liberal bourgeois ideology, which Niebuhr regards as in part a vice, holds that social harmony and general prosperity will result from the unimpeded pursuit by each individual of his own self-interest, but whatever social justice we have gained has been achieved in spite of that way of thinking. America's "experiences in domestic politics represent an ironic form of success. Our success in establishing justice and insuring domestic tranquility has exceeded the characteristic insights of a bourgeois culture." We have been pragmatists as well as believers in laissez faire, so that we have been able to transcend our own limitations. This is a genuine irony, although the usual terms are reversed. Our unconscious and automatic pragmatism is a "flaw" in our bourgeois liberalism, a flaw that unexpectedly furthers our success as a society.[8]

One of Niebuhr's major ironic perceptions involves American illusions about the nature of power within society, a question closely related to the main set of problems with which the book is concerned. Niebuhr argues persuasively that is has been characteristic of American society to ignore the realities of unequal social and economic power, and focus its attention only upon the obvious power of the state. In our history "the privileged classes tried to preserve the illusion of classical liberalism that power is not an important element in man's social life. They recognize the force of interest; but they continue to assume that the competition of interests will make for justice without political or moral regulation. This would be possible only if the various powers which support interest were fairly equally divided, which they never are." American "society regards all social relations as essentially innocent because it believes self-interest to be inherently harmless." This denial of power relationships within society did not produce the justice that it was assumed to foster; rather, it led to greater injustice owing to the imbalance of actual power.[9] Here is one of Niebuhr's best insights into the irony-inducing characteristics of American society, an insight that he did not consistently use. The restriction of the conception of power to the political, combined with the hostility to its exercise, fostered a blindness to the actual, unequal strength of Americans, inequalities that were largely economic in character in our bourgeois society. While Niebuhr was sensitive to how this blindness to the realities of power functioned in our national domestic life, he did not apply that vision to our relationship to other nations.

Niebuhr exposes a number of other contradictions in American society, several of them quite substantial, but some that he refers to as irony do not in fact fit his own pattern. He notes, for example, that although the predominant ideology of our early history aimed at an agricultural society, we have become a great industrial nation. "There is a special irony in the contrast between the course of American history toward the development of large-scale industry and Jefferson's belief that democracy was secure only in an agrarian economy." This contrast does not amount to ironic history in Niebuhr's own terms because it does indicate how Jeffersonian devotion to agrarianism contributed to the development of industry along with democracy.[10] This lack is characteristic of much of the book; Niebuhr often fails to apply his own vision of ironic history as a process of human intention actively producing unintended consequences over time. Instead, much of the book presents static pictures of contrasts and paradoxes that are neither genuinely historical nor effective in indicating human responsibility. The detailed analysis needed to show how specific ironies function has not been done in this highly generalized work.

*The Irony of American History* deals more with our foreign policy problems than with our domestic difficulties. Niebuhr points out the contrast between our security in the past when we were a minor country and our insecurity now when we possess great power:

> The element of irony lies in the fact that a strong America is less completely master of its own destiny than was a comparatively weak America rocking in the cradle of its continental security and serene in its infant innocence. The same strength which has extended our power beyond a continent has also interwoven our destiny with the destiny of many peoples and brought us into a vast web of history in which other wills, running in oblique or contrasting directions to our own, inevitably hinder or contradict what we most fervently desire.

Although this comment does not make it clear how the contradiction between our power and our security has been a product of historical choices we have made, it does relate the process of growing strength to the development of the conditions that make us feel insecure in spite of our strength. Our power was produced by the same factors that also created the international dilemmas that confront that power.[11]

Our problems as a major force in the world are compounded by our illusions of innocence, illusions that arise out of both the liberal assumptions of our time and our particular national history as the heirs of the Puritans and Jefferson. "Our pretensions of innocency . . . heightened the whole concept of a virtuous harmony which characterizes the culture of our era; and involve us in the ironic incongruity between our illusions and the realities which we experience." These illusions, although not entirely peculiar to the United States, are present here in an intensified form involving the idea "that our nation turned its back upon the vices of Europe and made a new beginning." This pretense to being innocent of the vices of older nations could result in an inability to act as we must and should in the complex international relations of our time. "The irony of our situation lies in the fact that we could not be virtuous (in the sense of practicing the virtues that are implicit in meeting our vast world responsibilities) if we were really as innocent as we pretend to be."[12] This statement brings us to Niebuhr's central concern in this book.

The irony with which the book begins, and that is discussed recurrently throughout, involves the moral dilemmas that arise from America's role as an atomic power. It is primarily in this connection that Niebuhr suggests that our past has caught up with us, as our traditional "innocence" has become markedly inappropriate to our "responsibilities": "Our age is involved in irony because so many dreams of our nation have been so cruelly refuted by history. Our dreams of a pure virtue are dissolved in a situation in which it is possible to exercise the virtue of responsibility toward a community of nations only by courting the prospective guilt of the atomic bomb."[13] While from Niebuhr's point of view this may be a genuinely ironic dilemma, it does not fit his own pattern for ironic history because America's predicament is not seen as a product of our past actions. By Niebuhr's account no fault of ours led us into that predicament, although our "innocence" is an element in the present situation that might lead us to fail to live up to our responsibilities in the future and bring about unintended consequences. This ironic dilemma is neither historical nor morally focused in that it ignores America's past role in generating its own present problems, a role that Niebuhr's own theory requires us to take into account.

One might argue that the United States was not responsible for the Cold War or the balance of terror that went with it, but such an argument would be out of place in a book entitled *The Irony of American History* if Niebuhr's definition of irony is used. I do not claim that Niebuhr explicitly makes this point, but he assumes a kind of innocent passivity on the part of the United States that implies that conception of the past. If he believed that we had no responsibility for the Cold War, he should not have attempted to apply his ironic concept of that issue. Niebuhr's failure here—in his own terms—is made more obvious by his application of his ironic theory to Cold War issues later in his life.

In his treatment of the problems of American power Niebuhr is most concerned with the dangers of isolationism, which he sees as the abandonment of the responsibility required by the possession of power. Isolationists "did not understand that the disavowal of the responsibilities of power can involve an individual or nation in more grievous guilt" than that which comes from the exercise of power. He recognizes the danger of imperialism but sees the United States as more subject to the temptations of isolationism because of a certain "moral advantage that we possess. "No powerful nation in history has ever been more reluctant to acknowledge the position it has achieved in the world than we. The moral advantage lies in the fact that we do not have a strong lust of power, though we are quickly acquiring the pride of power which always accompanies its possession." Niebuhr's apparent equation here between our "reluctance to acknowledge" the strength we have acquired in relation to other nations with a presumption of the lack of "a strong lust for power" on our part is rather surprising. As we have seen, Niebuhr was very sensitive to the tendency of our culture to deny the realities of power within our national domestic life, to focus its attention upon the overt power of the state while ignoring the realities of covert economic power. Here Niebuhr ignores the possibility that the same kind of self-deception may occur in our foreign relations. That we do not like to admit how much power we have can indicate not the lack of a "lust for power" but a pretense of innocence, in this case a pretense that Niebuhr seems rather to share as a participant in irony, defined in his own terms, than to expose as a historian of irony.[14]

In addition to isolationism, Niebuhr sees another possible peril stemming from our illusions of innocence and virtue; instead of retreating from the world, our pretensions to a peculiar virtue may lead us to act too precipitately. The dangers are that "either we will seek escape from responsibilities which involve unavoidable guilt, or we will be plunged into avoidable guilt by too great confidence in our virtue." In developing this theme Niebuhr reveals both the power of his theory and the weakness of his application of it to American history:

> Our moral perils are not those of conscious malice or the explicit lust for power. They are perils which can be understood only if we realize the ironic tendency of virtues to turn into vices when too complacently relied upon; and of power to become vexatious if the wisdom which directs it is trusted too confidently. The ironic elements in American history can be overcome, in short, only if American idealism comes to terms with the limits of all human striving, the fragmentariness of all human wisdom, the precariousness of all historical configurations of power, and the mixture of good and evil in all human virtue. . . . That idealism is too oblivious to the ironic perils to which human virtue, wisdom and power are subject.[15]

This statement curiously combines Niebuhr's perception of the ways in which vices are linked to their appropriate virtues in general with his reluctance to apply that perception critically to the United States. He asks Americans to shape their foreign policy in terms of a general awareness of the evil that may accompany benignly motivated actions at the same time that he himself gives expression to an illusion of specifically American innocence. Although it may well be true that there is a difference between "conscious malice" and an "explicit lust for power" on the one hand and "the ironic tendency of virtues to turn into vices" on the other, Niebuhr makes that difference too absolute, ignoring the way in which evil motives permeate virtuous ones that his own theory draws to our attention. His ironic vision demands that we recognize our own unconscious responsibility for the evil that may follow from actions consciously directed by virtuous intentions, but the separation he makes here in reference to American foreign policy between evil and benign motives has the effect of reinforcing our sense of being innocent of the evil effects of our actions. One of the main reasons why virtuously intended actions produce unintended evil is the intermingling of evil and virtuous motives, according to Niebuhr's own ironic concept. Although Niebuhr clearly recognizes "the curious compounds of good and evil in which the actions of the best men and nations abound"[16] as a general proposition, he does not apply that insight concretely to the ironic processes of American history. Yet, a history of America that would be true to Niebuhr's own ironic vision would have to reveal the moral mixture of intentions behind the actions of Americans as well as the mixture of benign and evil consequences.

The failure effectively to acknowledge the evil in American motives that his own theory requires us to recognize is symptomatic of a general tendency for Niebuhr to be uncritical of America in this book; because of that his irony loses its power. For example, his formulation of the irony discussed earlier in our achievement of a greater degree of social justice than our bourgeois ideology would allow involves the exaggeration of American accomplishments and a degree of blindness to our faults. Although this argument undoubtedly contains an element of truth, its implications are excessively comforting to American self-esteem and, what is more important, it ignores some of Niebuhr's own ironic insights into our relationship to our national wealth and the way we avoid acknowledging social conflict. It would be unfair to criticize Niebuhr for the exaggeration of the virtues of American political and economic democracy that was so common in the 1950s were it not for the fact that his own theory points out the error of taking credit for what nature or providence has given us. Niebuhr maintains that America "has established sufficient justice to prevent the outbreak of the social resentments which have wrecked the less healthy European nations and have created social acerbities exceeding our own in the best of them."[17] What he appears to be doing here is taking our relative lack of overt social conflicts as evidence of a high level of achievement in the area of social justice, ignoring his own insights into how our society and ideology function to minimize the visibility of social conflicts. Insofar as our relative lack of apparent internal conflict is a result of our great national wealth this comment also is an example of the self-comforting illusion of Americans that Niebuhr himself warns against, in that it assumes that we have earned something that is largely accidental.

In general it is the omissions that reveal most clearly the extent of Niebuhr's uncritical attitude toward American society at the time he wrote this book. He does not touch upon the profound irony of the continued existence of poverty in the midst of affluence. While it is true that Niebuhr was writing well before the rediscovery of American injustice and poverty in the 1960s, some recognition of the ironic situation of various oppressed groups might be expected in a book entitled *The Irony of American History*, even in the early 1950s. Blacks, for example, are almost totally invisible in the work, although the contradiction between their conditions in the land of freedom and equality and American values, a contradiction suggestive of irony, had been observed by others not long before the book appeared and later was to be a major source of Niebuhr's recovery of a critical perspective. In one indirect reference to racial minorities Niebuhr implies criticism of them, not of America, for the way they have been treated. He argues in passing that "members of minority groups invariably assume that racial arrogance is a peculiar vice of the group which causes their suffering."[18] It is irrelevant whether this comment is true or not. Its presence here, combined with the lack of any comments on the irony of white racism in egalitarian America, suggests Niebuhr's inability in this book to face certain crucial ironies in the American experience.

Niebuhr's lack of criticism of the United States is particularly evident in relation to the foreign policy questions with which he is most concerned. As noted earlier, he denies that we have a "strong lust for power." He sees our achievement of overwhelming strength as unintended. An "element of irony lies in the fact that our nation has, without particularly seeking it, acquired a greater degree of power than any other nation in history." His account of the role of innocence and illusions of innocence in our relation with others is confused in terms of his own theory because of his own reluctance to abandon these illusions. Niebuhr claims that "we lived for a century not only in the illusion but in the reality of innocence in our foreign relations," but he acknowledges that this does not adequately characterize the major foreign policy development during that century, our continental expansion: "We were of course, never as innocent as we pretended to be, even as a child is not innocent as is implied in the use of the child as the symbol of innocency. The surge of our infant strength over a continent, which claimed Oregon, California, Florida and Texas against any sovereignty which may have stood in our way, was not innocent. It was the expression of a will-to-power of a new community in which the land-hunger of hardy pioneers and settlers furnished the force of imperial expansion." This judgment is dubious and does not make sense in terms of Niebuhr's ironic framework. For example, it is difficult to see how the treatment of the Indians can be described as innocent in any but an entirely illusory sense without grossly distorting the moral reality of their destruction. Beyond that, when Niebuhr comments that "from those early days to the present moment we have frequently been honestly deceived because our power availed itself of covert rather than overt instruments" he reinforces rather than exposes irony-inducing illusions of innocence.[19]

Our "honest" failure to recognize our own aggressiveness could be clarified by the critical application of Niebuhr's own perception of our bourgeois denial of the realities of power relationships within our domestic market economy to the history of our foreign relations. But Niebuhr does not clearly recognize that what he presents is evidence not of honest innocence but of illusions of innocence. He has at hand a persuasive explanation of how it has been possible for us to seek vast power without ever admitting to ourselves that that was what we were doing. Niebuhr sees that the belief on the part of commercial societies that the relations between their members are balanced is an illusion; he knows that power inequalities and conflicts exist in such societies in spite of their denials. But he does not carry this insight beyond our borders and fails to recognize that the innocence of our foreign relations, like the innocence of our domestic market, masks power drives similar to those of other nations. This blindness is a result in large part of the same factor responsible for much of his overly favorable view of America in general: his demonic perception of communism.

Of course, the tendency to see communism as an absolute evil was widespread in the early 1950s and, in light of what we know of Stalinist totalitarianism, quite understandable. Niebuhr's anticommunism of those years is questionable, not because of his highly critical attitude toward the Soviet Union, but because an exclusive focus on Russian evil tended to prevent him from seeing the active role played by the United States in international conflict and to interfere with his recognition of evils within American society, thus blocking his application of his own ironic theory to the United States since that theory demanded the recognition of responsibility and partial evil in his subject. While the apologetic atmosphere of the Cold War was pervasive in America, it was not universal, and Niebuhr's irony rigorously applied could have given him a means of maintaining a critical view of both the Soviet Union and the United States.[20]

*The Irony of American History* begins with a clear statement of Niebuhr's feeling that communism is totally and unquestionably evil. "Everbody understands the obvious meaning of the world struggle in which we are engaged. We are defending freedom against tyranny and are trying to preserve justice against a system that has, demonically, distilled injustice and cruelty out of its original promise of a higher justice." Niebuhr seems to regard communism as the greatest evil that has ever existed: "we have to deal with a vast religious-political movement which generates more extravagant forms of political injustice and cruelty out of the pretensions of innocence than we have ever known in human history." In his eyes the unmitigated evil of communism is greatly compounded by its dynamic qualities and its efforts to expand. He says that "the world is confronted by a mania which represents the corruption of a characteristically historical tendency in man. Communism is compounded of Messianism and a lust of power." The West will have to confront communism as a unified, expanding force over a long period of time: "we must face the menace of the spread of tyranny in the non-industrial world for many decades to come."[21] Most of Niebuhr's references to communism treat it as dynamic and monolithic, absolutely evil, truly demonic.

In contrast, in a few places Niebuhr seems to imply that communism can be understood as an ironic extension of some of the tendencies of liberalism: "communism changes only partly dangerous sentimentalities and inconsistencies in the bourgeois ethos into consistent and totally harmful ones." He suggests that "the evils against which we contend are frequently the fruit of illusions which are similar to our own." The book concludes on a religious note, asking us to acknowledge "a sense of contrition about the common human frailties and foibles which lie at the foundation of both the enemy's demonry and our vanities." But a remark on the page preceding this directly contradicts it: "we are dealing with a conflict between contending forces which have no common presuppositions."²² It cannot be true both that communism represents the evil extension of certain tendencies in liberalism and that there are no common presuppositions between liberal America and communist Russia. Only in regard to the illusion that men can understand and control history, a pretension toward which Niebuhr has a particular hostility, does he consistently relate communism to some tendencies in Western liberalism. More often communism is seen as the alien enemy, a force with which we have nothing in common, a demonic reality in the world that conditions our ironic behavior, but not itself human enough to be perceived ironically.

The major ironic dilemma with which Niebuhr is concerned — the dangers inherent in our need to possess atomic weapons in order to ward off Soviet expansion — presupposes Russian guilt and American innocence in generating the situation we face. The ironic potential is that we will give in to our desire to escape from the tensions of the Cold War either by launching a preemptive attack or by letting our guard down and deluding ourselves that it is possible to compromise with the communists. Niebuhr's view of Russian evil is so strong that part of the logic of this ironic dilemma rests upon his assumption that we cannot negotiate peace.²³ Either by preemptive war or by compromise we would produce unintended consequences — in the former case a horrible postatomic world, in the latter, a Soviet victory. The whole dilemma is predicated upon the assumption that we face an absolutely evil enemy. It does not consider the truly ironic possibility that our actions may have contributed to the conflict with communism. To suggest this possibility is not to say that the United States and the Soviet Union are moral equals; it is only to acknowledge that we are all human, all the potential subjects of irony, and all motivated by both good and evil, perhaps to different degrees — in other words, to apply the vision of the human condition that Niebuhr's own theory suggests.

Insofar as Niebuhr sees the existence of communism as a source of our irony he violates his own definition of irony as the unintended consequences of human action, not something that is forced upon people by fate or the actions of others. He appears to do this when he defines the irony of our situation in terms of the evil into which the communists have turned our "harmless illusions." "There are so many obvious ironic elements in current history, particularly in our own national history, because a nation which has risen so quickly from weakness to power and from innocency to responsibility and which meets a foe who has transmuted our harmless illusions into noxious ones is bound to be involved in rather ironic incongruities." The power we have achieved is in part the result of our own actions, but we are not really at all responsible, in this view, for the world situation in which we exercise that power. In the very process of warning against the danger of fanatical anticommunism Niebuhr reveals how his vision of communism as demonic softens his conception of American irony. The existence of the communists is blamed even for our blindness to our own ironies. "One reason for our difficulty in sensing the ironies in which we are involved is our encounter with a foe the fires of whose hostility are fed by an even more humorless pretension."[24] To say that the existence of a pretentious external evil is a major reason for our problems in recognizing our own ironies and pretensions suggests an attempt to escape from seriously admitting that we too suffer from pretensions that blind us to our own evil; this is a form of the very self-righteousness that Niebuhr warns against. Here Niebuhr participates in irony rather than exposes it.

Niebuhr's extreme anticommunism is in part a reaction against the communist pretense to understand history and their efforts to control it. In theory he repeatedly emphasizes the need to balance our vision of human action with a recognition that human beings are also creatures of history, and argues that much of the difficulty of our time is a result of our overemphasis on the active role of people in making history. This theme is pushed by Niebuhr to the point where it seriously compromises his basic ironic vision, a vision that requires a balanced sense of the human capacity to act in history as well as of the limitations of human control. One of the greatest — if not the greatest — of evil pretensions for Niebuhr is the assumption "that some group of men has the intelligence to manipulate and manage the process" of history. Western liberals as well as communists have been the victims of this pretension, but other elements in liberalism have prevented it from becoming the source of demonic behavior. Liberals and Marxists share the hope "that man may be delivered from his ambiguous position of being both creature and creator of the historical process and become unequivocally the master of his own destiny." The Marxists are surer of themselves in this belief and much more ruthless in acting upon it. Niebuhr's argument implies that most of the evil in the world comes from the conviction of communists, and of some Western intellectuals (particularly social scientists), that man is an exclusively active agent in history, that he controls the overall processes of historical change.[25]

Niebuhr's emphasis on this theme is so strong that it leads him away from his own insight into the balance among activity, passivity, and unconscious responsibility in history. Having identified the exaggerated sense of human capacity to act with communism and with human evil, in contrast he tends to present a curiously passive picture of America. His call for the United States to accept a balanced, active, responsible role in the world in opposition to communism assumes our innocence and passivity in the previous development of the Cold War. To see the Russians as evil men acting out their pretensions to the knowledge and ability to control history, while perceiving America as a nation that has avoided such temptations, blinds us to any unconscious responsibility we may have for bringing upon ourselves the dilemmas we confront. It undermines a really ironical understanding of the Cold War, because in Niebuhr's own terms irony depends upon a recognition of the way in which a historical actor contributes unintentionally to his own problems. A truly ironic view would not obscure the difficulties the Soviet Union presents by its pretensions and actions, but would require us also to recognize how American behavior contributed to the development of the Cold War. This Niebuhr's application of his own concept fails to do.[26]

A particularly painful example of Niebuhr's attribution of a passive innocence to American actions in the Cold War can be seen in the contrast between his comments on our policies in two Asian nations. "Sometimes, as in Indo-China, strategic necessities in our conflict forced us into an alliance with a discredited French colonialism. In other cases, however, as in Indonesia, we may have acted more precipitately in favor of independence than was wise." The language of this quotation is revealing. In Indochina "necessities in our conflict forced" us to support the French. This does not amount to a mature acceptance of the need actively to do evil in the fulfillment of our virtuous responsibility for protecting the "free" world, the moral point that Niebuhr presumably wants to make. The terminology here suggests that our behavior is not the product of a responsible moral choice made in a difficult and ambiguous situation, but rather of an absolute necessity in which we are described as if we had no choice. This presentation undermines Niebuhr's argument for American responsibility and for our acceptance of the burden of irony. In contrast, in Indonesia where our policy was "moral"—that is, anticolonial—if unwise, it is described as an American action, something for which we bear responsiblity. The effect of the contrasting language in these two instances is to imply that we deserve the credit for our moral behavior but that when we act immorally we are merely responding to necessities created by communist pressure, that we are not really responsible for such actions. Instead of leading us to accept responsibility for evil actions that Niebuhr feels we should undertake, making us conscious of the irony in our situation, this has the effect of reinforcing our illusions of innocence and virtue. That this example of Niebuhr's participation in, rather than exposure of, American irony involves Indochina is a painful paradox in light of what subsequently happened in Vietnam and Niebuhr's own later conviction that our illusions of virtue played a terribly ironic role in the war there.[27]

## 2. The Irony of Niebuhr's Christianity

In this part I shall examine the ironic way in which Niebuhr's Christianity was at once the source of his greatest wisdom and worst errors. It led him to his ironic vision but also prevented him from fully realizing it. Niebuhr's hostility to human pretensions to control history and his extreme anticommunism are derived from his faith, as is his basic theory. He claims that a theistic perspective on the human predicament allows for a transcendence that no secular point of view permits: "everything that is related in terms of simple rational coherence with the ideals of a culture or a nation will prove in the end to be a simple justification of its most cherished values." Only through religious faith can we have "an experience of repentance for the false meaning which the pride of nations and cultures introduces into the pattern" of history. According to Niebuhr "the Christian faith tends to make the ironic view of human evil in history the normative one."[28] Yet when we look at how Niebuhr's own faith affects his historical interpretations, it seems as if Christianity may block as well as encourage ironic perceptions.

His hostility to the exaggeration of human knowledge and power that he sees both in certain liberal tendencies and in communism arises in great measure out of his Christian belief "that the whole drama of history is enacted in a frame of meaning too large for human comprehension or management. It is a drama in which fragmentary meanings can be discerned within a penumbra of mystery. . . . A sane life requires that we have some clues to the mystery so that the realm of meaning is not simply reduced to the comprehensible processes of nature. But these clues are ascertained by faith, which modern man has lost."[29] This expression of Niebuhr's belief in the limits of human understanding is hardly as humble as it may at first glance seem. His assertion that only faith can provide "clues" to the "mystery" that secular wisdom fails to comprehend can be read as itself a statement of intellectual presumption, justified on the grounds of religion. Its thrust is to cut down the presumption of the secularists while asserting the superior wisdom of Christianity. This is hardly the kind of "height which can only be grasped by faith," the height that offers a vision transcending the limitations of any culture or nation.[30] It is itself the expression of similar limitations, as can be seen in some of Niebuhr's specific comments on communism.

Much of his enmity to communism was the result of his perception of it as a religious movement diametrically opposed to Christianity. Of the communist Messianic vision of the working class Niebuhr says: "As a religion this faith generates what in Christian terms is regarded as the very essence of sin. It identifies the interests of a particular self or of a particular force in history with the final purposes of the God of history." That force is the proletariat mistakenly perceived as possessing a special historical mission. Niebuhr argues that "in the Marxist apocalypse one error is piled upon another with regard to the virtue of the poor." In his reaction to these errors we can see a clue to the narrowing effect of his Christianity: "All these errors enter into the monstrous evils of communism. It has transmuted religious truths, intended to warn against the element of pretension in all human achievements into political slogans, effective in organizing a political movement in which these very pretensions achieve a noxious virulence of unparalleled proportions."[31] The extremeness of this statement suggests that Niebuhr's anticommunism was in some measure owing to his feeling that communists had appropriated and perverted specifically Christian ideas such as the sanctity of the poor. In any event, it seems evident that his Christianity predisposed him to oppose movements like communism that emphasized the ability of human beings to understand and influence history in general to a degree that prevented his effective use of his own ironic concept in certain important contexts. Although it may well be true that Niebuhr's insight into human nature as inwardly divided owed much to his Christian sense of original sin, although his religion may have deepened his insight into the darkness of human intentions, it did not broaden his vision or increase his distance; it had the same narrowing effect he saw in other, purely secular, perspectives.

One is almost tempted to say that, in his exclusive claims for Christianity and in his identification of Christianity with the cause of the West, Niebuhr is guilty of a form of idolatry that he himself warns against in a later work:

> we must admit that there is no guarantee in any theology or form of worship that a community of faith, which intends to bring men into contact with the true God, may not be used for essentially

idolatrous purposes. Men may use it to claim a special alliance
with God against their foes. We must confess the significance of
the long history of religious fanaticism, and must admit that a
religion which has triumphed over idolatry in principle may in actual fact be made an instrument of partial and interested
perspectives.[32]

In addition to preventing him from seeing communism ironically,
Niebuhr's Christianity seems to have distorted his perception of
America and of the underdeveloped nations. In an extremely revealing passage Niebuhr compares the communists to Moslems. "The
rise of communism in our world is comparable to the rise of Islam
and its challenge to Christian civilization in the high Middle Ages."
His major point in making this comparison is to show the similarity
of the Western response to the two challenges, but he goes on to
compare the history of the two movements themselves. "The Islamic
power finally waned. It was destroyed not so much by its foes as by
its own inner corruptions. The Sultan of Turkey found it ultimately
impossible to support the double role of political head of a nation
and the spiritual head of the Islamic world. Stalin has the same double role in the world of communist religion." When we recall that
Niebuhr repeatedly refers to communism as "demonic," it is difficult not to see this assertion of the similarity of Islam to communism as an expression of a narrow, particularistic Christian
perspective. Surely we should have enough distance now on the Middle Ages to recognize the mixture of good and evil in both Islam and
Christianity, to see both, at least in part, in Niebuhr's own ironic
terms. Here his specific religious commitment seems clearly to deny
him the very "repentance" and "charity" that he claims it alone can
provide.[33]

Niebuhr's ethnocentrism is more distressing, and it more
significantly interferes with his ironic vision, when it is applied to
contemporary non-Western nations. His discussion of the Third
World consists mostly of attempts to defend the West in general and
the United States in particular against blame for the problems that
plague the underdeveloped countries. Although Niebuhr sees the
United States as particularly innocent of imperialism, he does indirectly acknowledge a certain hidden exploitiveness in our relations
with the Third World. "Ironically our own nation, which has
become the residuary legatee of these resentments, was not in the
forefront of the imperial venture. . . .Our economic power produced
a great deal of covert imperialism. But we did not seek to govern
other peoples politically."[34] Niebuhr's use of the term *ironically* here
is a perversion of his own concept. He specifically does not intend to

acknowledge that we are responsible for the resentments directed at us by the former colonies of the imperial powers. This is an irony in which we are innocent, unjustly accused, and hence in his terminology it is no irony at all, but merely a paradox. However, he does leave open the possibility of another interpretation of the situation when he admits that we have engaged in covert imperalism. We feel ourselves innocent of the charge of imperialism because the power we have exercised in the Third World has been largely covert and economic rather than overt and political. But if Niebuhr were to apply his own insight into how our attitude toward power functions in our domestic economic life to our relations to the Third World he might conclude that our conviction of innocence is an illusion, that our covert economic power is a form of imperialism. The irony in the situation then would become true to the Niebuhrian form; the resentment of the Third World toward us, which so inconveniences our policies now, would be seen as the unintended and ironic outcome of our exercise of covert economic imperialism, an imperialism in which we persist partly because of our illusions of innocence. Without coming to an ironic consciousness of how we brought this situation upon ourselves, without facing the fact that we have engaged in hidden imperialism, without abandoning our pretensions to innocence, we cannot deal with the situation. Instead of functioning as an ironic historian and exposing our illusions here, Niebuhr participates in the illusions himself.

The evasive ethnocentrism implicit in his treatment of the developing nations is one of the major failures of *The Irony of American History*.[35] At one point Niebuhr suggests how our encounter with the wider world, particularly the underdeveloped nations, might serve to expose our own ironies and pretensions: "The progress of American culture toward hegemony in the world community as well as toward the ultimate in standards of living has brought us everywhere to the limits where our ideals and norms are brought under ironic indictment. Our confidence in the simple compatibility between prosperity and virtue is challenged particularly in our relations with Asia; for the Asians, barely emerging from the desperate poverty of an agrarian economy, are inclined to regard our prosperity as evidence of our injustice." This perceptive remark is not developed. Niebuhr is well aware of the ironic potential in our assumption that our wealth, which is largely the result of fortuitous circumstances, is a product of our pretended virtues,[36] but instead of showing how contact with the Third World, in which the opposite assumption is made, might serve to make us conscious of our pretensions, Niebuhr chooses to defend us against the charge that our wealth is the product of the exploitation of others. This choice amounts to a decision not to use his ironic concept as a critical tool for understanding America. That Niebuhr fails to adopt the point of view of the underdeveloped nations either to expose the evil, if unintended, consequences of our economic and political relations with those nations or to develop his insight into our presumption that our wealth is a result of our virtues reveals the limitations of his ability to apply his own ironic concept.[37] While it may not be justifiable to blame his blindness in this respect entirely upon his religion, his remarks on Islam suggest that the non-Christian character of the Third World may have something to do with Niebuhr's inability to utilize its perspective as a means of revealing ironies of the Christian West.

Certainly Niebuhr's Christianity had a creative as well as a destructive function in this book: it was his faith that led him to his ironic vision of man. Niebuhr's claim that "the Christian faith tends to make the ironic view of human evil in history the normative one" may be accurate in the sense that the Christian God is conceived of as "a divine judge who laughs at human pretensions without being hostile to human aspirations." Niebuhr's ability to state a traditional Christian insight into the relationship between virtue and evil in human behavior in a form accessible to the modern secular mind was one of his major contributions. He may well be right to argue that only God is in a position to see the totality of human experience ironically. But historians generally do not deal with that totality and in commenting on parts of it they may very well be able to maintain the combination of sympathy and detachment demanded by irony. Their ability to do this is not dependent upon their belief in God. Niebuhr seems to attribute to Christians something of the advantage of the deity's vision.[38] This is highly presumptuous and is the source of much of Niebuhr's own failure as an ironic historian of America. The Christian conception of God's perspective on man may well place the deity in a position to see men ironically; the fact that a writer is a Christian gives him no special access to that perspective, and is certainly no guarantee that he will see men with sympathy and detachment similar to God's. Christianity as an earthly phenomenon is a particular set of values and human ideas. Although God may or may not be a Christian, no Christian is God. As one system of beliefs among others in the world, Christianity has no privileged access to the divine perspective; it can be as blind to its own weaknesses and vices and to the virtues and strengths of its enemies as any other system, as the ironic conception of the human condition itself suggests.

*The Irony of American History* is a deeply flawed book when judged in light of the very theory it presents. It offers a conception of irony that is highly appropriate to historical study in general and profoundly pertinent to the history of the United States in particular, but the application of that concept to the history of that nation is largely inadequate. Although there are in it many penetrating insights into American ironies, the book in general lacks sufficient specificity and is too ahistorical to be effective; above all, it is too uncritical of its subject to meet the demands of Niebuhr's own concept of irony.

Niebuhr's failure to gain sufficient ciritical distance from the United States is perhaps the most striking characteristic of this book. That failure is related to the Cold War atmosphere in which the book was written. Niebuhr's demonic view of communism interfered with his perception of America as a historical agent. He violated his own perception of the fundamental irony of the human condition in which good and evil are linked by presenting the world situation as one in which good and evil were polarized into America and the Soviet Union. Because he saw our central problems as flowing from the existence of the vicious, dynamic force of communism in the world, he did not focus on how we ourselves also have a responsibility for those problems, a focus required by his own theory. The core of his book—his concern that we adopt a strong, moderate, and consistent policy of resistance to communism—fails to take into account the possibility that the dilemmas of the Cold War were to some extent of our own making. (If Niebuhr felt that that possibility was irrelevant to the origins of the Cold War he should not have tried to apply his ironic concept to that development.) He presents us as victims in our confrontation with the active and demonic Soviet Union, a passive picture that tends to reinforce rather than expose our pretensions to innocence. While he is concerned that illusions of innocence, virtue, and power not lead us into future actions that might produce disastrous but unintended consequences, he largely ignores the way in which such illusions led us into the situation that presents such dangers, a perception that his own ironic history ought to open up. In the moral universe implied by this opposition of an active, demonic communism with a passive, responding America, the greatest source of evil is the humane pretense to be able to understand history and control events. Although Niebuhr recognizes a tendency to such pretenses in secular liberalism—he claims superiority for the Christian point of view in part because he holds that religion does not make such claims—he sees them mainly as characteristic of the communists. From such a perspective not only is activism a source of evil; the attempt to understand the world can also become one. The way in which Niebuhr presents his critique of human wisdom seems to have the unintended effect of supporting a certain kind of anti-intellectualism. The view that the wise men are fools, and that our national wisdom comes from the acceptance of our practical experience, tends to discredit and undermine the very kind of self-awareness that a writer using Niebuhrian irony would seek to enhance.[39]

Niebuhr's failure to make use of his own wisdom involves not only his nonapplication of some of the general principles of his own ironic concept, but also his failure to apply certain specific insights that he develops in other contexts in this book. Of these the most striking is his recognition that we suffer in our domestic life from the illusion that all power is political, that we fail to recognize the great power of corporations and other economic forces in our society. While he notes that in our foreign affairs we have frequently used covert economic power where others use overt political power, in that area he does not expose how our conviction of innocence is a dangerous pretense, how we have unconsciously but actively contributed to the problems we face by our failure to acknowledge the reality of the power we have exercised on others, conclusions to which his own insight should lead.

Niebuhr's Christianity seems to have played a role in his tendency to see the world as divided too sharply between the evils of communism and the virtues of America. It also appears to prevent him from recognizing the ironies that our expansion into the world at large, particularly into its undeveloped parts, exposes about ourselves. Niebuhr argues that the Christian faith offers a world view particularly appropriate to irony, but his own faith seems to block much of his ironic perception of America. As we have seen, he tends to confuse the breadth of vision that Christians attribute to God with the perspective that Christianity fosters in human beings. Niebuhr's concept of irony unquestionably is derived in large measure from his Christianity, not because that faith offers any particular breadth of vision toward mankind or any particular distance upon one's own culture, but because it does focus upon the relationship between virtues and vices within individual human beings. From it Niebuhr gains depth, but not, as he claims, breadth. His Christianity, which feeds his ironic insight into the pretensions of all men, seems also to block his recognition of some of the key pretensions of the West. Although Niebuhr does not explicitly identify the West with Christianity, it does obviously contain Christianity within itself in contrast to the communist world that is hostile to all religion. Christianity was a specific value system to which Niebuhr was committed and he was incapable of being ironic about it. In spite of Niebuhr's warnings against investing any earthly power with ultimate meaning, he does seem to surrender much of his willingness to stand critically apart from America and the West because he identifies their survival with the survival of Christianity in the face of a demonic and powerful enemy. Thus it would appear that Christianity functions as a Niebuhrian irony in Niebuhr's own book; it is at once one of the major sources of his brilliant ironic concept of history and a factor that prevents him from effectively applying that concept.

*The Irony of American History* not only compromises its own irony; it also tends to be a rather ahistorical book. Niebuhr does not deal with the ironic process, the way in which human desires produce actions that have consequences at variance with the original intentions, exposing the inconsistencies and self-contradictions in the historical actors and their purposes. Instead, his focus is on a static picture of ironic dilemmas, on the potentiality for actions in the present that could produce disastrous but unintended consequences. The book is in this sense not history at all, for it does not deal very much with the past nor does it move actively through time.[40]

This ahistorical character of the book has several unfortunate effects. It certainly contributes to weakening the application of Niebuhr's concept of irony that lends itself so naturally to presentation in historical terms as a process of intention, action, and unintended outcome over time. It reinforces his uncritical picture of American foreign policy by ignoring how our past actions have got us into our current problems, actions that Niebuhrian irony should highlight. It tends to present the United States passively since it focuses on a present dilemma that we confront passively. I also think that this ahistorical mode of presentation tends to undermine Niebuhr's purpose in this book. His intention is to warn against certain actions and to expose certain illusions that he thinks might lead us to act so as to produce awful consequences we do not wish to bring about. But his ahistorical and passive presentation leaves him with only a didactic or perhaps prophetic voice with which to warn us. He sacrifices the potential therapeutic power of irony, a therapeutic power in which he had a belief qualified by his Christian pessimism. He suggests in general how, by becoming conscious of the way in which pretensions have led a people to act so as to produce unintended consequences in the past (and conscious too of the relationship between their virtues and their vices), they may be led to see their own illusions, abandon them, and amend their actions in the future. This is the hope of ironic history; it is a hope that Niebuhr abandons in practice by his failure to present a critical and historical account of how American illusions have led us into our present dilemmas, an account that would expose the link between American virtues and American evil. While there is no guarantee that such a history would lead us to abandon our dangerous pretensions, his own theory implies that the relinquishment of illusions is more likely to follow from such an account (particularly if it is specific and if its criticism is permeated with historical empathy) than from the disembodied ahistorical warnings that he offers.

But the failures of *The Irony of American History* do not invalidate the utility of the concept of historical irony that it presents. Even in Niebuhr's own hands that concept could be turned to critical and therapeutic uses more in keeping with its own premises.

## 3.   American Historical Irony in Niebuhr's Later Works

In Niebuhr's vast output there are a number of works on history in general, and many on America, but few that purport to deal with American history. An examination of those writings and a few others on American subjects that appeared between 1952, when *The Irony of American History* was published, and 1971, when Niebuhr died, reveals some important changes in his application of irony to the American experience, particularly toward the end of that period.[41]

The only full-length book on American history produced by Niebuhr after *The Irony of American History* is a study of American national character he wrote with Alan Heimert entitled *A Nation So Conceived: Reflections on the History of America From Its Early Vision to Its Present Power* (1963). Written in the atmosphere of the early 1960s rather than of the early 1950s, the irony that does appear in this work is a bit more critical, truer to the theory, than that in the earlier book, although its view of the United States remains extremely favorable.

The central themes of our domestic history discussed by Niebuhr and Heimert are the rapid development of a "sense of national identity" among the highly diverse American people and the way in which industrialization emerged out of our "early agrarian innocence." In presenting the first of these themes, although more attention is paid to such unsavory facts as slavery in this book than in

*The Irony of American History*, Niebuhr and Heimert exaggerate the extent to which Americans have overcome their ethnic, racial, and cultural diversity.[42]

The second theme is developed with some sense of the cost of economic modernization and an awareness of ironic elements in the process. That cost was reduced by the fortuitous conditions, such as the availability of land and high mobility, under which industrialization occurred in America, but ironically "the very circumstances that moderated the impact of the industrial order . . . also fostered many an illusion that worked against a coherent national response to developments that made us, in the course of a century, the preeminent industrial power of the world." We persisted in conceiving of ourselves as an agrarian people long after we had become largely an industrial one, accepting an illusion that comforted us with the image of ourselves as unavaricious (avariciousness was considered in America to be a trait of nonagricultural peoples) while increasingly we gave ourselves to the pursuit of private wealth. Laissez faire was accepted in the United States as a path to communal well-being; what it "represented was a conversion of the nation to the faith that private interest — even private vice — would, whatever the incoherence of the moment, eventuate in a closer approximation of the public good than intelligent, cooperative forethought." The results of this policy were very different from this intention. The American who advocated complete free enterprise "barely glimpsed the possibility that *laissez faire* might create a new aristocracy and unequal happiness." Niebuhr and Heimert recognize the inequitable consequences of this policy. American farmers and workers "had been the victims rather than the beneficiaries of a system which promised justice through automatic balances in the market, but generated disparities of power in industrial enterprise itself." This view constitutes a critical application of Niebuhrian irony, but Niebuhr and Heimert exaggerate the extent to which these social wrongs have been rectified in the twentieth century.[43]

The Civil War played a crucial part in the process whereby agrarian America unintentionally transformed itself into an acquisitive industrial society, and Niebuhr and Heimert's interpretation of that war is suitably ironic. The war was the result of illusory self-images and false pictures of each other on the part of both the North and the South. Each section, "fighting as it thought for communal ideals and not for self, participated in what was a desperate *national* effort to recall the American spirit from the inexorable temptations of an acquisitive society." During the war itself there was a revival of public virtue, but the results of the war were quite the opposite of what had been intended: "the war had introduced America to the thought that conflict was the price not only of union but of progress. Within a decade of the Civil War, to be an American was to be, above all, an Ishmael, an entrant in a brutal competition in which, according to the most recent oracle, Darwin, only the fittest would survive."[44] A war fought in order to weld a more nearly perfect community among Americans and to preserve and extend civic virtue in the face of the growing acquisitive ethos of an industrial capitalism resulted in generating more competition and avarice. Since Niebuhr and Heimert see the reason for the disparity in the illusions of each side, this irony is critical and responsible in the best Niebuhrian sense.

*A Nation So Conceived* is also concerned, like *The Irony of American History*, with the development and dilemmas of American power. This theme is explicitly characterized as ironic, but the formulation here, as in the earlier book, is essentially passive. There was a contradiction between our expectations of how peace would be achieved and how it had in fact come about, but Niebuhr and Heimert do not indicate that our actions were responsible for that contradiction, so that in Niebuhr's own terms the situation is really a simple paradox; it does not have the moral significance of historical irony.[45]

In general this book is less preoccupied with foreign policy than the earlier work. Niebuhr and Heimert are not sympathetic with some aspects of nineteenth-century expansionism. They point to our "covert imperialism" more directly than did Niebuhr in the earlier work: "a nation of great economic strength like ours was bound to express itself in economic penetration of weaker nations— a form of covert imperialism which permits the expression of power without too obviously contradicting original ideals."[46] This would be an ironic formulation if it were stated more actively, but it is presented, like the ironic achievement of peace through a balance of terror, as if our exercise of hidden power over others were simply a historical inevitability for which we bear no responsibility.

In their account of the recent period of American foreign relations the authors do not carry over much of their criticism of our nineteenth-century behavior; it is colored by anticommunism but less obsessively so than in *The Irony of American History*. As in the earlier book, the most striking weakness of the treatment of our recent foreign relations is the failure to consider, as the ironic vision would suggest, what our intensive encounter with the rest of the world reveals about the limitations in our own assumptions, what it exposes about the illusions that have led us to act ironically, both internally and in dealing with others.[47]

In general then, although much of the apologetics that mars *The Irony of American History* persists in *A Nation So Conceived*, the later book does contain more criticism of America and is less obsessively anticommunist in spite of the continued presence of that theme. If there is not in fact much more critical use of Niebuhr's irony, there is more genuine history (as in the truly ironic account of the Civil War) and less of a tendency to see the past as simply preparation for present dilemmas. Certainly the fact that the book is less consistently focused on Cold War problems is one reason for the change. Perhaps the second author, Alan Heimert, is responsible for some of the difference; he is a literary historian, a student of and the successor to Perry Miller, and may have contributed to the more genuine concern with temporality in this book. I would conclude that in some marginal ways this book does represent a move a bit closer to the critical potential of Niebuhr's ironic concept, but that potential is not significantly fulfilled by it. That that kind of irony could serve to expose American pretenses in a far more cutting way, Niebuhr himself was to demonstrate in the last few years of his life.

Niebuhr's social and political ideas underwent numerous changes in the course of his long career. As has been noted, earlier in his life he had been a radical critic of American capitalism.[48] Between the end of World War II and the 1960s the Cold War limited his ability to perceive American evil, but before the end of his life he substantially recovered that ability. In the course of the 1960s he grew again increasingly critical of the United States, and apparently his Christianity became more completely detached from his image of America.[49] One development that moved him in this direction was the Civil Rights movement. Niebuhr was deeply affected by the way in which Martin Luther King and others used the essentially Christian method of nonviolent direct action to expose the evils of racism in American society, and he became more sensitive, as did many other Americans, to injustices within the nation that had seemed much less visible during the 1950s. Although Niebuhr took some pride in the role of King and other clergymen in the movement, and perhaps found in it a renewal of his own capacity for Christian social criticism, he also expressed dismay at the failure of the churches as institutions to meet the moral challenge of race relations and called for contrition and a renewed commitment.[50] In an article written in response to the report of the National Advisory Commission on Civil Disorders he asks us to "realize that the sheer helplessness of the black minority is due to a complacent self-satisfaction about our

American democracy." He points out how national illusions have fostered that complacency throughout our history, leading to the irony of the present time. "The climax of the contradiction in our national life which secured an affluent economy for the white man and increased misery for the Negro minority occurred in our own period, our industrial and technological era." Niebuhr acknowledges the failures of evangelical Protestantism, which he sees as an "ironic . . . source of complacence in the face of injustices which the Negro minority suffered at the hands of the white majority."[51] This essay, focused on racism, an issue almost ignored in *The Irony of American History*, reveals how a contemporary problem was rooted in illusions that arose out of our past; it is genuinely historical and ironic in terms of Niebuhr's own theory, and shows how his irony began to become a cutting, critical tool.

The last book that Niebuhr wrote (with Paul E. Sigmund), *The Democratic Experience: Past and Present* (1969), a work on government and not specifically on American history, acknowledged that the experience of the racial crisis had made him more critical of American democracy. The increased visibility of racial problems led Niebuhr to see the difficulties of democratic government in the West as more similar to those which confronted nations of the Third World than he had earlier thought. In addition to a more critical attitude on race relations in America this book also shows some reduction in Niebuhr's Cold War commitments. He did not abandon his belief that the West was fundamentally good and the communists evil, but his point of view toward both sides is more ambivalent in a spirit closer to the critical sympathy required by his ironic concept than the attitude that controls *The Irony of American History.* [52]

Finally, it was the Vietnam War that led Niebuhr to apply his ironic concept in a deeply critical way to the United States and to imply an ironic history markedly different from that which he had outlined in his original book on the subject.[53] An article published in 1967 reveals how the Vietnam War transformed Niebuhr's conception of the Cold War. While he continues to recognize the great differences between the internal social orders of the communist and Western nations, he comes much closer to equating their foreign policies. He reiterates his earlier recognition of the similar ideological denial of imperialism by the United States and the Soviet Union, but his perception of the dishonesty on the American side of this is much sharper. He applies this perception to history, and his presentation of past events takes on a new tone as exemplified by a comment on the idealistic rationalization of our entry into World War I. "The Wilsonian doctrine was an ideal moral fig leaf for a messianic nation in its first encounter with the problems of a nascent imperial dimension of power." He concludes that the result of Wilson's policy and rhetoric was not what was intended because of our illusions. He cites our continuing "myth of national purity" in spite of our continental expansion, involving as it did the Mexican War, and "our venture in overt, rather than covert, imperialism," the Spanish-American War, as evidence of "the capacity for self-deception, even on the part of democratic nations, in projecting mythical self-images to the world."[54]

In dealing with the Cold War itself Niebuhr goes much farther than before in equating American and Russian behavior:

> Ironies were compounded when historical providence made our innocent American democracy into one of the two imperial nations. Common sense certainly suggests that there were similar imperialistic impulses in both these powerful nations. But since both were by definition innocent of these impulses according to their own myths, both continued to proclaim their respective innocence. At the same time, the differences in their myths prompted them to cast each other in the role of the devil. We, as well as the Russians, are incapable of correcting or modifying our own national myths.

This reads almost like a critique of Niebuhr's demonic presentation of the Soviet Union in *The Irony of American History.* The retrospective shift in his perception of the Cold War seems to have been stimulated by the American experience in Southeast Asia. Niebuhr argues that our presence in Vietnam was the result of considerations of realpolitik but that as a nation we need government-invented "myths" to rationalize our involvement to ourselves. We justify our intervention by appealing to the "'right of self-determination' . . . we are told that we are only protecting a small nation from the 'aggression' of its neighbors," but "these myths and pretensions of our foreign policy are not sufficiently creditable to obscure our real hegemonial purposes." Niebuhr is highly critical of those myths and pretensions, but in this essay he is less clear-cut about condemning our action itself and its real motives than he is in attacking our illusory excuses for it.[55]

In another article, entitled "Vietnam: Study in Ironies," also published in 1967, Niebuhr is more explicitly critical of our policy itself as well as of our rationalizations for it. He sees our war aim as expressed in our peace proposals of that time as military victory under the cover of pretended compromise, an ironic situation because we were dishonest with ourselves as well as with our enemies as a result of deep-seated national illusions. "The contradiction between our ideal aims of a peace of conciliation and such an imposed peace, which only a defeated enemy would accept, can be understood only in the light of an ironic self-deception — ironic because we are the victims of our own ideology." Applying earlier insights in a more critical spirit, Niebuhr says that we deceive ourselves about the realities of our imperial behavior and actually damage our standing in the world as we seek to improve it because of illusions of innocence and our unconscious ideology. Our involvement in the war in Vietnam is "a mistake that has imperiled our imperial prestige. But in a democracy, particularly one with nostalgic visions of an early innocence, it is necessary to veil imperial and strategic interests behind 'democratic' and ideal goals. Hence, this war is interpreted as an ideological struggle between the 'free' world and the forces of communism."[56] The terms of the irony here are not new for Niebuhr. In his earlier work on American history he remarks upon our tendency to convince ourselves, and to try to convince others, that all our international actions were undertaken for the idealistic purpose of supporting democracy. The difference is that in the earlier work Niebuhr assumed that even if some self-deception had been involved in our actions in the last century and in the earlier part of this one, in the Cold War itself it was essentially true that we were protecting democracy. Our idealism became only a past and potential source of ironic behavior, not a form of present self-deception. The war in Vietnam seems to have been for Niebuhr the acting out of that potential and as such it sensitized him to the irony and evil in our actual behavior.

His changed perception of our international role, his acknowledgment that we did not simply protect freedom in our Cold War actions, is subtly suggested by the quotation marks around the word *free* in the last quotation, an emphasis that would not have appeared in his earlier work. Related to that change is his abandonment of his demonic view of communism. It became possible for Niebuhr to see American behavior with a more critical irony in part because he came to recognize concretely, not just theoretically, the ambiguous mixture of good and evil in our enemies, at least in the Vietnamese communists. He points out that, contrary to our ideological assumptions, "Ho Chi Minh is both a national patriot *and* a communist." Along with that recognition Niebuhr also abandons the monolithic view of international communism and observes that China and Russia compete in supporting the North Vietnames. He sees another irony or, perhaps more accurately, a paradox, in the juxtaposition of the Russian and American roles in

Vietnam: "the war has become a contest between two nuclear imperial powers, who are, or have been, ironically, the tacit partners to prevent a nuclear catastrophe" (which suggests the perception of a moral equality between the two nations absent from his earlier work).[57]

Niebuhr comments on the American conviction that we are incapable of imperialism and relates it to our belief that we are "also free of *any* ideological taint," an illusion that we share with the communists. That we in fact perceive the world through ideological glasses is most clearly revealed for Niebuhr by our tendency "to regard a free democratic government as a simple historical possibility for all nations in all continents and in every stage of cultural and economic development." This is another idea that can be found in *The Irony of American History,* but Niebuhr's application of it to our behavior in Vietnam makes it into a far more critical insight than it was in the earlier book because here it is applied to a situation in which we clearly play an active historical role derived from an ideology to which we are blind and that blinds us to the realities of the situation in which we act. This simplistic assumption about the universal possibility and desirability of democracy was an important factor in our involvement in Vietnam. In the service of that assumption we have sustained a government in South Vietnam that is "a perfect caricature of democracy, which corresponds to the caricature of communist propaganda." In support of that government and the imperial ambitions and ideological convictions it represents we have conducted a war that has destroyed many lives and ended our domestic reform.[58] The unintended consequences of our pretensions and ideologically induced illusions of defending democracy abroad have been to weaken our own democracy and to prevent its further development in our national life.

The crowning irony of our war in Vietnam, according to Niebuhr, is attributable to Lyndon Johnson. "The master politician in the White House has achieved a final irony in our 'democratic' foreign policy. He has ordered a massive bombing of North Vietnam in order to force our adversary into an 'honorable peace.'" This bombing has primarily domestic political purposes, but it "not only intensifies the odium in which we are held by the rest of the world, but also increases the danger of confrontation with either China or Russia." Niebuhr finds an added twist to this irony in its dependence upon our vast productivity. "A final ironic touch is given by the fact that only our plutocratic wealth allows us to commit these stupidities in international relations." In *The Irony of American History* Niebuhr comments upon the ironic potential of our assuming credit for our great wealth, which was really much more the result of chance, but here that wealth becomes a source of irony in a much more critical and immediate sense.[59]

We have here a brief account of a genuinely critical and historical irony of recent American history. In defending the "free" world against communism we have come to accept world responsibilities and develop imperial pretensions, but we fail to recognize those pretensions because of our illusions of virtue. We assume that all we are doing is protecting democracy, which we ideologically believe can flourish anywhere. In Vietnam we responded to a threat to our imperial pretensions that was perceived as a threat to the democratic world. In this response we ignored the nationalistic component of Vietnamese communism, seeing it as simply demonic. In our efforts to protect our prestige and further the cause of democracy we have in fact damaged that prestige in the eyes of the world, supported a phony democratic regime that tends to validate communist propaganda, weakened our internal democracy, and increased the danger of nuclear confrontation. All of these consequences are the unintended results of our acting under illusions of our own peculiar virtues, an exaggeratedly demonic perception of communism, and a false conception of our prestige. Niebuhr's vision in this short essay is definitely historical in the sense that the irony is perceived as the product of American action and not as the result of a static state or something that was done to us, as is the case with a number of the ironies in *The Irony of American History*. Although this essay builds upon insights in that book, it deals with a major irony of recent American history with more critical penetration than appears in relation to any of the situations dealt with in the earlier work.

By 1969 Niebuhr was able to acknowledge that his earlier call for "realism" was "excessively consistent" and to retreat from his criticism of Karl Barth's neutralism. The war in Vietnam had led him to recognize the dangers of anticommunism. "I must admit that our wealth makes our religious anticommunism particularly odious. Perhaps there is not much to choose between communist and anti-communist fanaticism, particularly when the latter, combined with our wealth, has caused us to stumble into the most pointless, costly and bloody war in our history."[60]

In other essays Niebuhr continued to use his ironic vision of America to criticize our role in Vietnam. The connection between these writings and *The Irony of American History* was made explicit in the case of an article entitled "The Presidency and the Irony of American History," which the editors of *Christianity and Crisis* prefaced with some quotations from the book defining irony. In this article Niebuhr sees the war as a product of our "pride of power . . . pride of virtue" and "pride of riches." He relates our uninhibited and unprofitable pursuit of pride in Vietnam to the ineffectiveness of the restraints upon the power of the president. He goes so far as to suggest that "our elected monarchs have become despots" and argues that our pursuit of pride could have been stopped only if presidential power had been effectively checked. Niebuhr concludes this highly critical article with some comments on how the war in Vietnam was ironic for America and how it was tragic:

> Since our difficulties in being involved in a pointless war may have sprung from our virtues, it might be said that the war represents a tragic chapter in our history. But since our boundless democratic self-esteem assumed these virtues without question, it would be more accurate to say we are anxious to draw to a close an ironic rather than tragic period. The well-known words of the Bible "whosoever exalteth himself shall be brought low" suggests that we are involved in an ironic error. Yet the death and destruction wrought by the war have made it a burden too heavy to be borne and tragic in its proportions.[61]

In a brief editorial column in the *New York Times* that Niebuhr wrote in 1970 he reiterated his sharp criticism of our Vietnamese policy and related it to pretensions that can be found throughout American history, particularly "the tradition of our self-righteous estimate of our own motives amidst the moral ambiguities of international power politics." In contrast to some of his earlier writing he here suggests much continuity in American pretensions and illusions in foreign affairs. He notes how old the idea of America as a "redeemer nation" is, and observes that "the hiatus, however, between our ideals and the ambiguities of power politics became more and more apparent when the young and small 'redeemer nation' became one of the two nuclear superpowers." In Woodrow Wilson he finds an example of how illusions and self-deceptions produced unintended consequences in American foreign policy in the past. Wilson called World War I "a commercial war" before we entered it but described it as a war "to keep the world safe for democracy" and one undertaken for the "right of self-determination of nations" when we joined it. Of the last phrase he observes that "Wilson had in mind not the independence of the Philippines, but the disintegration of the Hapsburg empire." Niebuhr's account of the consequences of Wilson's war policy is bitingly ironic. He notes that Wilson's fourteen points included a rejection of indemnities; that principle "was

contradicted by exacting a huge indeminity. Wilson had hoped that
the League of Nations would correct this; but meanwhile the war
debts wrecked the German economy, and sowed the seeds of Hitler's
despotic and immoral anti-Semitic reign. Isolationist revulsion
against the Versailles Treaty swamped our great nation in neurotic
neutralism." Niebuhr concludes this brief account of American
history with an enumeration of our foreign and domestic problems
and an appeal for a therapeutic ironic consciousness. "Our record as
a righteous nation has proved so filled with error that, obviously, we
must stop thanking God we are not like other nations. . . . Our overwhelming foreign and domestic problems must finally convince us
that the childish illusions of our infant days have come to an end."[62]
This short piece suggests how Niebuhr's ironic vision of American
history can be turned into a critical tool while offering the hope of
some resolution of national problems through a bitter acknowledgment of how our illusions have led us to contribute to our own problems.[63]


   The changes in Niebuhr's ironic perception of America toward
the end of his life might be regarded as a major reversal of his earlier
vision. The specifics of *The Irony of American History*, in contrast
to the general principles laid out in that work, suggested that irony
was applicable to the American past and a danger for the future,
but that in the present we were largely free of threatening illusions
and pretensions. The account of America there was mostly
ahistorical, in the sense that our role as a responsible actor in contributing to the development of our own difficulties was
understated. The Christianity that was the source of Niebuhr's
general ironic vision of how human evil is related to human virtue
ironically seemed to block his perception of American evil under the
conditions of intensive Cold War. The import of his last articles is
very different. In them Niebuhr presents American history in a continuity with the present; he sees us continuing to act under illusions
of innocence and power, acting so as to bring about evil, if
unintended, consequences. There are some similarities in particular
ironies presented in these two periods of Niebuhr's writings, but the
difference in tone and moral stance toward America is marked. Yet
I would argue that there is a deeper continuity of perception, that
Niebuhr's critical use of irony can best be understood as a fulfillment of the original implications of the idea imperfectly executed in
his earlier work on American history.
   The discrepancy between the theoretical parts of *The Irony of*

*American History* and the chapters that deal with substantive issues in the American past and present is striking. Those chapters were deeply colored by Cold War attitudes and assumptions that prevented Niebuhr from achieving the critical distance from America needed for irony. Niebuhr's perception of the communists as demonic obscured his vision of American evil. His apparent identification of Christianity with the cause of the West, in spite of his own warnings against confusing the realm of the absolute with any earthly power, reinforced his blindness to American evil. His view of the evil in communism as largely the result of a pretense to the ability to control history led him, in contrast, away from the recognition, demanded by his own theory, of the active role of the United States in contributing to the historical development of its own problems. On the other hand, the atmosphere of the Cold War may have sharpened Niebuhr's awareness of the close connection between evil and virtue in human action, an awareness that informs the theoretical parts of the book. The general description of irony there seems perfectly suited to the human, critical, and therapeutic study of the American past, although at that time Niebuhr himself was not in a frame of mind to apply it very effectively.[64]

It might be said, however, that history itself brought Niebuhr to the point where he was much better able to make use of his own ironic concept. Although these last articles do not constitute anything like a full ironic history of America, they do suggest how such a history might be written. They are critical of American actions without abandoning a basic sympathy with America. They seem, even more surprisingly, to be genuinely historical in implication, although they are too brief and too much focused on present problems to be really historical in substance. They suggest an image of America as suffering from illusions of innocence and power and as actively responsible for the evil consequences of its own actions.

Niebuhr's sensitivity to the way in which human evil is related to human virtue is the starting point for his most profound insights into the processes of history. As evil consequences of American action became more visible in the 1960s, Niebuhr was able to apply that sensitivity to the situation and history of his own nation without losing sympathy with it. The Civil Rights movement and the war in Vietnam may have led Niebuhr to disidentify Christianity with America so that he gained greater critical distance and was freed from the limitations that Christianity ironically had imposed on his irony. It is as if history fulfilled the implications of Niebuhr's ironic theory while at the same time undermining his earlier specific applications of that theory.[65] It is to his credit, and to our benefit, that it did so just in time for him to suggest some of the ways in which his concept of irony might be applied in a critical vision of the American past. An appreciation by Henry May of *The Irony of American History* might better be applied to that book along with Niebuhr's later and more critical comments on American history: "Niebuhr made us understand, that either innocent escape or durable victory was impossible. All triumph was illusory because of the dual nature of man. Good and evil, virtues and faults, were linked together. This was the ironical situation, true of all men, and especially poignant for Americans because of our tendency to insist on our own innocence."[66]

# V.  Irony and Consensus History

Reinhold Niebuhr was a crucial figure in the intellectual life of mid-twentieth-century America, but the direct impact of *The Irony of American History* on professional historians was limited.[1] His influence on historiography was largely indirect; he gave expression to and furthered the development of certain general attitudes in post-World War II America that affected the writing of history only as it affected other cultural activities. There undoubtedly were some historians among the mythic fraternity invented by Morton White called "Atheists for Niebuhr."[2] For example, Perry Miller, a major historical ironist, acknowledged a rather reluctant membership in that group saying that he was one of "those who . . . have copiously availed themselves of Niebuhr's conclusions without pretending to share his basic and to him indispensable, premise."[3]

This chapter will examine the relationship between consensus history and irony through a study of some of the work of three major scholars who produced general statements of the consensus interpretation of the American experience: Richard Hofstadter, Daniel Boorstin, and Louis Hartz. Although I shall argue that both Hofstadter and Hartz made use of ironic forms similar to those of Niebuhr, it is not my intention to attribute this to Niebuhr's direct influence. They arrived at their ironic views by paths that may have paralleled Niebuhr's, but they did not specifically follow after him.

## 1. Consensus History

A major shift in American historical attitudes occurred after World War II. The Progressive interpretation in one form or another had continued to color the writing of American history between the wars in spite of a growing sense of its inadequacies among some scholars. By the 1950s it had been replaced by a consensus, or post-Progressive, view. Instead of conflict between economic interest groups, agreement upon political fundamentals came to be perceived as the most distinctive characteristic of the American past. American history seemed to be marked by its continuity, by a gradual process of evolution, rather than by a series of sudden changes. Whereas Progressive historians had tended to see the forces that move history as hidden selfish motives, consensus historians were impressed with the role of principles and ideas. They were more ready to accept the statements of historical actors at face value, and when they looked beneath the surface they tended to focus on psychological forces rather than disguised economic motives.[4]

A number of factors conspired to bring about this shift in historical views. In part it was simply the result of the development of certain tendencies within Progressivism itself. When Charles Beard argued that there was a correlation between the ownership of public securities and support for the Constitution it was only a matter of time until historians would broaden the scope of the correlations and refine Beard's methods, with the result of exposing similarities between those who favored and those who opposed the Constitution. As the focus on conflict in the Progressive form became exhausted, it was natural for historians to think in terms of its opposite. As Gene Wise has argued, consensus or counter-Progressive history arose in part out of the anomolies in Progressive history, out of the ambiguities that that interpretive form could not comprehend.[5]

Ambiguity and uncertainty were pervasive in post-World War II America. Changes in the social and political climate within which historians worked had a profound effect on their vision of the past. In the 1940s Americans had seen fascism lead to a world war and in the later part of the decade the fear grew that communism might produce a conflagration. It seemed as if America, which had felt itself to be the great expanding power in the world for decades, no longer had the initiative. We were on the defensive against the rising tide of communism. The discovery of the horrors of Nazi and Stalinist concentration camps generated the feeling that the only alternatives to liberal, democratic capitalism led to evils far greater than those of that system. In addition, the development of the atomic bomb created great anxiety that another war would mean the end of mankind or at least of civilization.

This fearful picture of the world outside our borders was combined with a contrasting image of domestic prosperity. Contrary to widespread fears, the end of the war did not bring about the return of the depression. Instead, the standard of living of many Americans greatly improved. The reforms of the New Deal, the increased effectiveness of labor unions, and the practical acceptance of deficit financing seemed to produce general prosperity and put a cushion under the harmful effects of capitalistic economics. This combination of circumstances led to a tendency on the part of historians to focus upon that which was unique in the American experience, that which distinguished us from other nations rather than that which we had in common with them. The apparent stability of our politics appeared to contrast sharply with the ideological conflicts that had disrupted the history of Europe throughout the twentieth century. It came to seem that in addition to being new, our country was old in the sense that we had survived under the same constitutional structure longer than most nations of Europe. The conceptual framework through which Progressive historians had perceived the American past no longer seemed relevant to a changed American present.

The focus on American consensus and continuity, stability, and prosperity engendered by the sociopolitical circumstances under which historians wrote was reinforced by some cultural developments of the period. American thought came more directly under the influence of Europe than it had been in the nineteenth or early twentieth centuries. European thought in this period, where it was not dominated by one form of Marxism or another, was markedly disillusioned. Three European tendencies that affected American literature and ideas in the postwar period were existentialism, neoorthodox Christianity, and Freudian psychoanalysis. All of these have in common tendencies toward a pessimistic concept of human nature, negative views of human potential, and doubts about the power of human reason. The European influence was direct, in the sense that many European intellectuals emigrated to America, which, for example, had the effect of New York's replacing Vienna as the international capital of psychoanalysis. In addition, indirectly, Americans were more receptive to European ideas, more in touch with European attitudes and assumptions than before, more directly involved in the international dialogue, even, in the visual arts at least, leading Europeans in new, sophisticated ways. This close cultural communication with Europe contrasted with our tendency in this period to reject the relevance of European political precedents, to emphasize our uniqueness. What we were receiving from Europe were points of view themselves largely critical of European politics. The older, optimistic liberalism seemed generally discredited on both sides of the Atlantic, although under these conditions liberal democratic principles of government appeared more attractive in America than utopian hopes for a better world.

The process of disillusionment was centered in the arts in America. In most academic disciplines its effects were indirect, but nonetheless real. Historians and political scientists who came to believe that the end of ideology had been reached were restating in the pragmatic language of American thought attitudes very similar to those that underlay existentialism. In theology, under the leadership of Niebuhr and others, neoorthodoxy became dominant, and although academic psychology remained largely immune, psychoanalysis became the most widely accepted view of human nature among American intellectuals in general. Its impact was much deeper and truer to Freud's own hard-headed vision than the fashionable interest in psychoanalysis as a liberating doctrine in the 1920s.

The consensus interpretation of American history, which was a response of the historical profession to all of these influences, has been characterized in contradictory ways by critics and commentators. As it first developed, the new view of the American past was seen and praised in its own terms. The argument that the American past was characterized by an agreement upon fundamentals and marked by an unusual continuity of political institutions and ideas seemed persuasive. It offered comfort to a fearful but prosperous people.

Criticism of this approach soon began to appear. The Progressive view of America had arisen out of a commitment to reform, and much of the history written by Progressives was intended to serve the purpose of reform. Consensus history seemed without ethical purpose. Its view of the American past appeared to be bland, and its function in the present merely that of justifing the status quo.[6] Its pretense to objectivity was not so much an advance over Progressive relativism as a retreat to the scientific pretensions of late nineteenth-century historians. The change in the political atmosphere of the 1960s deepened and broadened the criticism of consensus history. Some historians questioned the basic assertion that American history has been marked by an agreement upon fundamentals, and others, who accepted that as a description of the American past, argued that, to the extent that there was such an agreement, it was a mark of the limitations of American politics, not its virtues. The assumption that relative prosperity had characterized the lives of Americans in the past was challenged as a result of the discovery of the persistence of poverty in the present, and the relative neglect by the consensus historians of the history of minority groups (in spite of their sympathy for the Civil Rights movement and their tendency to see the Civil War as a moral struggle over slavery) and of the common man and woman was criticized. The assertion by some post-Progressive historians that American liberalism was a political creed without an ideology was denied by those who saw an unacknowledged ideology underneath the seemingly pragmatic surface. The tendency of consensus historians to focus on ideas was challenged by those who insisted that social and economic life influenced thought. For some younger historians the consensus historians seemed to abandon faith in human reason as they sought psychological explanations for political behavior and discredited past radical movements.[7]

A rather different picture of consensus history has emerged from some of its defenders in recent years. While acknowledging weaknesses in the explanatory power of the idea of consensus and admitting that the emphasis on abundance and agreement has led to important omissions, they have argued nonetheless that consensus history represents a step forward. They have emphasized the way in which consensus history increased our sense of the complexity of the historical process in America, drawing attention to ambiguity and self-contradiction in American life. They suggest that post-Progressive history is not necessarily wedded to the nationalism that it seemed to serve in the 1950s, that in its very insistence upon American distinctiveness it draws our attention to the comparison of American history with that of other nations. In this view the abandonment of the bipolar vision of the American past held by Progressive historians opens up the possibility of seeing that past in more variegated terms, allowing us to use more sophisticated models. They argue that consensus history has been the handmaiden of new quantitative methods that make it possible for us now to recapture some of the history of the mass of Americans and oppressed groups that have been invisible in the conventional documentary sources previously relied upon by historians. They maintain that the focus on irrationality that some critics find so objectionable is a great virtue, pointing to new dimensions of historical inquiry. Finally, the defenders of consensus history claim that the assertion that American politics has been marked by an agreement upon fundamentals draws our attention away from political history, which has been the central concern of American historians throughout the history of American historical writing. They suggest that we are now free to devote more attention to the history of the ways in which Americans have actually lived, seeking in that to recapture more of the genuine past as well as finding deeper explanations for political behavior in nonpolitical factors more subtle than economic interest.[8]

Which of these pictures of consensus history (still perhaps the general view accepted by most professional historians who will admit to having a general view) is accurate? Perhaps they both are. It may be that consensus history has been for some historians essentially an apologetic approach to the American past, while for others it has been a way of revealing complexity. (There may be scholars in whose work it is apologetic in some contexts and critical in others.) Perhaps one historiographic movement has encompassed both a reassertion of comforting myths of unique American virtues and a maturation of historical consciousness, promising a deeper criticism than that of the Progressive historians, who did not abandon a fundamental faith in American exceptionalism. Irony is associated with a complex vision of the past, with a sense of ambiguity and contradictions. It is the antithesis of apologetic history—in spite of Niebuhr's tendency to use it that way. An examination of the use of irony by consensus historians differentiates the critical from the apologetic in the work of particular consensus historians and among consensus historians. While irony does not exhaust the ways in which the writing of American history has matured in the last few decades, it is a sign of that maturity.[9]

The historians to be examined in this chapter are the three major generalizers of consensus history, Richard Hofstadter, Daniel Boorstin, and Louis Hartz.[10] While it is true that the consensus point of view was established at least as much by work on particular problems and periods, sweeping studies by these three men played an important role in the acceptance of a new formulation of the American past in the post-World War II period. By examining the presence of irony—or its absence—in these works, we can gauge the extent to which the vision of an ironic pattern at the core of American history became part of the established interpretation of our past, an interpretation paradoxically perceived as supporting American beliefs in our unique innocence, virtue, wisdom, and success.

## 2. Richard Hofstadter: *The American Political Tradition*

Richard Hofstadter might be regarded as the original consensus historian. His *American Political Tradition and the Men Who Made It* (1947) was the first general book on American history (and one of the most influential) written from that point of view.[11] In defending consensus history against its critics twenty years later Hofstadter indirectly described this study as representing "the rediscovery of complexity in American history," including "the unintended consequences of political actions."[12] *The American Political Tradition* is a highly sophisticated work containing a consensus interpretation and Niebuhrian irony, both serving the purposes of critical history. My discussion of Hofstadter will focus on this book because of its originality, generality, and influence.

*The American Political Tradition* consists of a series of essays — most of them biographical studies of major individual statesmen — held together by the consistency of Hofstadter's concerns and perspective rather than by a continuous narrative line. His overall consensus interpretation of American history is expressed in the introduction, which Higham informs us was written after the body of the book was completed.[13] Hofstadter argues that historians have focused too much on conflict in the American past, obscuring our perceptions of deeper agreements on the fundamentals of democratic capitalism. "The fierceness of the political struggles has often been misleading; for the range of vision embraced by the primary contestants in the major parties has always been bound by the horizons of property and enterprise." Continuity as well as consensus marks Hofstadter's interpretation. He argues that these same basic principles were held by leading Americans from the end of the eighteenth century through the mid-twentieth century.[14]

Although Hofstadter characterized the American political tradition as one of consensus, he himself did not participate in that consensus. His critical approach toward American political culture is most obvious in some of his remarks on individual statesmen, an approach that he justified by the comment that "democratic society . . . can more safely be overcritical than overindulgent in its attitude toward public leadership."[15]

His criticism went far beyond the character and ability of American statesmen. Two decades after *The American Political Tradition* was published he himself suggested that his ability to recognize the American consensus arose out of the fact that he did

not share it. "My own assertion of consensus history in 1948 had its
source in the Marxism of the 1930s." He follows this with a quotation from his own earlier book to the effect that American
democracy "has been a democracy in cupidity rather than a
democracy of fraternity."[16] In an informative essay Arthur Schlesinger, Jr., remarks that, in contrast to Daniel Boorstin, "Hofstadter
perceived the consensus from a radical perspective, from the outside, and deplored it." Christopher Lasch, a student of Hofstadter's,
has recently described the radical milieu out of which *The
American Political Tradition* came. He relates Hofstadter to a
group of intellectuals around the *Partisan Review* who attacked the
Progressive intellectual tradition because it had become nationalistic and self-celebrating.[17] Although specific evidence of
Marxism is slight in the book, there are many indications that, while
Hofstadter respected some aspects of American democracy, he rejected the basic values of American capitalism when he wrote this
consensus history.

Hofstadter saw the preservation and expansion of capitalism as
the central concerns of American politics. "The sanctity of private
property, the right of the individual to dispose of and invest it, the
value of opportunity, and the natural evolution of self-interest and
self-assertion, within broad legal limits, into a beneficent social
order have been staple tenets of the central faith in American
political ideologies." As his remark quoted above on "democracy in
cupidity" suggests, when he acknowledges that America has been
democratic as well as capitalistic, Hofstadter implies a feeling that
the evils of capitalism have compromised the virtues of democracy.[18]
This theme reappears in various places throughout the book and
underlies one of its major ironies.

Another recurring theme in the book is the anachronism of the
ideas that make up the American consensus. Hofstadter suggests
that American politics were trapped in a set of assumptions bequeathed to us by the Founding Fathers that offered us no alternative to a dehumanized capitalism. "Modern humanistic thinkers
who seek for a means by which society may transcend eternal conflict and rigid adherence to property rights as its integrating principles can expect no answer in the philosophy of balanced government as it was set down by the Constitution-makers of 1787."
Neither does our two-party system function so as to foster diversity:
"party differences have rarely been profound and party structure
has been so rigid that minorities, instead of being focused on either
major party when it was out, have rather had to sunder their traditional party ties and—in most cases—drown alone in the political

seas." This statement reveals how in Hofstadter's hands the argument that American politics was based upon an agreement on fundamentals was critical and not apologetic.[19]

Hofstadter's critical attitudes toward capitalism and some other features of American life are aspects of a complex and in part ambivalent attitude toward American history in general, an attitude that is often expressed in paradoxes and ironies. Some of the paradoxes are benign, with a light cutting edge; others are more deeply critical.

His rhetorical irony is frequently very biting and sometimes quite amusing. A good example is his closing comment on Grover Cleveland: "this product of good conscience and self-help, with his stern ideas of purity, efficiency, and service, was a taxpayer's dream, the ideal bourgeois statesman for his time: out of heartfelt conviction he gave to the interests what many a lesser politician might have sold them for a price."[20]

In addition to rhetorical irony Hofstadter makes use of the Niebuhrian form. As we shall see, sometimes that irony is fully developed but at others it is not, usually because of his highly critical attitude. His treatment of William Jennings Bryan closely follows the Niebuhrian form but it is in the end too unsympathetic for irony. Bryan's great virtue and the source of his strength lay in his ability to articulate the ideas and feelings of the Western farmer, but this was also the source of his weakness because those ideas could not resolve the farmers' problems under the conditions that had developed by the late nineteenth century. Wedded too much to the past, Bryan could not accomplish that which he wished to do, to improve the farmers' lot in the present, in part because he was too close to those he wished to help. An added ironic twist appears when Hofstadter suggests that perhaps unconsciously Bryan's motives were confused; part of him really did not seek the power that he would need to accomplish his conscious intention of solving the farmers' problems through the application of the old values. As much as this sounds like irony, however, there is too much hostility in Hofstadter's attitude toward Bryan to regard this as really an example of Niebuhr's approach. He does not lead us to identify with Bryan's humanity as irony should. The flaws that Hofstadter sees in Bryan are too deep and general. Damningly, Hofstadter says that "the Commoner's heart was filled with simple emotions, but his mind was stocked with equally simple ideas."[21] Other writers might maintain sympathy for a man they regarded as stupid, but I do not believe that Hofstadter could. Similar ironies, incomplete for much the same reason, inform his chapters on the two Roosevelts and

Herbert Hoover. In general, Hofstadter had the sensitivity to perceive ironic patterns but was at times too critical as a historian to maintain a consistent Niebuhrian attitude. When he did maintain that attitude, however, his ironies were penetrating.

One such irony informs Hofstadter's account of Jackson's war with the Second Bank of the United States (BUS). Opposition to the bank was widespread among diverse groups, according to Hofstadter; farmers interested in land speculation; Southern, Western, and New York City bankers; labor; and small businessmen. A general resentment of the special privileges represented by monopolistic state corporation charters was frequently directed against the BUS and it was held responsible for many problems, some of which were none of its fault. A key point Hofstadter makes is that the bank was opposed by different people for contradictory reasons: "it was blamed by Western inflationists for deflationary policies and by Eastern hardmoney men for inflation."[22]

Jackson himself was deeply sympathetic "with the entrepreneurial impulse that gave Jacksonian democracy so much of its freshness and vitality." He perceived the bank in opposition to that impulse as "an instrument of great privilege and power." Hofstadter points out the unchecked public power that the bank really had but he judges that the BUS "had done a creditable job in stabilizing the currency and holding in check inflationary pressure from the wildcatters."[23] Although its director, Nicholas Biddle, tried to keep it out of politics, that was impossible. In spite of its beneficial effects, and in spite (or because) of its great potential power, Jackson, who had a distaste for all banks, decided to oppose rechartering the BUS. Biddle chose to force the issue himself and asked Congress for a rechartering bill, which was passed but vetoed by Jackson.

Jackson was successful in destroying a center of privilege but the economic effects that his attack on the bank produced were quite opposed to those he had intended to bring about. Hofstadter's summary of the consequences of the conflict is clearly ironic: "Pursuing the bank war to its conclusion, Jackson found defeat in victory." In fighting Jackson, Biddle brought about a short depression, but Jackson for his part produced a large-scale inflation followed by a major bust: "This had been no part of Jackson's intention, nor that of his hardmoney followers. . . . By destroying Biddle's bank Jackson had taken away the only effective restraint on the wildcatters. . . . He was opposed to both privilege and inflation, but in warring on one he had succeeded only in releasing the other . . . he had left the nation committed to a currency and credit system even more inadequate than the one he had inherited." Hofstadter argues that

Jackson, in bringing down the BUS, mixed legitimate fears about its undemocratic character with economic illusions, and thereby missed the opportunity of preserving a useful institution in a reformed and more democratic shape: "The popular hatred of privilege and the dominant laissez-faire ideology made an unhappy combination."[24]

This is a clear and significant ironic pattern. Jackson and his hard-money followers sought to destroy the BUS for two reasons: as a center of privilege, which it was, and as the source of paper money and inflation, which it was only in a restrained way. In destroying the bank they did end it as a center of privilege, but instead of creating a hard-money situation they increased the amount of paper money with inflationary effects, resulting in an exaggeration of the boom-bust cycle. This was not their intention, nor was it a price they were consciously willing to pay for the destruction of the bank's privileges. Neither was it necessary, in Hofstadter's judgment. He suggests that the reasons for this action were opposition to privilege and the laissez-faire ideology that assumed that, without such institutions as the BUS, money would return to its "natural" state, hard currency. Such an assumption was both false and self-serving. It is possible to infer from Hofstadter's account that Jacksonian hard-money beliefs and opposition to all banks were in a sense illusions of financial innocence, expressions of a desire not to be implicated in the monetary consequences of the entrepreneurial fever in which the Jackson men participated. There is also perhaps the element of a pretense on Jackson's part to a power he did not have. Hofstadter points out that Jackson did have the power to kill the bank, but he did not have the ability to return the country to a hard-money system while preserving and expanding entrepreneurial opportunities, although his pride of power was such that he seems to have imagined that he could do this. To the extent that Hofstadter suggests that Jackson imagined he had such a capacity, he operated under illusions of power as well as innocence. In any event, even if for some Jackson men — the inflationists — the bank war had intended consequences, for Jackson himself and for many of his followers those consequences were, in Hofstadter's account, clearly ironic.

Among Hofstadter's chapters on modern figures, the one on Wilson contains the most Niebuhrian irony. In spite of the comment that Wilson sought "a forward-looking return to the past," Hofstadter does not treat his domestic program ironically.[25] He regards that program as a temporarily successful effort to institute conservative reform, although he does say that the war and consequent reaction destroyed most of its acomplishments. But his accounts of Wilson's role in the period of American neutrality, in our entry into the war, and in the peacemaking are all permeated with Niebuhrian irony.

According to Hofstadter, anglophile sympathies and a fear of the consequences for the United States of a German victory were combined in Wilson with a wish to remain at peace and made it impossible for him to realize that wish. That combination "made real neutrality impossible. . . .and in the end" Wilson "became a prisoner of his own policies." Hofstadter suggests that he could have used the Allies' economic dependence on us to exert pressure on them rather than being drawn into the war by our need for trade with them. It was felt that Allied war orders staved off a depression in the United States so that when it became necessary to loan the Allies money to maintain their buying power, the ban on loans to belligerents was lifted. Hofstadter argues that Wilson thought that if Allied business was cut off, there would be economic distress; then the Republicans would come to power and "what chance would there be for peace or world leadership on a disinterested and elevated plane? No, the best course of action would be to keep the American people busy and prosperous at their peaceful wartime pursuits, the manufacture of munitions."[26] Hofstadter seems to be suggesting here that Wilson's illusions of his own virtue — as compared to men like Roosevelt and Lodge — played a role in steps that the United States took that led to war.

In Hofstadter's account, American entry into World War I was the unintended consequence of Wilson's policy of unneutrality. That policy was manifested not only in the war loans to the Allies but in the prejudicial way in which he dealt with German submarine warfare as opposed to the British blockade of Germany. When in 1916 he secured a German pledge limiting the use of submarines by threatening to break diplomatic relations, he planted the seeds of the crisis that was to bring us into war during the following year: "this concession had been won by a virtual threat of war, and Wilson had placed himself in a position that would require a declaration of war if the pledge should be withdrawn." In early 1917 Wilson was as committed to keeping the United States out of the war as he had ever been, but he was forced to face the unexpected results of his earlier action when the Germans announced the unrestricted resumption of submarine warfare. "In one instant Wilson reaped the whirlwind of unneutrality that he had sown in the first two years of the war. For the Germans . . . were calculating on American entrance into the war."[27]

Wilson, then, the man of peace, brought the United States into a

war that Hofstadter believes he did not wish and might have avoided. In assuming that the United States could remain the innocent
neutral while supplying arms to the Allies — and profiting from the
trade — Wilson led us "innocently" into war. Hofstadter suggests
that Wilson felt his responsibility for the unintended outcome of his
policy and subsequently acted like a man trapped in an ironic pattern:

> in accepting war he was forced for the first time to turn his back
> upon his deepest values. The man who had said that peace is the
> healing and elevating influence of the world was now pledged to
> use 'Force, Force to the utmost, Force without stint or limit.' Hav-
> ing given the nation into the hands of a power in which he did not
> believe, he was driven more desperately than ever before in his
> life to justify himself, and the rest of his public career became a
> quest for self-vindication. Nothing less than the final victory of
> the forces of democracy and peace could wash away his sense of
> defeat — and Wilson was conscious of defeat in the very hour in
> which he delivered his ringing war message in tones of such confi-
> dent righteousness.[28]

Wilson's illusions of innocence interfered with his ability to
achieve the type of peace he wanted, just as they had led him into
the war he did not wish. Hofstadter points out that he failed to
utilize American power, particularly economic power, to pressure
the Allies into accepting the kind of just peace he sought, just as he
had failed to use their economic dependence upon the United States
in the period before it entered the war. His failure to take account of
economic realities in his plans for peace was further evidence of his
lack of realism. Hofstadter argues that Wilson understood the role
of economic relations in causing the war, but failed to act on that
understanding in the program for peace that he presented because
of his return to illusions of innocence and virtue. In general, that
idea seems central to Hofstadter's presentation of Wilson's role at
Versailles.[29]

Although some of Hofstadter's comments on Wilson's behavior at
Versailles are quite critical, he retains enough respect for and sympathy with Wilson for his attitude to be described as ironic.
Hofstadter observes that Wilson worked under severe handicaps and
did achieve some mitigation of the terms of the treaty. He comments
ironically that among the circumstances that limited Wilson's
freedom of action at Versailles was the fact that he was "committed
by his belief in capitalism and nationalism to accept the major consequences of the disaster they had wrought." He believes that

Wilson had the realism to know how bad the treaty was, although he felt compelled to defend it, and furthermore "one thing, he believed might save the whole structure—the Covenant of the League."[30]

Wilson's struggle in support of American entry into the League, Hofstadter suggests, amounted to an effort to preserve his illusions of his own virtue: "The effort to save the League became a matter of the most desperate psychological urgency for him. His plans had been hamstrung, his hopes abandoned one after another, until nothing but the League was left. . . . If a lasting peace were not realized what justification could he find for having led his country into war? His sense of guilt hung over him like a cloud." Hofstadter's description of Wilson's behavior in the struggle over American entry into the League reads very like the description of a man acting out an ironic process and defeating himself: "By refusing to accept the mildest reservation upon American membership . . . he did as much to keep the United States out of the League as isolationists like Borah or partisans like Lodge. . . .During the fight over the treaty a sort of perverse cooperation underlay the hatred between Wilson and Lodge, which Borah recognized when he said that he and his irreconcilables were standing with Wilson—to have the treaty rejected."[31]

Hofstadter's summary of Wilson's career as an international statesman is equally ironic. He suggests that Wilson was a failure if judged by his own values and intentions, because his actions produced consequences sharply at variance with them:

> If he believed his fine statements with the depth and emphasis with which he made them, he may well have accounted his career as a world statesman a series of failures. He appealed for neutrality in thought and deed, and launched upon a diplomatic policy that is classic for its partisanship. He said that American entrance into the war would be a world calamity, and led the nation in. . . . He said that the future security of the world depended on removing the economic causes of war, and did not attempt even to discuss these causes at the Peace Conference. He declared his belief in the future of government ownership, and allowed his administration to close in a riot of reaction. He wanted desperately to bring the United States into the League, and launched on a course of action that made American participation impossible.[32]

This litany of paradoxes amounts to an ironic summary of Wilson's career because in Hofstadter's view Wilson's failures were in part the consequences of his virtues. When it was necessary for him to compromise his ideals in order to actualize a part of them, his sense of his own innocence prevented him from doing so. His great strength was his idealism and his great weakness was the illusion of unique virtue that was a part of that idealism.

Hofstadter's radical and critical perspective can be seen clearly in his ironic treatment of the relationship between democracy and capitalism. The theme of America as a democracy in cupidity runs through several chapters. Hofstadter points out how irony-inducing ambiguities were built into the American capitalistic and competitive conception of human nature from the beginning. The Founding Fathers did not admire human cupidity but they believed it immutable:

> The result was that while they thought self-interest the most dangerous and unbrookable quality of man, they necessarily underwrote it in trying to control it. They succeeded in both respects: Under the competitive capitalism of the nineteenth century America continued to be an arena for various grasping and contending interests, and the federal government continued to provide a stable and acceptable medium within which they could contend; further, it usually showed the wholesome bias on behalf of property which the Fathers expected. But no man who is abreast of modern science as the Fathers were of eighteenth-century science believes any longer in unchanging human nature.[33]

Hofstadter suggests here that the Founding Fathers unintentionally encouraged the flowering of types of human behavior that they disliked and sought to control, because their conception of what it was possible for human beings to be was too limited. By assuming a fixed human propensity to cupidity and competition they unintentionally contributed to shaping an American culture that fostered the development of these traits.

In a similar way Hofstadter points out the unintended consequences of Jefferson's advocacy of laissez faire. He failed to take sufficient account of the unequal power that wealth gave to some men and so contributed to the failure of the egalitarian democracy he wished to see in America. His laissez-faire economics, which he assumed would support such a democracy, came instead to contribute to the growth of inequality.[34] The source of the irony here is similar to the point Niebuhr makes about the tendency of Americans to ignore the differences in social power produced by differences in wealth.

Hofstadter also implicates Jacksonian democracy in the development of the inequities of American capitalism. He conceives of the

general population in the middle period as involved in the development of capitalism as well as democracy. Capitalistic values and activities were not confined to an elite, but rather found expression in
national character and behavior. "The typical American was an ex-
pectant capitalist, a hardworking, ambitious person for whom
enterprise was a kind of religion, and everywhere he found conditions that encouraged him to extend himself."[35] The assault on the
Bank of the United States, with its unfortunate economic consequences was in part a product of this widespread capitalist ethos of
expansion. Hofstadter argues that the long-run results of the Jacksonian fight for democratic capitalism are the inequities of late
nineteenth-century American society.

Lincoln as well as Jackson was implicated in the development of
American democratic capitalism. He shared "the traditional ideals
of the Protestant ethic: hard work, frugality, temperance, and a
touch of ability applied long and hard enough would lift a man into
the propertied or professional class." This ethic was "the legitimate
inheritance of Jacksonian democracy. It was the belief not only of
those who had arrived but also of those who were pushing their way
to the top. If it was intensely and at times inhumanly individualistic,
it also defied aristocracy and class distinctions." The values of
capitalism were held by the mass of Americans, who saw no contradiction between their democracy and that individualistic ethic.
Mobility reconciled egalitarianism and capitalism. Hofstadter has
an ironic view of the consequences of Lincoln's belief in "self-help"
and of the effect of his political actions undertaken in the intended
furtherance of that belief.

> If there was a flaw in all this, it was one that Lincoln was never
> forced to meet. Had he lived to seventy, he would have seen the
> generation brought up on self-help come into its own, build op-
> pressive business corporations, and begin to close off oppor-
> tunities for the little man. . . . He himself presided over the social
> revolution that destroyed the simple egalitarian order of the
> 1840s, corrupted what remained of its values, and caricatured its
> ideals. Booth's bullet, indeed, saved him from something worse
> than embroilment with the radicals over reconstruction. It con-
> fined his life to the happier age that Lincoln understood—which
> unwittingly he helped to destroy—the age that gave sanction to
> the honest compromises of his thought.[36]

This is high Niebuhrian irony. Lincoln believed in the ethos of the
self-made man and that opportunity was the key value of American
democracy, but unintentionally he contributed to the development

of a social order that increasingly constricted opportunity. By "the honest compromises of his thought" Hofstadter means Lincoln's efforts to reconcile his ambition — his own participation in the myth of the self-made man — and his moral idealism. His involvement in that myth — combined with his contributions to the destruction of the conditions sustaining its realization — constitutes the element of moral responsibility in Lincoln for the unintended outcome of his actions. That Hofstadter treats Lincoln as a kind of representative American in his participation in the self-destroying myth of the self-made man amplified this into a major irony of American democracy and American capitalism.

Hofstadter devotes much of his chapter on the Gilded Age to a discussion of the consequences of that irony. During this period the country was dominated by "the captains of industry" who had fulfilled the Jacksonian hopes for the self-made man with dramatic success. The corruption and inequity that resulted from that fulfill-ment were hardly what Jackson and Lincoln had intended. Hofstadter observes that the activities of the Gilded Age businessman were not inhibited by feelings of guilt, not because they had no moral sense, but because their values were such that they could believe that they were doing good. The ethos of their culture offered them many justifications. "Perhaps their primary defense was that they were building a great industrial empire. . . . Further, they stood squarely upon the American mythology of opportunity for the common man." Hofstadter argues that "such men could tell themselves and the world that their riches and power were the result of hard work and special talents, could hold themselves up to the ambitious American middle class as exemplars of an economy of magnificent opportunities."[37] The ironic fruit, then, of Jacksonian laissez faire was a rapacious industrial order that corrupted the democracy that the Jacksonians had sought to buttress with laissez-faire economics, and the unintended fate of the ideology of the self-made man was for it to become the rationalization of the men of great wealth and power who dominated that order and restricted opportunities for others.

This pattern of the irony of American capitalism is clear and significant, a democracy in cupidity rather than in fraternity, as Hofstadter points out. The expectation of the democratic Americans is that through laissez faire, self-help, and entrepreneur-ship a condition of equality of opportunity will be created in which ability, virtue, and hard work can enable common men to rise. But the results of laissez-faire capitalism are quite different. Some men become extraordinarily rich, wealth and power become concentrated in a few hands, and opportunity becomes restricted. Because the laissez-faire point of view is assumed to be democratic, it is retained at a time when it furthers the interests only of the wealthy few, not those of the many, whom it was expected to serve. Hofstadter sets the democratic intentions behind antebellum American capitalism against the consequences of capitalist development in the later nineteenth century. His perspective is ironic because he remains sympathetic with that democratic impulse at the same time that he is highly critical of the capitalist form in which it was expressed.[38]

Hofstadter's finest achievement in *The American Political Tradition* is the essay on Lincoln. It contains some of his best writing and the most profound irony in the book. Its title is itself a paradox, a serious play on words that condenses and implies a central theme of the chapter: "Abraham Lincoln and the Self-made Myth." Hofstadter shows how important the myth of the self-made man was in Lincoln's life on a number of levels. His career was an illustration of the rise of the common man through self-help; he was self-made in that sense. Lincoln clearly understood the role of the idea of self-help in the American public mind and effectively used his own life as a political asset, presenting himself as the self-made man he really was. His myth was therefore self-made. Lincoln not only exemplified and utilized the myth; he also profoundly believed in it, seeing America's distinctive virtue as the opportunity it provided for men of common origins to rise as he himself had. In Hofstadter's view this was the heart of the idealistic element in Lincoln's politics, as his ambition — "a little engine that knew no rest" — explains his opportunistic utilization of his own life as a political tool.[39] In one of his astute insights Hofstadter relates Lincoln's ambition to his political values and suggests that in itself it was a source of his ability to fulfill it since it gave him insight into common American aspirations. Finally, the idea of Lincoln as a self-made myth becomes deeply ironic as Hofstadter shows that the very sensitivity that enabled Lincoln to understand the public mind and project himself into it successfully, led him to the presidency, a position of power that could only make a sensitive man miserable.

Hofstadter begins his discussion of Lincoln by emphasizing the continuing hold of his legend on the American mind. It is interesting to note that in this demythologizing book no attempt is made to discredit the essential elements in that legend. Hofstadter summarizes it as "a drama in which a great man shoulders the torment and moral burdens of a blundering and sinful people, suffers for them, and redeems them with hallowed Christian virtues — 'malice toward none and charity for all' — and is destroyed at the pitch of his success." He observes that Lincoln has been compared to Christ and surprisingly does not mock the idea but merely says that it is "a comparison one cannot imagine being made of any other political figure of modern times." The Christian myth is only one source of the grip of Lincoln's life on the American imagination; the other is the self-help myth. The key to the irony, and tragedy, in Hofstadter's account of Lincoln can be seen in the contradictions between these two myths that he represented, and in which, in Hofstadter's view, he really participated:

> Humility belongs with mercy among the cardinal Christian virtues. . . . But the demands of Christianity and the success myth are incompatible. . . . The motivating force in the mythology of success is ambition, which is closely akin to the cardinal Christian sin of pride. In a world that works through ambition and self-help, while inculcating an ethic that looks upon their result with disdain, how can an earnest man, a public figure living in a time of crisis, gratify his aspirations and yet remain morally whole? If he is, like Lincoln, a man of private religious intensity, the stage is set for high tragedy.[40]

As Hofstadter makes clear, the major moving force of Lincoln's life was political ambition. In addition, Hofstadter observes that no other American leader "has combined with the attainment of success and power such an intense awareness of humanity and moral responsibility."[41] The fulfillment of his success drive, leading him as it did to the presidency in a time of great national disaster, brought him not the sense of accomplishment that the self-help myth implies, but rather the agony of a sensitive man who finds himself responsible for war and suffering.

Lincoln's drive for success was satisfied with the attainment of the presidency: "his external and worldly ambition was quieted when he entered the White House, and he was at last left alone to reckon with himself." Hofstadter suggests that Lincoln may have felt some guilt for his contribution to the sectional crisis, but in any event he "shouldered the moral burden of the war," and his pride was diminished by it. "The great prose of the presidential years came from a soul that had been humbled. Lincoln's utter lack of personal malice during these years, his humane detachment, his tragic sense of life, have no parallel in political history." The agony of the war pained him enormously because he had retained his human feelings throughout his climb to power. Hofstadter is deeply impressed with the way in which Lincoln responded to the agony he found in the presidency: "Here, perhaps, is the best measure of Lincoln's personal eminence in the human calendar—that he was chastened and not intoxicated by power."[42]

Quoting the poet biographer of Lincoln, Hofstadter points to the unanticipated consequences of the successful pursuit of the myth of the self-made man by one so sensitive: "Sandburg remarks that there were thirty-one rooms in the White House and that Lincoln was not at home in any of them. This was the house for which he had sacrificed so much!" In the end, Hofstadter suggests, after his ambition was realized so bitterly, Lincoln himself came to see how that drive contradicted his own inner being: "Now he could see the truth of what he had long dimly known and perhaps hopefully suppressed—that for a man of sensitivity and compassion to exercise great powers in a time of crisis is a grim and agonizing thing. Instead of glory, he once said, he had found only 'ashes and blood.' This was, for him, the end product of the success myth by which he had lived and for which he had been so persuasive a spokesman. He had had his ambitions and fulfilled them, and met heartache in his triumph."[43]

I have quoted at such length from the last part of Hofstadter's chapter on Lincoln because it stands as one of the finest examples of Niebuhrian irony in American historical writing. Lincoln successfully pursued the myth of the self-made man, pursued it to its highest political level, the White House. But once he was there, the consequences of his success were extremely bitter. All his rough life in politics had not removed his sensitivity; all his compromises had not eliminated his human idealism. But he was president in a time of great crisis. The fulfillment of his responsibility to his office, and to the principles of freedom, opportunity, and union in which he believed, demanded that he conduct a great war, a war that caused him immense agony because he retained his deep compassion and an acute feeling of personal responsibility in such a position of power. The consequences of his pursuit of his ambition were indeed ironic. The irony is deepened if we can regard the sensitivity to the suffering of others that caused him such pain as president as one of the factors that enabled him to fathom so perceptively the public mind and to appeal to it so effectively. The very trait that caused him to suffer as president had been a characteristic of his that had enabled him to fulfill his driving ambition. We might say that the flaw in Lincoln's personality that led him to act so as to contradict his own intentions was the very combination of ambition and sensitivity that had made it possible for him to succeed and necessary for him to suffer in his success. Hofstadter implies that that flaw was his suppression of the knowledge that for one so sensitive the power of the presidency would mean agony, knowledge suppressed so that he would not have to abandon his ambition.

There is tragedy beyond irony in this account of Lincoln. Hofstadter's description of the misery that Lincoln's success brought him is ironic, but his comments on Lincoln's behavior as president reveal tragedy. Lincoln became conscious of the contradiction between his pursuit of success and its consequences and, rather than hardening himself against those consequences, he remained open and conscious. As president he pursued a war that brought him much misery, knowing with marvelous ironic awareness that the war was in large measure evil, and not justifying the evil by the ends, although pursuing those ends nonetheless. No longer driven by ambition, he retained his sensitivity, accepted his responsibility, and consciously did evil for what he believed was a good purpose although it brought him continued pain. This is how tragedy can emerge out of ironic consciousness.

If we take Hofstadter's account of Lincoln as whole we can see that the irony, if not the tragedy, encompasses more than Lincoln himself. Hofstadter repeatedly states that Lincoln not only experienced and believed in the myth of the self-made man; he also exemplified it. He was sympathetically and emblematically connected with a large segment of the American people, the risen common man and the common man who hoped to rise. As such, the implication of Hofstadter's account of the misery that Lincoln found in his success certainly has a broad resonance. Throughout *The American Political Tradition* Hofstadter raises implicit questions about the moral worth of the self-made-man ethos that he finds so central to the American experience. In the conclusion to the Lincoln chapter he seems to be suggesting that in human terms the struggle for success is not worth the effort. Lincoln, the symbol of the myth, in finding bitterness in the fulfillment of his ambition, does not cease to be symbolic of the human condition in America. There is, I believe, no deeper criticism to be made of America than the one that Hofstadter suggests here: To fulfill the myth of the self-made man, to find that success which the culture promises but only rarely provides, is to discover how empty that success is, how humanly unsatisfactory. Hofstadter implies that what is wrong with America is not that there is more failure that success, not simply that opportunity has become more restricted, but that success itself, defined in American terms, brings emptiness and misery.

*The American Political Tradition* is a profoundly humane as well as a deeply critical work of history. Because it is composed of essays integrated by perspective and not by narrative structure it does not offer a general ironic interpretation of American history. Although Hofstadter certainly was a historical generalizer, his generalizations did not take the form of explicitly stated overall interpretations. Rather, they emerge out of the wide-ranging themes of his particularized studies. One of those themes in this book is the contradiction between the democratic hopes behind the development of American capitalism and the undemocratic consequences of that development. That theme is presented through Niebuhrian irony here, revealing how such irony can provide a sharply critical perspective on American history. In addition, Niebuhrian irony informs some of his accounts of individual statesmen; his essay on Lincoln in particular demonstrates how humanizing and profound Niebuhrian irony can be.

This book makes an interesting contrast to Niebuhr's *Irony in American History*. As we have seen, Niebuhr's application of his own concept in American history is compromised by his inability to maintain sufficient critical distance on America under the conditions of Cold War. The conflict between Russia and the United States was almost as great in 1948 when *The American Political Tradition* appeared as it was to be when Niebuhr wrote his book, but Hofstadter's work does not suffer from a similar defensive loss of the capacity to criticize America.[44] Indeed, his use of Niebuhrian irony is most often limited by the intensity of his criticism and not by any apologetic stance. Although his differences from Niebuhr's book may in part be due to the contrast between the theologian's concern with American foreign policy in the atomic age and the historian's with the development of American ideology, Niebuhr's decision to focus a presumably general book on *The Irony of American History* in that way could itself be regarded as an indication of how his attitude was shaped by the Cold War.

*The American Political Tradition* was a pioneering work of consensus history and long has been recognized as such. In it Hofstadter describes that consensus critically; his own position at this time lay outside it, and it might be argued that only from the outside could it be recognized. The combination of irony and consensus history in this work indicates how critical both of those points of view can be.

Hofstadter's ability to stand outside the American consensus was related to his cultural position, unusual for an American historian. As Schlesinger has suggested, he "was one of the first major American historians to come out of the cultural life of New York City." In a sense he bridged the gap between the professional world of the historian and the literary world of New York. The interests of no previous American historian, except, significantly, Henry Adams and possibly Carl Becker, had been so broad. Hofstadter was involved in literature and the social sciences as well as history. His literary concerns affected more than just his style, as Schlesinger suggests.[45] American literary culture has long been more sophisticated, certainly more critical, than American academic culture. In moving between these two worlds Hofstadter contributed greatly to the maturation of the historical profession. His easy use of critical irony indicates how much a literary consciousness could contribute to historical writing in America. In concluding this section I shall quote, as I did in beginning it, from *The Progressive Historians*. Hofstadter ends that book with a defense of the cultural value of history in sentences that well can be applied to his own work, particularly *The American Political Tradition:* "As practiced by mature minds, history forces us to be aware not only of complexity but of defeat and failure: it tends to deny that high sense of expectation, that hope of ultimate and glorious triumph, that sustains good combatants. There may be comfort it in still. In an age when so much of our literature is infused with nihilism, and other social disciplines are driven toward narrow positivistic inquiry, history may remain the most humanizing among the arts."[46]

## 3. Daniel Boorstin: *The Genius of American Politics*

Hofstadter refers to Louis Hartz and Daniel Boorstin as "the two leading consensus theorists."[47] He modestly does not include himself, perhaps accurately, because he was not a theorist in the same sense as Hartz and Boorstin, but the three are surely the most important consensus generalizers. Each wrote a broad history of the United States published between 1948 and 1955. These three studies were focused upon the history of American political thought and they all argued in different ways that the outstanding characteristics of that thought were its agreement upon fundamentals and its continuity over time. However, they did not all have the same attitude toward that consensus. As we have seen for Hofstadter, at least in *The American Political Tradition,* and as we shall see for Hartz, it was regrettable that American political thought had been so narrow. For Daniel Boorstin the American agreement upon fundamentals was an unmitigated blessing. Both Hofstadter and Hartz made extensive use of Niebuhrian irony whereas Boorstin did not; indeed, his basic categories were incompatible with that form of irony.

These differences among the consensus generalizers suggest a connection between the use of Niebuhrian irony and the expression of a critical version of consensus history.

In addition to interpreting American history in consensus terms, Boorstin and Hofstadter share other traits. Unlike Hartz, both are interested in historical particulars, Hofstadter primarily in the psychology of leadership and Boorstin in the specifics of past social life. Among historians, Boorstin and Hofstadter are both outstanding stylists. They rely especially on paradox, although only in Hofstadter is that paradox extended to morally responsible irony. As similar as they are in some ways, the differences between them are deeper. Whereas Hofstadter illustrates the critical sophistication and sense of complexity that can characterize consensus history, Boorstin exemplifies the uncritical acceptance of an ultimately simple and happy picture of the American past that also can be found in that interpretation.

Boorstin might be regarded as the archetypical consensus historian, particularly in his most general statement about the American past, *The Genius of American Politics*. He emphatically insists that the vast majority of Americans have shared the same fundamental political beliefs throughout our history, emphasizing continuity as well as agreement. His central argument in this book is that we have failed to produce significant theory, that our agreement upon fundamentals has made it unnecessary for us to articulate political philosophy in the way that Europeans have. Instead of political theory we have had what Boorstin calls a sense of "givenness." " 'Givenness' is the belief that values in America are in some way or other automatically defined: *given* by certain facts of geography or history peculiar to us." The idea of givenness consists of three basic notions: "our values" are "a gift from the past" and also "from the present" and "a belief in the continuity or homogeneity of our history. It is the quality of our experience which makes us see our national past as an uninterrupted continuum of similar events so that our past merges indistinguishably into our present." Because of these ideas "the American is . . . prepared to find in *all* experience — in his history and his geography, in his past and his present — proof for his conviction that he is equipped with a hierarchy of values, a political theory." Boorstin recognizes, and emphasizes, that this concept of givenness amounts to the argument that Americans have believed that they could find the normative in the descriptive. He speaks of "the recurrent tendency in American history to identify the 'is' with the 'ought,' to think of values and a theory of society as implicit in facts about society."[48]

Boorstin's version of the consensus interpretation is both extreme
and uncritical. His treatment of the Revolution consists of an exaggerated version of the widely held view that it did not involve profound social transformations,[49] but his account of the Civil War
reveals even more clearly how far he carried his consensus interpretation. He presents that great break in the continuity of
American history as affirming constitutional continuity because it
did not result in any fundamental rethinking of our institutions.
The bloody conflict itself is seen as expressing consensus in that both
sides appealed to different versions of the same past and both relied
upon "facts" to justify their values.[50] While the specific points that
Boorstin makes are defensible — it is plausible to argue that the Civil
War did not fundamentally change American constitutional
thought or political institutions — the overall impact of his view is
distressingly out of joint with the bitterness of division during the
war and the contrast between that episode of the American experience and most other conflicts that did not result in anything like
such national warfare. It is grossly distorting to argue that a bloody
breakdown in the federal system can best be understood as evidence of
the continuity and vitality of that system. If Boorstin offers an insight of sorts by arguing that the Civil War can be understood from
some perspectives as a sign of the health of the American political
system, he creates a greater distortion by ignoring the much more
obvious ways in which it represents a failure of that system. If differences in historical interpretations can be understood as different
forms that focus our perceptions on certain features of the past
while obscuring others, Boorstin's view of the Civil War can be seen
as one that draws to the center of our attention true but secondary
characteristics of the war while its more important features lie outside his field of vision. Many consensus historians regard the war as
an exception to their basic interpretation of American history; that
Boorstin forces it into that pattern reveals clearly how exclusive his
commitment to that interpretation is.

Boorstin's treatment of the Civil War as an affirmation of the
American consensus also suggests how uncritical his version of that
interpretation is. *The Genius of American Politics* is a highly
apologetic work that supports the idea of American uniqueness.
Boorstin regards our lack of political philosophy not as a possible
flaw but as a great virtue: "it is a hallmark of a decent, free, God-
fearing society." His nationalism is most evident in his hostile
response to European criticism of America. American intellectuals
have been particularly guilty of accepting critical foreign views of
the United States, and too reluctant to celebrate our virtues.

Boorstin argues that if we look at ourselves from an American rather than a European perspective we may discover unique advantages in our culture. He denies that such an attitude would be apologetic, but his very claim that we are self-critical winds up as a call for an awareness of our peculiar virtues.[51]

Boorstin really seems to regard American history as a great and unique success story. In denying that "the isolated utopian communities in American history" constitute "anything like a great tradition of utopianism in the mainstream of our thought," he makes the astounding statement that "the whole American experience has been utopian."[52] Since it is a basic premise of his argument that Americans have not been utopian in the sense that they have characteristically not pursued utopian goals, the only possible meaning of this statement can be that Boorstin regards America as itself in fact utopia.

Boorstin's conservative and uncritical attitude comes out with particular clarity in the discussion that concludes this book of how we can best fight the ideological cold war. He urges us to present ourselves as a model to the rest of the world, not to try to export particular institutions peculiarly appropriate to our conditions or an ideology that we do not have. "We have traditionally held out to the world, not our doctrine, but our example. . . . .It was life, and not thought, which would excel here. . . .It is our experience, not our dogma or our power, that may be the encouragement and the hope of the world." Boorstin argues that the fact that our model for the world is our life and not our thought "has perhaps taken some of the sting of arrogance out of our consciousness of destiny" but the logic of this whole argument presumes a belief in American virtues that it is difficult not to see as arrogant. Simply by showing other nations what we are and how we live, we can most effectively oppose communism. The assumption here is that what we are and how we live are so obviously good that if we do not confuse the issue by trying to export inappropriate philosophy or institutions, other peoples will recognize in our way of life such great virtues that they too will adopt our concept of givenness.[53]

The conservative and apologetic nature of Boorstin's version of consensus history is demonstrated by the implications of that fundamental idea of givenness itself. The claim that Americans have believed that their values were given to them by their forefathers and their environment amounts to the assertion that America is a traditionalist and conservative country, as Boorstin himself recognizes. Implicit in the idea of givenness he finds "a sense for the 'seamlessness' of experience. Aspects of experience which are elsewhere sharply distinguished here seem to merge into each other: the private and the public, the religious and the political, even. . .the 'is' and the 'ought,' the world of fact and the world of fancy, of science and of morals." Boorstin finds this sense of seamlessness to have both a spatial and a temporal dimension. In general, according to him, "to us institutions have appeared as a natural continuum with the non-institutional environment and the historical past."[54]

It is important to recognize that Boorstin is not merely arguing that Americans have believed that their values were given to them by their past and their environment. One could make such an argument critically, as does Louis Hartz, who sees our belief in the "natural" origins of our political values and ideas as an illusion. Boorstin appears to go beyond this, arguing that not only do we believe that our values are given by history and circumstance, but that they really are so given. In addition, he maintains that this is a good thing, that our virtues as a people are in part owing to the way in which our values have been given to us by our seamless experience of the past and the environment. Initially his statements about givenness seem to be comments on what Americans believe about their history and their nation, observations on American self-perceptions, but when he slips from describing givenness as our belief that our past and our environment have given us our values to describing those values as if they really had been given to us in that way, he moves from the position of a historian describing givenness as an American belief to that of an American who believes in givenness. On the same page he moves from describing his effort "to underline the ways in which peculiarities of our history have encouraged our belief in 'givenness'" to the statement that "we have drawn values out of 'facts.' " Similarly, Boorstin moves easily between the statement that Americans have believed that they possessed common values and the claim that in fact such basic agreement exists. In describing the habit of Americans of trying to express in vague and high-sounding phrases the essence of American faith, Boorstin assumes that the common faith is really there, not that Americans merely believe that they have a common faith. "Whether all this talk is capable of *producing* agreement is really not too important, if, as I have suggested, the agreement is there all the time. . . .The tendency to gloss over differences and construct a kind of generalized American religion, and the tendency to talk a great deal about what we believe without feeling the obligation to sharpen our definitions — both of these express a unity in American life." He speaks of "the genuine community of our values."[55] Finally, his con-

cluding argument that we present ourselves to the world as an example of the benefits of letting history and circumstances dictate values
seems to assume that our values are uniform and have in fact come
from our past and our circumstances.

Boorstin would probably argue that it makes no difference
whether we say that Americans have believed that their values were
given to them or we say that they really were. From his point of view
that position makes sense. His main concern is to deny our reliance
upon explicit political theory and that is as defensible whether we
regard givenness as a belief or a fact. But from my perspective it does
make a difference. If we argue only that Americans have believed
that our values have come out of our experience it is possible to
speak of that belief as an illusion and to suggest that in fact our
values have other sources; such an illusion of givenness may have
ironic consequences. On the other hand, the claim that our values
have really come from our experience collapses the distinctions between value and fact and cuts off the possibilty of critical irony. If
our values are really the product of our experience, then they must
be appropriate and not pretentious or illusory; then our intentions
must fit our situation.

Although Boorstin is ambiguous as to whether givenness is a belief
or a fact, he obviously believes that it is good. The last chapter of the
book is addressed to what he sees as the problem of a decline in our
faith in givenness during this century. He sees this as a particularly
serious problem because our great power in the world places us in
the role of the main opponent of communism in the Cold War. He
rejects the idea that the solution is either to develop an explicit
political theory or to use our particular institutions themselves as
models for the rest of the world. Instead, he urges us "to try to bring
to the surface those attitudes which have been latent in the notion of
'givenness' itself, to discover the general truths about institutions by
which we have actually lived." This suggests that he regards givenness as a virtue, for why else would he regret its decline and advocate
making it explicit as a means of spreading our influence? When
Boorstin asks, "why should *we* make a five-year plan for ourselves
when God seems to have had a thousand-year plan ready-made for
us?", his tone suggests the possibility that he may find the widely
held belief that God has special plans for America plausible. When
he argues that "it is our experience, not our dogma or our power,
that may be the encouragement and the hope of the world,"
Boorstin not only implicitly accepts the idea that America has some
unique virtue but he also suggests that that virtue is to be found in
the characteristic he calls givenness.[56]

Boorstin, then, presents a thoroughgoing and consistent consensus interpretation of American history. He sees the American past as marked by an inarticulate agreement upon political fundamentals, an agreement that arises from the way in which we believe our values are given to us by our past and our environment. Not only does he describe this belief; he also shares it, suggesting that in fact our values have come to us naturally out of our history and our environment. He finds in this a peculiar American virtue that he urges us to recognize and conserve. From this givenness we derive traditionalism, pragmatism, and environmentalism, American characteristics that Boorstin praise. But this extremely sympathetic approach to the American past blocks our perception of failure, defeat, and evil in our national experience and obscures the recognition of our deepest social problems. In discussing our given and unarticulated values, nowhere in *The Genius of American Politics* does Boorstin consider the possibility that those values have included such vicious things as racism. This book ignores those who have suffered under American virtues: blacks, Indians, Spanish-speaking people, women, and those Americans who believed the promise of opportunity only to encounter the real limits of possibility.[57]

Boorstin's vision of America is profoundly nonironic, even anti-ironic. Much of what Boorstin writes in *The Genius of American Politics* sounds like irony, but the essential element is missing — a critical focus on how illusions have led Americans to act so as to contradict their intentions.

There is much use of paradox in the book, but these paradoxes do not become ironic because they are purely descriptive and do not involve contradictions between intentions and consequences. Neither do they have the critical bite of many of Hofstadter's paradoxes. Boorstin draws our attention to some of the benign incongruities in American history and not, like Hofstadter, to the moral and intellectual inconsistencies of American statesmen.

In *The Genius of American Politics,* when Boorstin does suggest moral responsibility in historical actors whose behavior might be understood ironically, he generally suggests that they do not really belong in the mainstream of the American tradition, that they are uncharacteristic. The abolitionists, for example, are presented as "absolutist and abstract." In Boorstin's account, when they based their case on the assertion " that slavery was a moral evil," they could be regarded as setting in motion a possible ironic pattern, but he treats them as atypical and relatively unimportant, as outside the mainstream of American history.[58] Their potential irony merely serves to confirm his tendency not to see American history as ironic.

Boorstin also finds irony in the way that Europeans, like the Puritans, were changed into Americans in spite of their intentions when they settled here, in how, in the words of *The Americans: The Colonial Experience*, "dreams made in Europe — the dreams of the zionist, the perfectionist, the philanthropist, and the transplanter — were dissipated or transformed by the American reality."[59] In *The Genius of American Politics* he sees the original Puritans as people of high expectations who came to American planning to build a particular type of godly community. They did not fit at all into Boorstin's vision of what it meant to be American. "Of all people in modern history, these early Puritans could be least accused of confusion about their ends or of that inarticulateness which I have described as a characteristic of American political thought." Significantly he notes that "Puritanism was a European product, brought here in its nearly finished state."[60]

Boorstin points out how suited this European movement at first seemed to be to the conditions of unsettled America, but the failure of the Puritans arose precisely out of the success that resulted from the match between their dogmas and the traits needed in a people who would conquer the wilderness. The Puritans succeeded in the sense that they established their orthodox community and that that community was continuous with later American culture, upon which it exerted a powerful influence. "Puritanism in New England was not so much defeated by the dogmas of anti-Puritanism as it was simply assimilated to the conditions of life in America."[61] Their success, then, lay in their becoming American; their failure, in their ceasing to be Puritan.

Boorstin's account of the process by which that success led to that failure is close to the Niebuhrian pattern and he explicitly refers to it as ironic. In the early years the uncertainties of life in the New England wilderness had confirmed the Puritans' sense of dependence upon God's Providence, but as they established control over the wilderness the basis for that feeling of dependence was eroded.

A distinctive and paradoxical feature of the American story was that the decline actually came in part from the removal of many of those perils which had earlier confirmed the Puritan dogmas. The more secure the Puritans became on this continent, the more meager and unimpressive became the daily proofs of their dogma. At the same time, success nourished their pride and gave them a community to which they could point as the embodiment of their philosophy. In all this we shall see how the New England story re-enacted one of the familiar ironies of history: in the very act of establishing their community, they undermined the philosophy on which it was to have been founded.[62]

By being successful in America, the Puritan ceased in important ways to be Puritan. He was transformed into an American, a creature who had some of the features of the Puritan but not his commitments.

As Boorstin points out, Puritanism began as an effort to remold the world in terms of an explicit religious concept of community. The Puritans were people who had a deep feeling that they should remake that which was into that which ought to be. But Boorstin argues that their effectiveness in building their community in the New World turned them into Americans, into people who identified the ought with the is. As the Puritans "succeeded in building Zion in the wilderness, they were increasingly subject to those influences which were to persist in American history. We can see the growing sense of 'givenness,' the growing tendency to make the 'is' the guide to the 'ought,' to make America as it was (or as they had now made it) a criterion of what America ought to be." In a very revealing passage Boorstin emphasizes the ineffectiveness of the articulation of Puritan ideals in dealing with the practical problems they had to confront in establishing their community.

> The mastery of nature depended on the ability to understand rather than on the ability to persuade. The Big Lie could not help against a snowstorm; it would kill no wolves and grow no corn. Therefore, it was less important to make a grand plan, to make generalities glitter, than to know what was what and how to control the forces of nature. . . .the second and third generation of New England Puritans. . . became more and more responsive to the values which seemed to emerge from their daily lives. The Puritan experience thus shows some persistent characteristics of American history which have encouraged belief in the implicitness of values. Already in that earliest age we see a growing sense of 'givenness.'
>
> There is a subtler sense in which the Puritan experience symbolizes the American approach to values. For the circumstances which have nourished man's sense of mastery over his *natural* environment have on this continent somehow led him away from dogmatism, from the attempt to plan and control the *social* environment.

In America, unlike in Europe, "nature had to be mastered before society could even survive."[63]

More is involved in Boorstin's ironic account of Puritan history than the transformation of a people with an articulate and deep sense of commitment to transcendental values into Americans with a sense that their values were given by their environment. Boorstin is also describing the transformation of a people with the aspirations, expectations, and illusions that produce ironic action into a people who do not behave ironically because they seek only to do that which can be done. Irony flows from the separation between human hopes and what it is possible for human beings actually to do. It is directly dependent upon a sense of disjunction between the is and the ought. If, as Boorstin argues, Americans are a people for whom the is and the ought are blended, then they are a people who do not behave ironically. In becoming Americans, by his account, the Puritans lost those characteristics — their sense of mission, of being called by God to establish in the world a kind of community that did not previously exist, their aspirations and values that extended beyond the given — which made them subject to ironic action. Irony, for Boorstin then, is unAmerican. It is something to which Europeans, with their ideologies, utopias, and reformations, are subject. In becoming American the Puritans ceased to be European and thus ceased to be potential ironic actors. The effect of Boorstin's ironic account of the New England Puritans is to read irony out of American history.[64]

None of this should be surprising. The characteristics that Boorstin finds typical of America are deeply incompatible with irony. His basic idea of givenness collapses the distinction between values and realities and makes irony impossible; it denies the contradiction between human aspiration and the circumstances under which people live. As John Diggins has observed, "one finds in *The Genius of American Politics,* and in many of Boorstin's other works, no wise and courageous losers, no agonizing second thoughts about might-have beens, no brooding over historical alternatives to the given. What happened, happened; those who survived, survived."[65] When Boorstin describes America as a land in which the ' "is' and the 'ought,' the world of fact and the world of fancy, of science and of morals"[66] collapse into one another, he is in effect asserting that the tensions in the general human condition between aspiration and realization, between hope and fulfillment, do not apply to Americans. Niebuhrian irony requires those tensions. To say that we do not suffer them is tantamount to saying that we are a people who do not experience irony.

Boorstin repeatedly and explicitly affirms this view of America as a land in which men do not pursue unrealizable dreams. He argues that American hopes have been shaped by what it was possible to do in America, that they did not run beyond the limits of the possible, that it has been the very extent of those possibilities, the richness of opportunity in America, that has made Americans cease to be dreamers like Europeans. "Political dreamers in Europe in the eighteenth and nineteenth centuries *had* to lead a rich fantasy life, precisely because their *real* political life was so frustrating. But America was the land of dreams-come-true; for the oppressed European, life in America was itself fantasy. It was not necessary here to develop theory to prove that man could begin anew, that decent community was possible; life in America seemed itself sufficient proof." Boorstin emphasizes how the fact that in America men could build anew taught its people how limited human freedom really is, because what Americans have built has not really broken very much with the past: "Because we in America, more than other peoples of modern history, *seemed* situated to start life anew, we have been better able to see how much man inevitably retains of his past. For here, even with an unexampled opportunity for cultural rebirth, the American has remained plainly the inheritor of European laws, culture, and institutions." He argues that in general "the American experience itself has been a providential solvent of romantic illusions. Only when men were forced to live out their illusions did they see how illusory they really were."[67] Rather than a land of heightened expectations, for Boorstin America is the country of chastened dreams, disillusioned and realistic. Without illusions and aspirations irony is impossible.

Like all historical interpretations, Boorstin's can be viewed as a device for focusing our attention on certain features of the past that of necessity at the same time obscures our perception of other factors. In his case among the factors that are obscured are those that foster irony. Boorstin's concept of givenness, as an American belief about and not a factual description of, the source of our values, has considerable plausibility when applied to political theory. It is certainly defensible to argue, as Boorstin does, that we have been a peculiarly untheoretical people. But he sets his argument up as if a desire to make a theoretical system is the only kind of heightened purposefulness that a people can exhibit. He implicitly denies that Americans suffered from exaggerated expectations, like all other human beings, when he claims that "what one *could* build on this continent tended to become the criterion of what one ought to build here." However accurate this may be as a description of the development of our political institutions, it has no obvious application to other dimensions of life in America. If the is and the ought have blended in American politics, they have been clearly distinguished in some areas of our collective life — in our sense of mission, for example — as well as in the private aspirations of most

Americans, where the mark of our people in contrast to Europeans has been the refusal to accept their present situation as setting the limits of their future possibilities. The desire to implement grand theories is just one type of heightened hope. Personal ambition, the desire for self-improvement, the effort to be "a city on the hill," to expand over a continent, to fulfill a "manifest destiny," to increase national production, to conquer nature, to make the world safe for democracy, to contain communism — all are efforts that express grand human dreams. By focusing only on political theory, Boorstin makes plausible his claim that America has characteristically not been a land of high aspirations. He draws our attention away from those large areas of life in which Americans, individually and collectively, have dreamed and struggled to realize their dreams, actively shaping history and producing intended *and* unintended consequences.[68]

In general, then, *The Genius of American Politics* is a book that has the effect of denying the possibility that America can be understood ironically. When Americans seem to have aspirations that would tend to make them ironic actors, Boorstin reads them out of the American tradition. The Puritans enter that tradition only by ceasing to have the goals and values that characterized them as Puritans in the beginning. Boorstin's basic categories are set up so as to exclude irony. Givenness denies the fundamental human conflict between values and expectations on the one hand, and the circumstances under which men act and the actual consequences of their actions on the other. He explicitly denies that America is a land of dreamers, of men of high aspiration. This denial is given plausibility by his focus upon political theory, an area within which it makes sense to claim that Americans have been highly pragmatic and traditional. But by that focus he draws our attention away from the factors in American life — the very possibilities and opportunities that Boorstin celebrates — that have encouraged high expectations, expectations that have frequently outrun the possibilities. All in all it is hard to imagine an interpretation of American history farther removed from Niebuhrian irony than that of Daniel Boorstin.

It is no accident that the book that presents this extraordinarily nonironic interpretation also contains a conservative and extreme version of consensus history. Boorstin's purpose is to reveal American uniqueness and virtue. His approach to history is explicitly uncritical. Like all consensus historians he emphasizes the role of continuity and fundamental agreement in American political development. Unlike some others, such as Hofstadter and Hertz, he regards these characteristics as unalloyed virtues and turns away from any formulation of his own concepts as critical tools, as when he denies that our lack of political theory is "a refusal of American statesmen to confront their basic philosophical problems" and when he urges us not to try to unravel the meaning of our basic agreement because such an effort might produce conflict rather than more agreement.[69] Whatever the virtues of this book, and they are considerable — it is for one thing written in a style that few historians can equal — and however understandable Boorstin's defensive posture is in light of the Cold War conditions under which he wrote the book, it is hard not to agree with critics of consensus history in regard to his work. It does homogenize our past, blurring whatever real political and social conflict has existed, as well as the more fundamental distinction between values and actualities. It is conservative not only in that it advocates respect for traditions, but also more fundamentally in that its logic requires that we renounce the possibility of human effectiveness in history. It is apologetic in praising American virtues; it also ignores most American faults. It focuses on American uniqueness to the point where our participation in common humanity is obscured.

It is important to recognize the features, attributed by some to consensus history, that *The Genius of American Politics* does not exhibit. One thing pointed out by radical critics of that view is a focus upon irrationality, upon human evil, that they see in consensus historians.[70] But Boorstin does not emphasize the irrational. Passing remarks about Europe in contrast to America suggest that he might see Europeans in psychological terms, but he does not see Americans that way. He does deny the effectiveness of rational planning in American history, but that is not the same thing as an emphasis on irrationality. What he does in effect is to appropriate the pragmatic tradition for his conservative vision of our past. Americans are not irrational, nor are they rational planners. They are men who respond to circumstance, molding their goals to their history and their situation. A real focus on irrationality opens up the possibility of criticism, a possibility that Boorstin does not seek to open.

Those who defend consensus history do so on the grounds that it represents a recovery of complexity in American historical thought, that it represents the mature recognition by American historians of the intricate ways in which evil and virtue have been intertwined in the American experience. Boorstin encompasses complexity but his achievement is to simplify it. There is no evil mixed with the virtues of his pragmatic Americans. The concept of givenness represents the antithesis of a complex view of history that requires above all an understanding of the contradictions inherent in the human condition. What we have in Boorstin, rather, is an account of American history in which paradox and contradiction are recognized but dissolved in a simple but comprehensive pattern.

In all of this, how incompatible a certain kind of consensus history can be with an ironic vision of our past emerges in reading *The Genius of American Politics*. It is too committed to our virtues and our uniqueness to have the distance required for irony. The very categories through which its author sees America—givenness and the merging of the is and the ought—deny the tensions on which an ironic history is based. In fact, Boorstin's conception of the function of history is diametrically opposed to that of an ironic historian. For such a scholar history is a means to try to free people from the repetition of ironic patterns by exposing the illusions that led them to act so as to contradict their intentions. Boorstin not only denies the existence of such illusions and contradictions in America; in effect, he urges scholars to refrain from exposing whatever contradictions and illusions there are. The task he sets for himself as a historian—and performs with consummate skill—is the articulation of the myths that he feels underlie American virtues. As we shall see, an ironic version of consensus history can make use of a comparative framework so as to expose the limits of American self-perceptions through contrasts with other countries and through the use of external perspectives. Boorstin does make a number of comparative statements, but they all underline the legitimacy and virtue of that belief in givenness which he finds to be the feature that distinguishes America from Europe. Comparison thus serves Boorstin only as a way of reinforcing his conviction of American uniqueness, not as a means of locating our distinctiveness in relation to that of other nations, of placing us in a context in which the ways that we are similar to them are clarified along with the ways in which we differ from them. Ironic history above all functions to place the historian in a position where he can act as a moral critic without judging people of the past, without becoming partisan. Boorstin's version of consensus history implicitly and explicitly asserts a judgment—that of America's peculiar virtue—without providing the basis for a moral focus on past human action. Unlike Hofstadter, he does not place us in a position to understand how fallible human beings made moral choices in a world in which values conflicted with realities, as irony assumes is the human condition.[71]

## 4. Louis Hartz: *The Liberal Tradition in America* and *The Founding of New Societies*

The third major generalizer among consensus historians is Louis Hartz, a political scientist who has written much history. Two of his works, *The Liberal Tradition in America* and the parts of *The Founding of New Societies* that he wrote himself, present a powerful, if theoretical, statement of the consensus view of the American past, an interpretation that intersects with irony in interesting ways. The outlines of Hartz's argument are familiar to all historians of America. His presentation of his basic idea is inviting: "There is a kind of Biblical irony here. European liberalism, because it was cursed with feudalism, was forced to create the mentality of socialism, and thus was twice cursed. American liberalism, freed of the one was freed of the other, and hence was twice blessed."[72]

Although Hartz maintains that American political thought can best be characterized as an agreement upon the fundamentals of traditional liberalism, he takes care that emphasis on consensus does not obscure the reality of conflict. In effect Hartz argues, as Hofstadter did, that the agreement upon fundamentals in American politics has not generally been recognized by American political leaders. Rather, that very agreement has led them into greater conflict over relatively minor issues. If, in Hartz's terms, American history has been limited to the conflict between Whig liberals and democratic liberals, that conflict has been bitter in spite of the deep assumptions that Whigs and democrats have shared.

Hartz's version of consensus history, like Hofstadter's, is indeed critical. He explicitly recognizes the dangers inherent in the limitations of American political conflict. He devotes more attention to those dangers than to the virtues, such as stability, that also are presumed to result from consensus politics. Hartz refers repeatedly to the "absolutism" of American liberalism that has "the sober faith that its norms are self-evident. It is one of the most powerful absolutisms in the world." He observes how in America Locke's imaginary state of nature and social contract, intended as normative models, became the actual conditions of political life. His statement of this could certainly be subject to an ironic reading: "It was a remarkable thing—this inversion of perspective that made the social norms of Europe the factual premises of America. History was on a lark, out to tease men, not by shattering their dreams, but by fulfilling them with a sort of satiric accuracy. In America. . .there was a frontier that was a veritable state of nature. There were agreements, such as the Mayflower compact, that were veritable social contracts."[73] Liberalism in America has been so universal, so lacking in other ideas with which to contrast it, that it has not been recognized for what it is, but has been held onto irrationally. Hartz emphasizes the dangers that liberal absolutism, irrationality, and unconsciousness pose for both domestic civil liberties and a rational foreign policy.

For present purposes it is particularly important to recognize that Hartz explicitly introduced the idea of national evil into his conception of the American past. He perceives that that dimension of history was omitted by most earlier scholars. In the Progressives' "demonology the nation never really sinned: only its inferior self did, its particular will, to use the language of Rousseau. The analyst of American liberalism is not in so happy a spot, for concentrating on unities as well as conflict, he is likely to discover on occasion a national villain, such as tyrannical force of Lockian sentiment, whose treatment requires a new experience for the whole country rather than the insurgence of a part of it."[74]

Although *The Liberal Tradition* is sensitive to American evil, like the other early consensus works it is not so critical of America as many historians would be today. Although there is some discussion of slavery, in general blacks, other minority groups, poor whites, and women are neglected. There may be some excuse for this in the fact that Hartz is not writing a general social history but rather a broad study of the history of American political thought. Still, at times he does seem to assume a uniform social background of middle-class prosperity. He refers to "the fact that Americans were 'all of the same estate,' " as if he regards it as an accurate description of the status of Americans as well as an article of American faith.[75] While being of the same estate is not necessarily the same as living under the same conditions, this does nonetheless suggest an insensitivity to such realities as exploitation, poverty, and discrimination. Yet, in at least one important context, he does show a keen awareness of the contrast between the image of American life encouraged by our national beliefs and the realities under which many Americans live. Implicitly he recognizes the reality of failure in America by exploring the psychological burden the Horatio Alger ethos imposes upon those who do not succeed.[76]

Other observations that have critical implications in regard to internal American conditions concern social blindness induced by American liberalism. He notes that the idea of social freedom, the basic presumption that such freedom characterized American life, was the starting point for the political ideas of Americans. Like Niebuhr, Hartz observes that this assumption has made it difficult for Americans to perceive certain important realities, particularly in regard to the nature of capitalism which, when it was regarded as an evil, was frequently blamed on the state.[77]

Hartz's book, then, reveals an attitude toward America appropriate for irony. He is deeply sympathetic with the political tradition about which he writes, but by no means so sympathetic as to be blinded by its flaws. He has a reasonable amount of critical distance, in most ways more than Neibuhr, at least more than Neibuhr had in the 1950's. As one might expect from this perspective, there is much irony in *The Liberal Tradition in America,* although some of it does not precisely fit the Neibuhrian pattern.

The book is shot through with the term *irony,* which is applied to numerous fundamental and peripheral points, sometimes in ways that relate to Neibuhr's use of the word and other times in ways that do not. Most commonly he uses the term to describe situations that might better be called paradoxical, although some of those have implications suggesting Niebuhrian irony.[78] More significantly, that specific form shapes the major historical theme of Hartz's book — his account of the evolution of liberalism from high Whiggery to democracy and the interaction of the two kinds of liberals, Whigs and democrats. In that account the Whigs and the democrats are seen as successively contributing each to his own defeat in a twofold ironic pattern. The very manner in which the Whigs, as Federalists, secured the passage of the Constitution prepared the way for their replacement by democrats: "For the very solidarity which supported the Constitution meant that Whig elitism would be isolated as the democratic tide of the nation asserted itself once more. . . .In this sense the mistaken views of American life that the Whigs cherished cost them heavily." The Whigs perceived America as if it were Europe and attacked the democrats as if they were European radicals leading a mob. This "conservative denunciation of the people not only becomes suicidal, since it is precisely the people who are sure to shatter them, but loses much of its connection to reality." Hartz makes clear that in his view the Whigs themselves contributed unintentionally to their own defeat. They could have used a different strategy, one suited to American, not European conditions. Eventually, they were able to do this and to regain power by adopting the Horatio Alger myth that all Americans could be capitalists: "This was the law of Whig compensation inherent in American life."[79]

The irony of the American Whig is intertwined with that of the

American democrat. The latter's popularity stemmed in part from his ability to attack the Whig as an aristocrat, ignoring the extent to which in America both Whigs and democrats were liberals, and obscuring those of his own characteristics which would in the end make him vulnerable to the Whig as Horatio Alger capitalist:

> above all, the historic petit-bourgeois dilemmas of the Western world remained: individualist fear despite a faith in the majority, capitalist hunger despite talk of 'monopoly.' These drives, as we know, ultimately enchained the American democrat to the very Whigs he was able to shatter in 1800 and 1828. . . .the American democratic giant bought his strength at the price of weakness, his power to defeat Whiggery at the price of losing to it in the end. Here was American's law of Whig compensation mirrored in reverse.

The American democrat "is too thoroughly torn by inner doubt, too constantly in danger of selling out to his opponent, for a warrior legend ever successfully to be built around him." He is "a Hercules with the brain of a Hamlet."[80]

The interlocking drama of the American Whigs and democrats underlies Hartz's conception of consensus politics in America. In language strongly suggestive of Niebuhrian irony he characterizes his "central point": "the weakness of the American democrat was a part of his strength, his defeat a part of his victory. America isolated Whiggery by making the entire nation as liberal as it was, and this was also the reason that the entire nation, in the end, fell for its liberal fears and capitalist dreams."[81]

Although certain antebellum developments such as the election of Harrison in 1840 and Lincoln in 1860 foreshadowed it, the era of Whig triumph through the Horatio Alger myth came in the period between the Civil War and the Great Depression. It was not owing merely to the success of capitalist industrialization, which occurred elsewhere, but to the way that success occurred in the context of liberal America. The American democrat "was able to smash Whiggery in the age of Hamilton when it tried to use the European techniques, but he was a pushover for its democratic capitalism, its pot of American gold, when it gave those techniques up." The Whig effort to identify his capitalism with Americanism and to label the democrat as a socialist reinforced the appeal of his Alger promise. "We see here how ironically the new era has turned the tables on the American democrat. In the time of Jefferson he was able to isolate the Whig from the American world: now having 'discovered America' they [sic] are able to isolate him." Among other tricks the

Whigs reversed their position on state economic action and adopted the laissez-faire policies that the antebellum democrats had succeeded in identifying with Americanism, using "the ancient arguments of the American democrat himself." The democrat "in assailing state action, had opposed 'monopoly,' which meant particularly the corporate charter. Indeed, lacking any real understanding of social oppression he had defined all nonpolitical tyranny in terms of inequitable political decisions. Now, with the corporate charter universally accepted, due in part to his own ultimate drive for general incorporation, and with a huge trust growth being built upon it, he found himself confronted in his efforts to solve a real social problem with the very symbols he had used." The Whig "sounded 'Jeffersonian' indeed: state action was the root of inequity, it took away from one man and gave to another. If a massive confusion of political traditions took place in general when Hamilton absorbed Jefferson and Horatio Alger emerged, this was its most vital spot, the issue of economic policy."[82]

We have here a major irony of the dialectic of Whig and democrat in America, and by implication a major source of weakness in American public policy. The democrats had succeeded in identifying the idea of the exercise of state power in economic life with the idea of privilege. As economic power grew increasingly concentrated in post Civil War America, the Whig was able to use this identification to protect that power against the use of the state to limit it. Underlying this was a basic failure of Americans to recognize the reality of social power that was expressed by means other than overt state action. As Hartz says, the only tyranny that Americans recognize is the tyranny of the state. That is why our greatest problems with power have come not from the state but from private concentrations of power, which we have been reluctant to use the state to check because the state itself is seen as the only possible source of tyranny. This insight into American blindness to the realities of social power is one critical link among Niebuhr, Hofstadter, and Hartz.

The irony of the dialectic between right and left wing liberals continues in the twentieth century in various progressive movements; it can be seen "in the imperfect knowledge they have had of the enemy they face, above all in their failure to see their own unwitting contribution to his strength." The Americanist argument has been repeatedly thrown against them and they have unintentionally validated it by accepting a form of Americanist Algerism themselves.[83]

These tendencies for Progressives both to present themselves in

terms of Alger-like American values and to internalize them were
carried further by the New Deal. The key to its success was a "happy
pragmatism which usually refused to concern itself with moral issues
at all." This pragmatic approach shielded the New Deal from attacks upon its Americanism but it also had the unanticipated consequence of easing the eventual transition back to the opposite party:
"by defining New Deal policies in amoral terms and hence making it
easy for the Republicans ultimately to accept them, Roosevelt
helped to save the Republican party. In this sense he was a better
friend of Dewey and Eisenhower than Hoover himself."[84]

Finally, Hartz observes how the Progressive and New Deal traditions have contributed to their own problems with McCarthyism. "If
the mission of the anti-Communist hysteria is in significant part to
discredit the American Progressive movement, still that movement
has always contributed heavily to its ultimate strength. . . .It is
ironic that the Progressive tradition should be discredited by an
'Americanist' tide of which it was itself a part." In this Niebuhrian
irony Hartz's critical position stands in sharp contrast to Niebuhr's.
Neibuhr deplored the tendency in American liberalism to "social
planning" and applauded its pragmatism. Hartz sees that
pragmatism and the absolute assumptions behind it far more
critically. He calls for what amounts to a therapeutic, ironic
historical consciousness of how Progressivism has sustained its
enemies by its Americanist opposition to social theory. "If the Progressive tradition is to become a fighting weapon against the red
scare hysteria, against American conformism in its current frighten-
ing phase, the soul-searching that leads to an understanding of this
facet is an experience it has got to go through."[85]

A key to that soul-searching comes, in Hartz's view, from
America's involvement in the larger world. His attitude toward that
involvement is critical, particularly in contrast to Niebuhr's. In
discussing Hartz's comments on American foreign policy I shall
compare them to Niebuhr's in order to reveal the former's more
critical use of irony. Hartz observes, like Niebuhr, the paradox of
isolated America emerging as the leading anticommunist power in
the mid-twentieth century, but for Hartz this is an incomplete statement of the problem: "Fully as significant as the fact that modern
America finds itself in the big wide world while the Founding
Fathers managed to escape from it is the tradition that modern
America brings to its new role — the tradition of escape itself, of a
nonrevolutionary nation as compared with a Europe that has emerged out of revolution and an Asia that is now undergoing it." Hartz
argues that the content of our political thought — "a colossal liberal

absolutism" — not only distorts our domestic politics; it also seriously weakens our capacity for rational international action. He finds no real inconsistency between the isolationism he sees in earlier American history and how

> in the twentieth century, "Americanism" has also crusaded abroad in a Wilsonian way. . . .Embodying an absolute moral ethos, "Americanism," once it is driven on to the world stage by events, is inspired willy-nilly to reconstruct the very alien things it tries to avoid. . . .Americans seem to oscillate between fleeing from the rest of the world and embracing it with too ardent a passion. An absolute national morality is inspired either to withdraw from "alien" things or to transform them: it cannot live in comfort constantly by their side.[86]

Hartz points out that at the time of the Spanish-American War the antiimperialists were able to present themselves as the real Americanists, but in the twentieth century this has changed. "What the World War and its Russian Revolution aftermath did was to color American policy with the conscious ethos of the American liberal faith and thus to take away from its opponents any real polemical grip on 'Americanism.' Of course, this made America's intentions finer. . . .But this very shift had the effect of projecting the limitations of the American liberal perspective onto the world scene and at the same time, by generating the national moral passion, striking hard at the lone dissenting spirit." The key figure in this transformation is Wilson, of whom Hartz is quite critical. His presidency is particularly important because "there the mechanism of American liberal absolutism can clearly be watched at work, preparing for the responses that the current expansion of the Russian Revolution have evoked. And it is, of course, that Revolution which has fixed the categories of modern ideological war."[87] In contrast to Niebuhr, Hartz here implies criticism of actual American participation in the creation of the Cold War.

In Hartz's view Wilson's foreign policy was a direct outgrowth of the domestic Americanist tradition, original only in its worldwide application. His errors, his "inner contradictions" had philosophic roots, but also were products of American history. "If he missed the enormous social upheavals that were impending in Europe. . .this was half due to the fact that the concept of social upheaval was alien to the American mind. If he exalted national self-determination, he did so not only because he worshipped Bright and Mill but because for a nation 'born equal' the Declaration of Independence symbolized the essence of liberation." The unintended consequences of

Wilson's activism were the result of these philosophic and historical limitations of his thought. Hartz reiterates a telling point made by Hofstadter. Not only was Wilson limited by American thought and experience in general; his failure was also conditioned by the way in which "Wilson's world policy reflected his domestic Progressivism. . . .Wasn't Wilson smashing the Austro-Hungarian Empire into bits much as he would smash an American trust? Wasn't he depending on an automatic harmony as clearly in the one case as he was in the other? Actually Wilson's enslavement to the American experience reflected not only its original nature but the very stage of its internal development."[88]

The international application of Americanism may have begun with Wilson but it did not end with him. As we turned from isolationism to intervention in our response to fascism in the 1930's our policy "took on the Wilsonian logic in which 'Americanism' when it does not retreat, goes abroad." Hartz suggests that "on the whole it was chastened 'Americanism' that was projected onto Europe with America's entry into the war. . . .but it is the battle against the Communist revolution in its current phase which has brought to the fore the peculiar orientations of a nation 'born equal.' " He sees the Cold War as having "brought into plainest view America's psychological pattern." Part of his description of this pattern sounds similar to Neibuhr's description of our dilemma: "One of the issues it involves is the issue of a social 'message' to compete with the appeal of Communism in various parts of the world. Since the American liberal creed is a submerged faith, even in its Alger form, it is obviously not a theory which other peoples can easily appropriate or understand. Its very absolutism depends of course on this aspect of its character." But Hartz is more critical of the consequences of this unconscious, absolute liberalism than was Niebuhr. "At the same time this is not antithetical. . .to a crusading 'Americanism' based on the absolute mood which this very character of American thought inspires." The aspect of our past that most weakens us in dealing with the rest of the world under mid-twentieth century circumstances is our lack of a revolutionary tradition. This lack is what leads us "to interpret even the democratic socialism of Europe in terms of our own anti-radical fetishism" and to "tend to interpret even reactionary regimes as 'democratic.' We fail to appreciate non-political definitions of 'freedom' and hence are baffled by their use." All of this makes us weaker in dealing with an ideological opponent presented by Hartz as an enemy, not necessarily a demonic one, because "Russian Communism. . .grave as is the threat it poses, is nonetheless a genuine ideology of social revolution."[89]

Although all of this is stated in terms of the same problem to which Niebuhr addressed much of his book—the problem of how our past experience weakens us in our struggle with communism—it is perhaps intentionally open to a broader interpretation. Our absolute, messianic, liberalism can easily be seen as a cause not only of our unintended ineffectiveness in fighting the Cold War, but perhaps of the Cold War itself. Although Hartz does not address himself to the issue of the origins of that conflict, his interpretation of the basis of our ideological disadvantages in that struggle could also be seen as a description of the ways in which we as well as the Russians may have contributed to its origins. Although it might be said that Neibuhr's ironic interpretation of America could also be turned into an instrument for arguing American as well as Russian responsibility for the Cold War, that argument would have to be made in the face of Niebuhr's specific characterization of communism as demonic and his clear assumption that our role has been purely defensive. Hartz does not portray Russia as demonic and leaves open the possibility that we have been active in our liberal messianic way in contributing to international conflict. I am not arguing here that Hartz anticipated New Left historians in blaming America for the Cold War, but only that his approach has greater distance than Niebuhr's and allows for a more critical and more genuinely ironic view of America.

Hartz's interest in the world outside America has a critical and therapeutic purpose. We must allow an awareness of that world to inform our sense of ourselves if we are to overcome our narrow absolutist liberalism, in a process that has some analogies with the development of an ironic historical consciousness. Comparative history is the only approach that can expose the limitations imposed by our uniqueness. Our increased involvement in the outside world both intensifies our need to adopt a comparative perspective and provides an added opportunity and incentive to do so.

We could use our uniqueness as an excuse for evading its study so long as our world position did not really require us to know much about it. Now that a whole series of alien cultures have crashed in upon the American world. . .we need desperately to know the idiosyncrasies which interfere with our understanding of Europe. . . .But the issue is deeper than foreign policy, for the world involvement has also brought to the surface of American life great new domestic forces which must remain inexplicable without comparative study. It has redefined, as Communism shows, the issue of our internal freedom in terms of our external life. So in fact it is the entire crisis of our time which compels us to make that journey to Europe and back which ends in the discovery of the American liberal world.[90]

In contrasting the mid-twentieth century with the earlier part of the century Hartz observes how our increased involvement with the rest of humankind pushes us toward a more critical understanding of our national self: "We know the meaning of world involvement, as the age of Alger did not know it, and this is the real force driving us toward objective national analysis." Hartz argues that it is only intensive contact with the outside world that can free us from the narrowness of our experience, free us to act rationally in relation to that world. In a nice ironic insight he points out how our involvement with the rest of humanity is at once a major source of our problems, or of the increase of already existing problems, and our only hope for overcoming them:

> For if that involvement intensifies nationalist blindness in some, it serves to educate others. . . ."Americanism" is at once heightened and shattered by the crashing impact of the rest of the world upon it. And so, curiously enough, the answer to the national blindness that the new time produces is the national enlightenment that it also produces: the race between the two is a fateful one indeed. Which is to say that America must look to its contact with other nations to provide that spark of philosophy, that grain of relative insight that its own history has denied it.

The development of an awareness of how the American Progressive tradition has contributed to its own defeat, an awareness that is needed if that tradition is to be relevant to present and future needs, depends upon the opening up of our self-awareness through foreign contacts. Hartz is not at all sure that American involvement in the world will produce the enlargement of vision needed rather than increased blindness, but the issue is crucial. "What is at stake is nothing less than a new level of consciousness, a transcending of irrational Lockianism, in which an understanding of self and an understanding of others go hand in hand."[91]

Irony, then, plays a crucial role in *The Liberal Tradition in America*. Hartz's attitude toward the United States is an appropriate blend of criticism and sympathy. His account of the dialectical process whereby Whigs and democrats successively brought defeat out of success fits the Niebuhrian pattern. His interpretation of American foreign policy is based upon a critical recognition of the role of our illusion of uniqueness in many of the problems we face and the purpose of his book is to expose that illusion by making us conscious of how we interact with other nations that are both similar to and different from us.

This call for America to become conscious of the limits of Americanism through comparative self-understanding induced by world contact is very similar to the idea of ironic historical consciousness freeing America from the illusions that lead us to go on acting ironically. This therapeutic idea is carried into a more explicit comparative framework and given a clearer historical dimension by Hartz's later book, *The Founding of New Societies,* an even broader work than *The Liberal Tradition.* It goes beyond Hartz's earlier book in that it seeks to develop the comparative perspective that that earlier work argues for, and places the limitations of the American liberal absolutism in relation to both Europe and other colonies peopled by Europeans.[92]

In *The Founding of New Societies* Hartz treats the United States and the other colonial areas as offshoots (he calls them "fragments") of Europe. As such they take on the character of the historical force that was dominant in their founding: for example, French Canada, feudalism, the United States, bourgeois liberalism or "Whiggism," Australia, working-class radicalism. The subsequent development of the fragments differs from that of Europe because the colonies lack the complexity of conflicting classes and historical forces that arose in Europe after they are founded. Instead, the development of the fragments is governed by the working out of the internal logic of the one major stream that controlled their initiation. The liberal absolutism of America described in Hartz's earlier book thus takes on a deeper historical dimension and broader comparative meaning: it is the manifestation of European bourgeois tendencies when they are freed of the dialetical necessities created in Europe by the pressures of other powerful classes and other ideologies. The American experience is also placed in a dialectical frame of its own; the working out over time of the tendencies in bourgeois liberalism involves the generation of conflicts implicit within liberalism, conflicts that in Europe are contained by the greater conflicts with other groups. All of this takes on a larger meaning in comparison to the histories of other European fragments. The substance of their politics and political thought differs greatly from the American because of the different point of origin of each fragment, but all are similar in form because they have all experienced the process of fragmentation. Above all, what Hartz's approach in this later book does is to provide us with a perspective that exposes the limitations of Americanism, which reveals that Americanism is merely a fragment; its highest aspiration is to undo the effect of America's fragmentary character by making us conscious of that fact.

*The Founding of New Societies,* written in 1964 from a comparative perspective, does contain more criticism of America than the earlier book. The main weakness of that work in this regard was its failure to take account of racial problems or poverty in America. Hartz's later book does deal with racism as one of the main factors in the "internal turmoil" of the bourgeois fragments. Racism is not, in Hartz's view, a mere imperfection in liberal society. It is intrinsically related to the mechanism by which bourgeois fragments develop. "The very experience of fragmentation is relevant, for. . .the racial detachment mirrors the primitive detachment from Europe, itself a kind of apartheid. If the mechanism of separation can be used in connection with decadent old Europe, why should it not be used in connection with the Negro? Here is 'flight' within the very context of exploitation." That racism is a fundamental and not a peripheral contradiction in America for Hartz is revealed in his comments on the explosive quality of the black movement of the 1960s. That quality exists because the black militant "is working with what has always been the one 'revolutionary' factor in the national history." Hartz also acknowledges the application of racism to the Indians. He comments on the "destruction of the aborigine" in the liberal fragments and makes an interesting point about our lack of historical consciousness of American Indians, accurately predicting that "as the comparative view of United States history gradually develops. . .the history of the American Indian will rise markedly in importance."[93] One function of Hartz's approach, then, will be to make visible the history of those whose past has been hidden by the exclusiveness of the traditional liberal approach, in America a major critical function.

Niebuhrian irony appears in several key places in *The Founding of New Societies,* for the most part in contexts similar to those in which it appears in *The Liberal Tradition.* The ironic dialectic between Whiggish and democratic liberals is restated in terms of the "fragment" theory. The isolation from other forces, which allowed for the unimpeded triumph of the American Whigs, leads to their replacement by the democrats, who represent the fulfillment of the logical tendencies of Whiggery itself. The Whig is able to return to power by holding out the promise that every man can be a bourgeois. When the hollowness of this promise is made particularly obvious by depression, the Whig is replaced by the democrat. Throughout this pattern sources of strength become sources of weakness with the passage of time.

As is the case with the concept of liberal absolutism in his earlier book, the irony of Hartz's fragmentation theory becomes most acute when it is applied to the recent history of America's foreign relations. It is here that the deeper penetration of the later approach becomes apparent. The escape from Europe that had been a source of strength to the fragments now resulted in an inability to deal effectively with the world. "The fragments. . .are involved. . . in one of the strangest issues of change that the world impact of the modern era has produced. For it is the irony of that impact that it has hurled back at the fragments, after centuries and from wholly unexpected angles, the very Western revolution they originally fled. Their escape has turned out to be an illusion."[94]

It was one of the major strengths of the fragment (as well as the source of the absolutism of its liberalism) that it provided its citizens with a world view that canceled out the consciousness of being a fragment of a larger whole. This lack of consciousness of its fragmentary character "is the reason for the peculiar trauma of the fragment as it is suddenly forced back, through the world events of our time, into the context of revolution. It does not return as an ideology. It returns as a world, a nation, as a way of racial life." This last is a statement of absolutism as it appears in a larger context. The world revolution of our time is inescapable.

> We can see now, with a kind of sudden Hegelian retrospect that inherent in the whole legendary process of 'escape' from Europe there were mechanisms cancelling out its results. . . .As the globe contracted, the Western revolution that the fragments escaped was spreading through it with increasing rapidity, so that ultimately it was bound to overtake them from a distant place suddenly made near. If Holland was left behind, there was still Russia, China, the awakening states of Africa.

To the extent that the fragments rely upon the mechanisms that had worked for them before, their response is inappropriate to the situation, in a typically ironic pattern.[95]

More painful even than the discovery that the world revolution moves in directions the man of the fragment cannot understand is the response of his own young to those changes. This irony is one that was visible in 1964 in ways that it had not been in 1955. The sons of the liberal fragment "will reject the proposition that 'Americanism' is the instinctive emotion of all humanity. . . .Indeed they will go a step further. They will recapture the memory of Europe itself, and in the very teeth of the fragment hysteric, they will expose the relativity of his ethic. They will announce outright

that the fragment is a 'fragment'. . . .the fragment world passes,
destroyed by the same 'honest' response to experience which created
it."[96]

The "fragment" character of America produces a specific blindness to that which we most need to understand in the present world:
the attraction of collectivism in its communist form. In this book as
in the earlier one, Hartz writes "of socialism fading in America
because feudalism has been left behind" as a feature of our experience that was a great source of strength. But that source of
strength has become in contemporary times a source of weakness:
"The United States and the other modern fragments. . .are destined
to deal with a world they cannot out of their experience understand
and for which they cannot out of their own experience prescribe.
That world. . .must achieve modernity through methods other than
the *Mayflower* voyage." Hartz finds that our inability to understand
collectivism makes our world role ironical. "There is more than a
touch of irony in the fact that circumstances of national power
should have made America the leader of the resistance to the
Bolshevik revolution. . . .For a fragmented liberalism is of course the
most powerful manifestation of the bourgeois tradition that can be
found. But more than this, even among the liberal fragments. .
.America stands out as the purest form of the 'capitalist democracy.'
"[97] The sources of the stability of the liberal fragment, the narrow
range of its political discourse and its rejection of any explicitly collective formulations, ironically make it impossible for the United
States to deal effectively with the world in which it has become the
greatest power because much of that world is turning to a collectivism that our traditions prevent us from understanding.

The most important advance in *The Founding of New Societies*
over *The Liberal Tradition* is in the expansion of Hartz's concept of
the function of historical consciousness, an advance that brings his
later work closer to the hope that through ironic awareness people
may be freed from the compulsive limits that their historical experience puts on their thought. Hartz finds in the contemporary
world an enlargement of consciousness within the fragments, a
breaking up of the limits of their vision. "The exposure of the fragment universe by the world impact of the present time, reversing the
history of the fragment, is bound to be traumatic. But it brings with
it a moral liberation, an enlargement of consciousness, which for its
own sake would well be worth the struggle." Hartz argues that the
"fragment"-comparative approach to history itself can contribute to
that enlargement of consciousness. He asks:

Is not comparison the true historical "experiment?" In American historical work, we have spoken much of "objectivity." But this concern has actually masked the deeper plunging of historical study into the fragment interior. The theory of the fragment, at the very moment that it illuminates our national dilemmas, promises in a new sense the fulfillment of that "objectivity". . . .It is the Hegelian virtue of our necessity that the difficulty of the present time drives us toward a new enlightenment.[98]

To enlarge our consciousness beyond the limitations of the fragment we must develop a historical awareness of the fact that we are a fragment. Only knowledge of the illusions that lie behind irony can free us from irony.

In addition to containing much irony, *The Founding of New Societies* also presents a conception of the therapeutic possibilities of comparative history that is very similar to the hope that ironic history may help to free us from some of our illusions. Although irony is not primarily a comparative method, it meets Hartz's objections to noncomparative approaches to the American past, that such approaches reflect "forgetfulness" and "subjectivity," because irony places at the center of the American experience a universal human pattern that is peculiar in America only because of its intensity.[99] In Hartz's work we have a powerful and critical wedding of consensus and ironic history. He perceives the American consensus as the result of a pretension to uniqueness, a pretension that an ironic and comparative historical consciousness can hope to dissolve.[100]

## 5. Irony and Consensus History

The three ironic generalizers examined in this chapter have different relationships to ironic history. Daniel Boorstin, perhaps the most extreme consensus historian, does not apply Niebuhrian irony to the American past in his broadest work, *The Genius of American Politics*. Since he does make extensive use of other literary devices such as paradox, and describes the Puritans in ironic terms before they became American, his failure to use that form in his account of American history is significant. To be American, in Boorstin's view, seems to be equivalent to not being ironic. As people become American they cease to have the characteristics that induce ironic behavior. His concept of the givenness of American values and his argument that in America the is and the ought are typically collapsed into each other are incompatible with an ironic version of

American history. Since Boorstin's version of consensus history is the least critical among the three historians examined here, his nonironic interpretation suggests the incompatibility of that form with an apologetic version of consensus history.

Both Hofstadter and Hartz, on the other hand, offer a more critical and ironic vision of the American consensus, although their social criticism is limited by the climate of opinion in the late 1940s and 50s. They differ from each other in the kind of history they wrote and in the function of irony in that history. In Hofstadter's *American Political Tradition* it is an important part of his sensitive appreciation of the contradictions in American culture. The Niebuhrian pattern appears in his perceptive accounts of how particular statesmen acted so as to bring about consequences inconsistent with their intentions. It provides him with a device for focusing moral attention in his discussions of such intricate personalities as Wilson and Lincoln. Irony also informs his account of the conflicts between American democracy and American capitalism. *The American Political Tradition* shows the importance of irony in a highly critical and complex kind of consensus history.

Hofstadter and Boorstin have in common a great sensitivity to the contradictions in American culture. They are both extraordinarily fine writers, and they use such techniques as paradox very effectively in dealing with those contradictions, but they use them to different ends. Boorstin seeks to resolve the tensions in a comprehensive, lucid, and simple theory of American history. Hofstadter, on the other hand, accepts contradiction and paradox as integral to the human and American condition. His style serves to make us aware of human complexity and the ironies of America. He does not offer a comprehensive theory but rather a series of linked insights into the contradictions and ironies of the American experience.

Hartz does offer a theory but, unlike Boorstin, it is one that seeks to expose the complexities of America in an ironic and dialectical pattern rather than to resolve them. If Hofstadter uses mostly an irony of character, Hartz uses an irony of process. He offers an overall interpretation of American history in which irony is a key part. His irony can be seen primarily in his account of the history of American politics, in which he perceives various kinds of liberals engaged in conflicts with each other and often drawing defeat out of victory. The key to that ironic behavior lies in the illusions of American uniqueness that Hartz exposes. His purpose is to indicate the need for Americans to overcome those illusions, to arrive at a comparative consciousness of the limitations of American political thought. In a direct contradiction, Boorstin's concept of givenness (if it is understood as offered as fact and not illusion) can be seen as an expression of that very forgetfulness which Hartz seeks to expose and transcend. In his call for us to recognize that we are but a fragment, in his efforts to expose our pretensions to uniqueness, and in his exposure of how we have mistaken our fragmentary perspective on the world for a realistic vision, Hartz demonstrates how critical, ironic, and therapeutic consensus history can be.

# VI.  Irony, Maturity, and Critical History in America

If the human condition tends to induce ironic behavior, the American situation exaggerates those aspects of that condition which foster that behavior. We are linked to humanity by the irony of our history and distinguished from other peoples by the extent of that irony. Illusions of innoncence, virtue, power, and wisdom, a pretension to having been divinely chosen, and heightened expectations — all have encouraged Americans to act as individuals and as a nation in ways that frequently produced unintended consequences. A history of growth and wealth has at once encouraged our pretensions and obscured our perception of our ironic behavior. Most of our historians, focusing on that growth and wealth and the virtues of our democracy, sharing our common illusions, have not perceived our history ironically until the disillusionment of the mid-twentieth century made irony visible to a number of our more sensitive scholars.

Irony has been used by European historians virtually from the dawn of historical writing. If the conditions of European life have been less conducive to ironic behavior than American conditions, the consciousness of Europeans has been more suited to ironic perception. European experience and culture have encouraged a deep awareness of the contradictions within human beings, a sense of the complexity of history, and a recognition of the difficulties people encounter when they seek to fulfill their intentions in action. Since for the most part European historians have tended to see the masses of people as relatively passive victims of history, their applications of irony have been largely confined to the study of active elites. American historians have long treated the common American as a relatively active creator of his own life. This was a feature of the democratic optimism of much earlier historical writing. When American historians came to see the consequences of American actions in a darker light, they were better prepared than the Europeans to visualize the whole people as caught in irony.

The story of the use of Niebuhrian irony in the writing of American history is an account of how a peripheral way of perceiving our past became an integral part of that perception. Although irony was applied to a few isolated incidents of our history by some of the tougher-minded nineteenth-century historians such as Hildreth, or to those who opposed the mainstream of American development by a romantic like Parkman, it was in general incompatible with the optimistic and progressive core of most historical writing of that century. Irony played a major role in Henry Adams's work, but Adams was also distinguished from most other historians of his time by his relative pessimism. Although he was among the greatest — perhaps the greatest — of American historians, he was hardly typical. Early in the twentieth century Progressive scholars developed a more critical way of looking at the American past, but their criticism did not cut very deep. They remained attached to some of basic American illusions and could not develop a comprehensive ironic vision, although hints of such a perception appeared in the work of Carl Becker and in that of the typical Progressive, Vernon Parrington, when he contemplated the fate of the agrarian democracy he loved in the industrial America of the Gilded Age. Only after the two world wars and a great depression, during the fearful prosperity of the Cold War, did the leaders of a generation of historians come to utilize Niebuhrian irony as a central part of their perception of the American past.

Reinhold Niebuhr himself wrote the most explicitly ironic interpretation of American history. Impressed with the irrationality and self-deception of human beings, Niebuhr saw the pretensions of Americans as generally conducive to ironic behavior, but his demonic conception of communism prevented him from maintaining a stance sufficiently critical to allow him to present the specifics of American history in an ironic form true to his own concept. As the Cold War waned, and as some of the evil consequences of our anti-communist policy became clear, Niebuhr was able to regain his critical perspective and suggest how irony could serve as a tool of critical history.

Richard Hofstadter and Louis Hartz, writing from within the historical profession, earlier demonstrated the critical power of irony. Hofstadter used it to great effect in exposing the subtle connections between virtue and evil in such figures as Wilson and Lincoln. Hartz presented a general interpretation of American history in which illusions and unintended consequences played a major role. His comparative approach had the same therapeutic purpose as ironic history—to dissolve the pretentious tendency to perceive our particular national experience as if it were the norm for the whole world. Both Hofstadter and Hartz wrote with that blend of sympathy and criticism appropriate to irony. Unlike Niebuhr in his *Irony of American History,* they were able to maintain a critical stance toward the United States in spite of the Cold War. Although, like Daniel Boorstin, they emphasized the agreement upon fundamentals that they saw as the distinguishing characteristics of American politics, they did not find in that agreement a cause for celebration. In their work we can see the connection between irony and the critical version of consensus history.

The generation of historians to which Hofstadter, Hartz, and Boorstin belong might be regarded as one in which the American historical profession underwent considerable maturation, and they might well be seen as representative of that mature profession. The broad consensus interpretation that Hofstadter and Hartz, along with Boorstin, presented can also be found in a more particularized form in the work of most historians of that generation, and the ironic vision informs much, although by no means all, of that work.[1] Both consensus and ironic history might be called mature scholarly positions, but in very different ways. The writings of Boorstin are mature in the sense that they are the work of a man who has made his peace with the world around him. Hartz and the early Hofstadter are mature in the way in which a person who has detached himself from narrow commitments is mature; their work is pervaded by a critical sense of the complexity and contradictions in human life and in the historical process. It is, to use Hartz's term, cosmopolitan. The confusion between the critical spirit of ironic history and the apologetic function of some consensus history may in part be owing to the fact that both can be regarded as symptoms of professional maturation. This confusion may also have represented the state of mind of most American historians at that time. Recognizing in some ways that America had lost its innocence and simplicity, they were still unwilling to give up the illusion that somehow we remained a nation apart. All too often in those years the evil and irrationality that scholars were rediscovering in human nature were projected onto the world outside America.

Most of the historians discussed in this book share not only a general ironic vision of American history; there are in addition similarities in the flaws they find in America and Americans that led us to act so as to bring about unintended consequences. In general these flaws involve illusions and pretensions to exaggerated virtues that America may in fact possess, above all the claim to being in some sense a people apart, a nation with a special destiny.[2] A particular illusion of a past golden agrarian age, an illusion that obscures American perceptions of social reality, plays a part in a number of these interpretations.

Most significantly Parrington, Niebuhr, Hofstadter, and Hartz all find in varying ways and to varying degrees that capitalism and its ideology have been major sources of ironic behavior in American history. The belief, sustained by the reality of many examples, that in America it was possible for common men to rise to wealth and status has fostered costly illusions of individual freedom and power among the American people, who have focused much of their energies on the effort to imitate the heroes of Horatio Alger, often without the kind of success they sought. The widely accepted capitalist assumptions that the marketplace would provide a just distribution of goods and that private selfishness would lead to public good have frequently led America into disaster. Blindness to the realities of economic power in a capitalist society and hostility to the exercise of political power have made it difficult for the mass of Americans to act effectively in their own collective interest. Although Americans have believed that their democracy and their capitalism reinforced each other in the world of Horatio Alger, these historians have exposed the ways in which that capitalism has distorted democracy. This is an irony of the whole people, because American capitalism has been democratically supported, as Hofstadter's penetrating comment on America as a "democracy in cupidity" suggests. In seeking the freedom and opportunity to advance in the world, common Americans have contributed to the growth of an industrial-capitalist system that restricts freedom and opportunity.

I am suggesting, then, that these historians have fulfilled at least in part the moral responsibility of ironic history. They have exposed some of the illusions and pretensions that, flowing out of our past, continue to lead us to act so as to contradict our best intentions. All of these ironic historians have been critical of American capitalism. In that sense they have been radical. Yet their criticism, their maturity, certainly their radicalism, are incomplete. Writing in the midst of the fearful prosperity of the Cold War, Hofstadter and Hartz were remarkably able to achieve critical distance, but the climate of opinion in that time limited their insight into American evil. In the 1960s a generation of historians appeared who saw that evil with a much sharper eye. Generally the work of these New Left historians is regarded as antithetical to consensus history, and much of it certainly is. Some of it is not at all ironic, either. Too many New Left historians were afflicted with conspiracy theories, with the desire to find happy precedents for their own radicalism, or with a simple view of the consequences of human action as the direct result of human intention. The kind of demonic history written by a few New Left scholars, in which the United States was portrayed as a uniquely evil nation, actually affirmed our sense of chosenness and perpetuated our illusions. Yet, perhaps it would be worthwhile to recognize the continuities between such older scholars as Hofstadter and Hartz and other New Left historians. The major weakness in Hofstadter and Hartz's histories was the failure adequately to recognize American social evils, the failure to deal with racism, sexism, poverty, and "democratic imperialism." These, of course, were the major concerns of many New Left historians. This difference of focus has been seen as evidence of the repudiation by the younger historians of their predecessors, but if we shift our angle of vision perhaps it might be possible to see New Left history as a further development of post-progressive history. A number of the New Left historians utilized Niebuhrian irony.[3] Their vision of the American past, although far more explicitly critical than that of Hofstadter and Hartz, can be seen as a further development and maturation of aspects of their predecessors' work. If irony does represent the maturation of American historical consciousness, that maturation is a process that continued to go on in spite of changes in the political climate of opinion.

In the 1970s the study of our past has become less overtly political and has largely transcended, or bypassed, the debate between consensus and New Left historians. Arising in part out of some of the concerns of the latter, the most dynamic movement in recent historical scholarship has been a shift of attention away from the political activities of American leaders to the social lives of ordinary Americans. New methodologies are being used to study those lives, and new questions are being asked. This social history already shows some of the developments characteristic of earlier historical schools in America. It arose out of a critical concern for the inarticulate, who had been left out of previous studies of our past; that concern remains, although it may well be losing its critical edge. Nonetheless, a number of the new social historians resist the drift toward optimism so common in the history of American historical writing, and perceive that past in ironic terms.[4]

Niebuhrian irony runs like a thread through much of the recent writing of American history, drawing attention to the link between American evils and American virtues, and to the unconscious responsibility of Americans for those evils. But irony is not the end of maturity. It is an important step in a process of cultural maturation; it is not the final product of such a process. Because it focuses our attention on aspects of life that people can hope to control, it leaves out important dimensions of the human condition, particularly death. Beyond irony there is tragedy. Although the relationship between life and death might be viewed ironically, since death flows from its opposite, life, death is absolute, final, and no product of human intention. There has been little tragedy in American historical writing, except occasionally in the work of a few historians of the South. I suspect that the American historical profession is no more ready to deal with tragedy than American culture is to deal with the reality of death, but as we mature in our ironic vision of our past, as the larger evils that that past has bequeathed to the present continue to grow, it seems reasonable to expect the development of a tragic vision. In the meantime irony remains peculiarly suited to our situation; it is the perception of our past most compatible with our deepest understanding of historical complexity and the most useful in the present in our efforts to free ourselves from the burden of those illusions, rooted in the past, which continue to lead us to act so as to contradict our own best intentions.

# Notes

## Preface

1. Paul Fussell, "The New Irony and the Augustans," *Encounter* 34 (June 1970): 68. If we are not the first generation to experience such contradictions, we seem to confront more of them than did most previous generations. Stanley Hopper finds our drama to be particularly characterized by irony ("Irony — The Pathos of the Middle," *Cross Currents* 12 [1962]: 31-40). Douglas Muecke in his comprehensive study sees Western culture since the eighteenth century as increasingly ironic in its perception of the human condition and the world at large (*The Compass of Irony* [London: Methuen, 1969], p. 123). He documents the rapid short-term growth in the interest in and use of irony during recent years from a study of the entries under that title in the *International* (later *Social Science and Humanities*) *Index*, (ibid., p. 9). Fussell's most recent book is a sensitive study of how the experience of war has made irony a dominant mode of literary perception in the twentieth century (*The Great War and Modern Memory* [New York and London: Oxford University Press, 1975]).

2. David Levin, *In Defense of Historical Literature* (New York: Hill and Wang, 1967), particularly "The Literary Criticism of History," pp. 1-33.

3. (Stanford, Calif.: Stanford University Press, 1959), particularly pp. 163-228.

4. *Metahistory* (Baltimore and London: Johns Hopkins University Press, 1973). White's analysis of the literary forms of historical writing is exceedingly complex and rigorous, involving modes of emplotment, argument, and ideological implication, each divided into four types, as well as his four basic poetry tropes. White's exploration of the relationship among these various modes and tropes is intricate and subtle, and his formalist argument is developed with a great richness of detail.

5. *Style in History* (New York: Basic Books, 1974). For a recent statement of a "realist" position similar to Gay's see David Hackett Fischer, "The Braided Narrative: Substance and Form in Social History," in Angus Fletcher, ed., *The Literature of Fact* (New York: Columbia University Press, 1976), pp. 109-33.

6. Gene Wise, *American Historical Explanations* (Homewood, Ill.: Dorsey Press, 1973), p. 51. Wise discusses the relationship between historical explanation forms and Thomas Kuhn's more familiar concept of scientific paradigms. Ibid., pp. viii, ix, 123-26, 223-95. For an examination of the relevance of Kuhn's concept for history to see David A. Hollinger, "T. S. Kuhn's Theory of Science and Its Implications for History," *American Historical Review* 78 (1973): 370-93.

7. There is no comprehensive study of the use of irony in historical writing in English, nor is there any general book on the literary forms used by American historians, although Levin's *History as Romantic Art* admirably fulfills that function for one period.

# Chapter 1

1. My definition is a slight modification of Wise's: "an ironic situation occurs when the consequences of an act are diametrically opposed to the original intention, and the fundamental cause of the disparity lies in the actor himself, and his original purposes." *American Historical Explanations* (Homewood, Ill.: Dorsey Press, 1973), p. 300. See also Wise's "Implicit Irony in Perry Miller's *New England Mind,*" *Journal of the History of Ideas*[29] (New York: Charles Scribner's Sons, 1952); hereafter cited as *Irony.*

2. Ibid., p. viii.

3. *A Grammar of Motives* (New York: Prentice-Hall, 1945), p. 515.

4. Niebuhr, *Irony,* p. viii. Robert W. Corrigan suggests the difficulties of defining tragedy and offers a broad statement of its more general trait: "The moment we try to establish a general definition of tragedy in terms of some set of formal characteristics we are sure to come a cropper. The constant in tragedy is the tragic view of life or the tragic spirit: that sense that life is, as Scott Fitzgerald once put it, 'essentially a cheat and its conditions are those of defeat.' " *Tragedy: Vision and Form* (San Francisco, Calif.: Chandler Publishing Co., 1965), p. xi.

5. *Irony and Drama* (Ithaca and London: Cornell University Press, 1971), pp. 225-26.

6. Douglas Muecke, *The Compass of Irony* (London: Methuen, 1969), p. 14.

7. *The Concept of Irony with Constant Reference to Socrates,* trans. Lee M. Capel (1841; reprint ed. Bloomington and London: Indiana University Press, 1965), p. 261.

8. Muecke, *Compass of Irony,* p. 7. This chapter on "Ironology," pp. 3-13, provides the best account of the scholarship on irony that I have found anywhere.

9. Ibid., pp. ix. 14. See G.G. Sedgewick, *Of Irony Especially in Drama* (Toronto: University of Toronto Press, 1948) for a discussion of how the historical development of the term has led it to take on "a confusing variety of shape" (ibid., p. 4).

10. Wayne Booth, *A Rhetoric of Irony* (Chicago and London: University of Chicago Press, 1974), p. ix.

11. Hayden White, *Metahistory* (Baltimore and London: Johns Hopkins University Press, 1973), pp. 37, 38. I have discussed the differences between White's conception of irony and Niebuhr's in greater detail elsewhere. See "The Use of Irony by Historians and Vice-Versa," *Clio,* 6 (1977):275-88.

12. Rhetorical irony itself is a broad term covering a number of forms and implications. See Norman Knox, *The Word Irony in Its Context. 1500-1750* (Durham, N.C.: Duke University Press, 1961) and A. E. Dyson, *The Crazy Fabric* (New York: St. Martin's Press, 1965) for studies confined to irony as a rhetorical device.

13. Northrop Frye, *Anatomy of Criticism* (Princeton, N.J.: Princeton University Press, 1957), p. 34.

214. Burke, *A Grammar of Motives,* p. 514. Sedgewick has almost the directly opposite attitude toward romantic irony: "To the romantics. . .sympathy and detachment are not mutually exclusive terms" (*Of Irony Especially in Drama,* p. 16). On the irony of superiority Paul de Mann argues that "the so-called superiority merely designates the *distance* constitutive of all acts of reflection" ('The Rhetoric of Temporality" in Charles S. Singleton, ed., *Interpretation: Theory and Practice* [Baltimore, Md.: Johns Hopkins University Press, 1969], p. 195.

15. States, *Irony and Drama,* p. 14.

16. Frye, *Anatomy of Criticism,* p. 237.

17. Burke, *A Grammar of Motives,* pp. 514, 515.

18. Niebuhr, *Irony,* p. 237.

19. In another sense it is a concept of the middle. According to Randolph Bourne "irony is . .

.a cure for both optimism and pessimism." "The Life of Irony," *Atlantic Monthly* 111 (March 1913): 364. De Mann would disagree with the main thrust of my argument here and elsewhere. For him "irony engenders a temporal sequence of acts of consciousness which is endless." It is the opposite of narrative temporality: "irony appears as an instanteous process that takes place rapidly, suddenly, in one single moment" ("The Rhetoric of Temporality," pp. 202, 206). However accurate this may be as a statement of the implications of irony as seen by both de Mann and the nineteenth-century writers he follows, it does not prove that irony cannot also be a process through time moving from intention, through action, to consequences. His reductive logic would deny that this process is really temporal, but we are under no compulsion to follow that logic to the extreme to which de Mann carries it.

20. Robert Merton, "The Unanticipated Consequences of Purposive Social Action," *American Sociological Review*,[1] (1939):895. For other discussions of irony and unanticipated consequences by sociologists see Severyn T. Bruyn, *The Human Perspective in Sociology* (Englewood Cliffs, N.J.: Prentice-Hall, 1966), pp. 150-55; David Matza, *Becoming Deviant* (Englewood Cliffs, N.J.: Prentice-Hall, 1969), pp. 69, 70, 77-85; Louis Schneider, "Dialectic in Sociology," *American Sociological Review* 36 (1971): 667-78; Schneider, *The Sociological Way of Looking at the World* (New York: McGraw-Hill, 1975), pp. 3-58; and Schneider and Charles M. Bonjean, eds., *The Idea of Culture in the Social Sciences* (Cambridge: At the University Press, 1973), pp. 62-63, 138-43.

21. Quoted by Eric Heller in *Thomas Mann: The Ironic German* (Cleveland and New York: World Publishing, 1961), p. 231, from *Meditations of a Nonpolitical Man*.

22. *The Use and Abuse of History*, trans. Adrian Collins (New York: Liberal Arts Press, 1957), pp. 28, 54, 55. On Nietzche's desire to transcend ironic historical consciousness see White, *Metahistory*, pp. 334, 371-72. For comments on the social and political dangers of the "ironic contemplation of intangible values" see Charles Child Walcott, "Irony: Vision or Retreat," *Pacific Spectator* 10 (1956): 365.

23. White, *Metahistory*, p. 38.

24. States, *Irony and Drama*, pp. xvii-xviii.

25. Muecke, *Compass of Irony*, pp. 243, 246, 247.

26. I am indebted to Robert Benson and Louis Mink for the idea that works of history may be compared to a Bildungsroman.

27. David Levin, "Literary Criticism of History" in *In Defense of Historical Literature* (New York: Hill and Wang, 1967). White demonstrates how works of history can be analyzed as literature in all of these terms and more.

28. "History and Fiction as Modes of Comprehension," *New Literary History* 1 (1970): 551. Of course, this is not the only contemporary position on the nature of historical knowledge. See ibid., pp. 542-58 (particularly the notes) for a statement of the argument between advocates of a modern positivistic concept of historical knowledge and those who, like Mink, hold that history is an autonomous form of knowledge.

29. *The Concept of Jacksonian Democracy* (New York: Antheneum, 1964), p. 337.

30. This problem is related to the methodological dilemma in intellectual history between the intrinsic treatment of ideas in purely conceptual terms and the intrinsic study of the social conditions under which they develop. Irony also helps us deal with this dilemma by focusing our attention on the interaction between ideas and values and the world in which people attempt to actualize them. On the intrinsic-extrinsic dilemma see Robert A. Skotheim, "The Writing of American Histories of Ideas: Two Traditions in the XXth Century," *Journal of the History of Ideas* 25 (1964): 257-78; Skotheim, *American Intellectual History and Historians* (Princeton, N.J.: Princeton University Press, 1966) and Rush Welter, "The History of Ideas in America: An Essay in Redefinition," *Journal of American History* 51 (1965): 599-614. Gene Wise has recently illuminated this issue by applying Kenneth Burke's concept of ideas as strategic responses to situations. *American Historical Explanations*, pp. 142-46.

31. This process is more complex than this description indicates. Ironies overlap in time, and goals and values change. Irony, like any kind of historical structure, when applied to any particular problem tends to freeze and isolate it from the flow of events of which it is a part. The only thing we can do about this is take it into account and avoid slipping into the relativist attitude that because history as actuality is more complex than any account of it, any one account is as good as any other.

32. Niebuhr, *Irony*, p. 156. See Wise's comments on the critical stance required of the historian who would use Niebuhrian irony. *American Historical Explanations*, p. 311.

33. Hayden White, "The Burden of History," *History and Theory* 5 (1966): 13.

34. Niebuhr, *Irony*, p. viii. See also p. 168. This line of argument assumes too much power for history. I do not know how much professionally written history affects public consciousness, although I think it is true that images of the past deeply influence politics. Robert J. Lifton suggests a possible ironic relationship between the liberal older generation and the radical youth of the 1960s. "The formative fathers of the young rebels are the middle-aged members of the intellectual left. (I recently heard one articulate young rebel say as much to an audience made up mostly of university professors: 'we are your children. You taught us what American society is like')" (*History and Human Survival* [New York: Random House, 1970], p. 355). If Lifton is right, it may be that the radicalization of students in the 1960s had something to do with the kind of history they were taught. The ironic view of our past — even in its consensus form — could have had the effect of sensitizing students to the discontinuities between our stated national values and our actual behavior, could have made them aware of our faulty pretensions to innocence, virtue, and limitless power, and led them to a determination to turn the country around and make it face and repudiate its ironies. Unfortunately, their ironic consciousness did not go deeply enough; they were not freed of their own illusions of innocence, and the result was the ironic history of the New Left.

35. Neither is there any guarantee that if people of a nation came to a contrite understanding of some of their collective ironies they would be able to change their nation's behavior when they tried. It is perhaps a basic article of American democratic faith that if such an understanding became general the people could bring about such changes, but it is by no means certain that the power structure is that flexible.

36. See chapter 3.

37. De Mann takes account of the view that irony can be therapeutic and denies it: "at the very moment that irony is thought of as a knowledge able to order and cure the world, the source of it runs dry. The instant it construes the fall of the self as an event that could somehow benefit the self, it discovers that it has in fact substituted death for madness" ("The Rhetoric of Temporality," p. 200). This argument is based upon the logic of de Mann's conception of irony as instantaneous rather than temporal. The present book about the use of irony by American historians does not claim to be an ironic work with the therapeutic power to dissolve irony-inducing illusions, but some works examined in it do have such power and in the conclusion I point to some of the specific national flaws and illusions that they suggest lie behind some of our national contradictions.

38. White, "The Burden of History," p. 134.

39. See chap. 4 for a more extensive discussion of Niebuhr.

40. Perry Miller, "The Influence of Reinhold Niebuhr," review of *Pious and Secular America, The Reporter*, May 1, 1958, p. 40.

# Chapter 2

1. I wish to thank present and former colleagues in European history for their advice on this chapter, particularly Sidney Bolkosky, Marvin Bram, Francis J. M. O'Laughlin, and Nancy

Struever. They have, of course, no responsibility for any inadequacies and are particularly innocent of any blame for the obvious incompleteness of my coverage; had I followed up all of their suggestions I would have written a book on irony in European historiography.

2. Herodotus also used irony, but it was more an irony of fate than a Niebuhrian irony. See J. A. K. Thomson, *Irony* (London: George Allen and Unwin, 1926), pp. 116-34 for an account of irony in Herodotus.

3. *History of the Peloponnesian War,* trans. Rex Warner (Harmondsworth, Middlesex: Penguin Books, 1954), pp. 481, 372, 367-86.

4. Ibid., p. 488.

5. Ibid., p. 7.

6. John H. Finley, Jr., *Thucydides* (Ann Arbor: University of Michigan Press, 1963), pp. 248, 249. The way in which democracy functioned so as to bring about Athenian failure involved repeated situations in which the city refused to accept favorable terms when an end to hostilities would have been in its interest because of "the unwillingness of a popular leader to risk his continued power by making peace" (ibid., p. 248). Thomson finds "tragic irony" in Thucydides and describes it in terms that suggest the Niebuhrian pattern. Thomson, *Irony,* pp. 135-53.

7. *The Language of History in the Renaissance* (Princeton, N.J.: Princeton University Press, 1970), pp. 32, 133, 134.

8. See Leo Braudy, *Narrative Form in History and Fiction* (Princeton, N.J.: Princeton University Press, 1970), pp. 12, 13, 46, 76, 214 on Hume and pp. 12, 13, 216, 245-55 on Gibbon, as well as A. E. Dyson, *The Crazy Fabric* (New York: St. Martin's Press, 1965), pp. 49-56 on the latter. White emphasizes the ironic character of most history written during the Enlightenment and points out the close relationship between irony and satiric attitudes in Hume and Gibbon. Metahistory (Baltimore and London: Johns Hopkins University Press, 1973), pp. 53-55. Peter Gay also discusses Gibbon's irony. *Style in History* (New York: Basic Books, 1974), pp. 40-56.

9. *The Decline and Fall of the Roman Empire* (New York: Random House, The Modern Library, 1932), 1: 382-444.

10. *An Inquiry into the Nature and Causes of the Wealth of Nations* (New York: Random House, The Modern Library, 1937), p. 423. Robert Merton sees this "doctrine of classical economics" as an example of "the unanticipated consequences of purposive social action" ("The Unanticipated Consequences of Purposive Social Action," *American Sociological Review* 1 [1939]): 902. On the use of the idea of unintended consequences by Hume, Smith and other figures in the Skotish Enlightenment see the comments and selections in Louis Schneider, ed., *The Scottish Moralists on Human Nature and Society* (Chicago and London: University of Chicago Press, 1967), pp. xxix-xlvii, 97-119.

11. *The Philosophy of History,* trans. J. Sibree (New York: Dover Publications, 1956), pp. 27, 30, 33.

12. *Hegel: Reinterpretation, Texts, and Commentary* (Garden City, N.Y.: Doubleday, 1965), p. 174. Hegel was quite aware of various uses of irony by Greek philosophers and by Kant. See *The Logic of Hegel,* trans. William Wallace (London: Oxford University Press, 1963), p. 149. White finds irony to be characteristic of historical consciousness in Hegel's thought, a form of consciousness that while higher than most others, is itself transcended. *Metahistory,* pp. 96, 102-3, 127, 131.

13. (New York: International Publishers, [1934]), pp. 58, 59, 60, 61.

14. Karl Marx and Friedrich Engels, *Correspondence, 1846-1895* (New York: International Publishers, 1935), pp. 475-77.

15. Harold Rosenberg in his *The Tradition of the New* (New York: Horizon Press, 1959) finds irony in Marx's *The Eighteenth Brumaire of Louis Bonaparte.* Marx observes how during the French Revolution the bourgeois revolutionaries identified with Roman Republicans,

finding in this "the self-deceptions they needed in order to conceal from themselves the bourgeois limitations of the content of their struggles" (Karl Marx, *Eighteenth Brumaire* [New York: International Publishers, n.d.], p. 14). Rosenberg comments on the irony of this process of self-transformation through self-deception: "Since it changes men into themselves by making them seem something else, history is ironical. But it is ironical only with regard to their consciousness of events and of themselves. The objective irony of Greek tragedy, Reversal of the Situation, 'a change by which the action veers around to its opposite' (Aristotle), does not rule over historical events" (Rosenberg, *Tradition of the New*, p. 158). The irony here is confined to the disjunction between the expectation of men and the way in which history moves. But Rosenberg's perceptive distinction does not focus on the role that the consequences of the actions of individuals may play, unintentionally, in the movement of history. On irony in the *Eighteenth Brumaire* see also Eugene Goodheart, Culture and the Radical Conscience (Cambridge, Mass.: Harvard University Press, 1973), pp. 105-110.

There is an implicit irony in the interpretation of history in *The Communist Manifesto*, particularly in regard to the role of the bourgeoisie as suggested in the following: "not only has the bourgeoisie forged the weapons that bring death to itself; it has also called into existence the men who are to wield those weapons — the modern working class — the proletarians" (Karl Marx and Friedrich Engels, *Basic Writings on Politics and Philosophy*, ed. Lewis Feuer [Garden City, N.Y.: Anchor Books, 1959], p. 13). White carefully unpacks the historical irony in this, but he concludes that here, as in his conception of history generally, Marx goes beyond irony. *Metahistory*, pp. 311-17. In a close analysis of some of the images in *The Manefesto*, Marshall Berman perceptively outlines the irony in Marx's vision of the cultural consequences of capitalism and points to a possible irony in Marx's own action as a writer (" 'All That Is Solid Melts into Air:' Marx, Modernism, and Modernization," *Dissent* [1978]: 54-73). For a reading of Marx that emphasizes the role of human action and unintended consequences in his historical thought see Jean-Paul Sartre, *Search for a Method*, trans. Hazel E. Barnes (New York: Random House, 1963), particularly pp. 85-166.

16. *The Protestant Ethic and the Spirit of Capitalism*, trans. Talcott Parsons (New York: Charles Scribner's Sons, 1958), pp. 89, 90. I emphasize Weber's awareness of the religious motivations of the reformers because some of his critics have argued that, since the Reformation was a religious movement, Weber is wrong in seeing any connection between it and capitalism. Such an argument seems to display a specific blindness to the ironic relationship between intention in one area of life and unintended consequences in another. For a summary of the arguments against the relationship between a branch of the Reformation and various aspects of modernity see Leo F. Solt, "Puritanism, Capitalism, Democracy and the New Science," *American Historical Review* 73 (1967): 18-29.

17. Weber, *The Protestant Ethic and the Spirit of Capitalism*, pp. 90-92.

18. The openness of Weber's universe and the ambiguities in his concept of causality are noted by Philip Rieff in a comment in which Weber's approach to history is specifically referred to as ironic in terms reminiscent of Niebuhr. In the course of a comparison of the attitudes toward the relationships among ideas, psychic states, and events on the part of Marx, Freud, and Weber, Rieff says: "Weber. . . .is a causal pluralist, asserting the autonomy of the three levels." This leads him to "his most delicate evasion, in a lifetime of delicate evasions, in the problem of social causation: the irony of history, the surprising thrust of the unintended consequences, so much ignored and despised by other sociologists but nevertheless crucial to Weber" ("The Meaning of History and Religion in Freud's Thought," in Bruce Mazlish ed., *Psychoanalysis and History* [Englewood Cliffs, N.J.: Prentice-Hall, 1963], pp. 37-38). Niebuhrian irony could certainly be described as a "delicate evasion" of the problem of causality.

19. Marianne Weber, *Max Weber: Ein Lebensbild* as quoted in Louis Schneider, "Dialectic in Sociology," *American Sociological Review*, 36 (1971): 674.

20. Merton, "The Unintended Consequences of Purposive Social Action," p. 903.

21. Ibid. At least since Weber's time there has been an ongoing debate among scholars as to the relationship between the rise of Protestanism and modernity. Irony and unintended consequences have been found in aspects of that relationship in addition to the rise of capitalism. Merton argues, for example, that "it was the *unintended and largely unforeseen consequences* of the religious ethnic formulated by the great Reformation leaders which progessively developed into a system of values favorable to the pursuit of science" ("Puritanism, Pietism, and Science," in *Social Theory and Social Structure*, enlarged ed. [New York: Free Press, 1968], p. 651). See also Merton, *Science, Technology and Society in Seventeenth Century England* (New York: Howard Fertig, 1970), particularly p. ix. Louis Schnieder discusses the irony of unintended consequences in both Weber and Merton and presents the idea as a central one for sociology in general. See particularly *The Sociological Way of Looking at the World* (New York: McGraw-Hill, 1975), pp. 37-42. For a discussion of the unintended political consequences of Calvinism and Puritanism as fostering a freer social order based upon internalized restraints see Michael Walzer, *The Revolution of the Saints* (New York: Antheneum, 1968), particularly p. 306. The ironic connection that William Haller finds between the rise of Puritanism and the development of religious toleration is related to the general question of the unintended modernizing effects of the Reformation. See below.

22. Although Freud was less directly concerned with history and historical processes than were Hegel, Marx, and Weber, he is another nineteenth-century social thinker whose work is related to irony. The image of humankind in Freud as internally in conflict and often self-defeating lends itself to ironic perceptions. Specific Freudian concepts such as projection, displacement, and the return of the repressed are highly suggestive of Niebuhrian irony. The argument I have made about the therapeutic power of ironic historical consciousness to free people to act more consciously and effectively by exposing their illusions, which arise out of the past, parallels the therapeutic hope of psychoanalysis to liberate individuals from the unconscious power of their childhood by recovering to consciousness repressed experiences. Both seek to enhance human control over their future by increasing awareness of the past. For some general comments on the relationship between irony and psychoanalysis see Douglas Muecke, *Compass of Irony* (London: Methuen, 1969), p. 142. A number of explicit applications of psychoanalysis to historical problems suggest the relationship between Niebuhrian irony and psychohistory. See, for example, Erik Erikson's comparison of Luther and Freud in *Young Man Luther* (New York: W. W. Norton, 1962(, pp. 251-53, also Lucien w. Pye, "Personal Identity and Political Ideology," in Bruce Mazlish, ed., *Psychoanalysis and History*, p. 168. Several important recent psychohistorical interpretations of American history point out the ways in which white Americans have tried to define their identity by projecting onto others their unacceptable sexual and aggressive feelings. This interpretation becomes ironic when it emphasizes the cost to white Americans themselves of this process of self-rejection. Winthrop Jordan's *White Over Black* (Chapel Hill: University of North Carolina Press for the Institute of Early American History, 1968) established the basic pattern for this combination of psychoanalytic and ironic history. Jordan also, incidentally, suggests the therapeutic power of historical consciousness in a way that also exposes the compatibility between these two approaches. ibid., p. 582. See the comments on Peter Loewenberg's work on young Nazis below for further consideration of the relationship between psychoanalysis and ironic history.

23. Alexis de Tocqueville, *The Old Regime and the French Revolution*, trans. Stuart Gilbert (Garden City, N.Y.: Doubleday Anchor, 1955), pt. 3, chap. 5, p. 180; hereafter cited as *Old Regime*. For a study of this book and its place in his thought see Richard Herr, *Tocqueville and the Old Regime* (Princeton, N.J.: Princeton University Press, 1962).

24. Tocqueville, *Old Regime*, pp. 180, 181.

25. Ibid., pp. 181, 182.

26. Ibid., pp. 187, 185.

27. Ibid., pp. 182, 180, 186.
28. Ibid., pp. 183, 185.
29. Ibid., pp. 188, 189.
30. Ibid., pp. 189, 190.
31. Ibid., p. 192.
32. Ibid., pp. vii, x.
33. Ibid., p. xi. This interpretation is mentioned but not developed in *The Old Regime*, which is devoted primarily to an examination of the roots of the revolution, not its consequences. Tocqueville presents his remarks on how the revolution aimed at creating more freedom but instead led to greater tyranny as an indication of the theme of a second volume on the revolution, one that he did not live to complete.
34. White sees Tocqueville as falling from his earlier tragic vision into irony in *The Old Regime*. His reading of that irony is somewhat different from mine. *Metahistory*, pp. 192, 215-18. According to White, Burkhardt is more consistently ironic than Tocqueville: "Burkhardt's historical vision began in that condition of irony in which Tocqueville's ended" (*Metahistory* p. 234). White considers Burkhardt an ironic historian in part because he "abandons any effort to construct a diachronic narrative of events, structures and processes that make up his account of the Renaissance" ("Interpretation in History," *New Literature History*, 4 (1973): 297 n., 298 n. Since it is precisely a "diachronic narrative"—allowing the reader to follow or constitute for himself a temporal account in which the action flows from intention and consequences from action—that Niebuhrian irony requires, it is clear that White is using the term differently. For White's comments on Burkhardt's narrative see *Metahistory*, pp. 250-51.
35. I deal with Haller not only because of the importance of his work and its close relationship to the ironic pattern, but also because he provides an interesting parallel to Perry Miller, another professor of literature who made an enormous contribution to historical understanding. Miller was one of the important of American historical ironists. On Miller's irony see Gene Wise, *American Historical Explanations* (Homewood, Ill.: Dorsey Press, 1973), pp. 296-359 and "Implicit Irony in Perry Miller's *New England Mind*," *Journal of the History of Ideas* 7 (1968). Although they share a common ironic interpretation of Puritanism, there are subtle differences between them, the most suggestive of which has to do with where their greatest sympathies lie. Miller, without being in any ordinary sense religious, clearly empathizes more with the original, communal intention of the Puritans. As much of his work shows, he had very ambivalent feelings about the modernity and the America that were the unintended outcome of New England Puritanism. His irony, then, is touched with tragedy and a sense of failure, of an opportunity lost. Haller, on the other hand, is more sympathetic to the consequences of Puritanism, to a modernity in which freedom and individualism are valued, than he is to the original Puritan impulse. For him the unintended consequences are in part, at least, beneficent, better than the intention.
36. William Haller, *The Rise of Puritanism* (1938; reprint ed. New York: Harper and Row, 1957), pp. 6, 127.
37. Ibid., p. 14.
38. Ibid., p. 173.
39. Ibid., pp. 174-79.
40. Ibid., p. 375.
41. Ibid., pp. 224, 225.
42. Ibid., pp. 49, 50.
43. William Haller, *Liberty and Reformation in the Puritan Revolution* (New York and London: Columbia University Press, 1955), pp. 352-53.
44. Haller and Miller were not the only historians to interpret Puritanism ironically. Among others, there is Max Weber whose vision of the consequences of Protestanism in general and

of Puritanism in particular also fits that pattern, as we have seen.

45. Hannah Arendt certainly sees the Nazis as demonic, but there is also a hard irony in her vision of the self-destructive aspect of the behavior of many of the Nazi's victims. There is also a kind of irony in her perception as pathetic rather than demonic of many of the men who did the most horrible things imaginable while thinking of themselves simply as order-following bureaucrats. See *The Origins of Totalitarianism* (New York: Meridian Books, 1959) and particularly *Eichmann in Jerusalem* rev. and enl. ed. (New York: Viking Press, 1964).

46. John Wheeler-Bennett, *The Nemesis of Power* 2nd ed. (London: Macmillan, 1964), pp. 182, 285.

47. Ibid., p. 285.

48. Ibid.

49. Peter Loewnberg, "The Psychohistorical Origins of the Nazi Youth Cohort, *American Historical Review* 76 (1971), 1501.

50. Ibid., pp. 1501, 1502.

51. James Billington, "Six Views of the Russian Revolution," *World Politics* 18 (1966): 469, 470, 471.

52. Ibid., p. 473.

53. (New York: Vintage Books, 1966). See, for example, his treatment of Muscovite attitudes toward the West, pp. 590.91.

54. Ibid., p. 592.

55. Ibid., pp. 592, 593.

56. Ibid., pp. 595, 596.

57. Isaac Deutscher, the biographer of Trotsky, presents an ironic interpretation of Stalinism different from Billington's. It falls more into the category of "the irony of fate" and does not clearly suggest that the unintended consequences of Stalin's actions were owing to his own flaws. "The Irony of History in Stalinism," in his *Ironies of History* (London: Oxford University Press, 1966), pp. 233-39.

58. A recent review of three German books on Western imperialism in Africa suggests how widespread ironic perceptions of European history may be. Wolfe W. Schmokel's summary comment on these works strongly suggests Niebuhrian irony: "These monographs illustrate effectively one of the central ironies of turn-of-the-century colonialism: European states and their colonial civil servants, professing capitalist-individualist ideology and objectives, consciously strove to remake the societies and economies of Africa by revolutionary methods of social engineering. While they did so entirely in the supposed interest of the mother countries' economies they unleashed dynamics in Africa's previously conservative societies that necessarily undermined the bases of European rule" *American Historical Review* 77 (1972): 559.

59. Some of the "new" social history in France and England may represent an exception to this. George Rudé, for example, is interested in studying the history of the common people as active agents. Rudé emphasizes the defensive - even perhaps conservative - nature of the crowds' goals, but the consequences of their actions were anything but conservative. *The Crowd in the French Revolution* (Oxford: Oxford University Press, 1959), pp. 9, 222, 225, 226.

Not all the French social historians focus, as does Rudé, on the active historical role of the common people. An examination of two collections of translated articles from the great French journal of social history, *Annales*, suggests that although these historians were concerned with getting at the conditions under which the masses of the past lived, they perceived them as the victims of broad structural forces and not creative participants in their own lives. Peter Burke, ed., *Economy and Society in Early Modern Europe* (New York: Harper and Row, 1972) and Marc Ferro, ed., *Social Historians in Contemporary France* (New York: Harper and Row, 1972). In a review of a translation of the first volume of Fernand Braudel's *The Mediterranean and the Mediterranean World in the Age of Phillipp II*, J. H. Elliott suggests that the great work may suffer from a disjunction between the structural analysis of the "impersonal forces" that shape the lives of people and the presentation of the sources of historical movement and change. "Mediterranean Mysteries," *New York Review of Books*, May 3, 1973, pp. 25-28. It is interesting to note that American social historians— some of whom were inspired by the French— tend, in contrast to most Europeans, to focus on private action, on such questions as the participation of individuals in social and geographic mobility. Even Rudé, who does perceive the masses as active, is concerned with public, collective activity under unusual, revolutinary conditions and not, like the Americans, with the ongoing role of ordinary human beings in the private creation of their own lives.

# Chapter 3

1. For a discussion of the role of irony as one party to a three-faceted dialogue with "hope" and "nostalgia" in nineteenth-century American literature see W. R. B. Lewis, *The American Adam* (Chicago: University of Chicago Press, 1955).

2. The question of the extent of fulfillment of American expectations is highly complex and debatable. In regard to the lives of most individuals it is closely related to social mobility. For a case study of America in which social mobility in the nineteenth century is perceived in part ironically see Stephen Thernstrom, *Poverty and Progress* (Cambridge, Mass: Harvard University Press, 1864). For a profoundly ironic account of how the American belief in the possibility of personal advancement produces unintended consequences see John William Ward's review essay on Alexander Berkman's *Prison Memoirs*, "Violence, Anarchy and Alexander Berkman," *New York Review of Books*, November 5, 1970, pp. 25-30.

3. "The American Search for Self-Understanding" in Roger L. Shinn, ed., *The Search for Identity* (New York: Harper and Row, 1964), p. 1.

4. Reinhold Niebuhr, *The Irony of American History* (New York: Charles Scribner's Sons, 1952), pp. 17, 7.

5. Ibid., p. 24.

6. Ibid., p. 28. C. Vann Woodward also has written about "the national myth that America is an innocent nation in a wicked world" ("The Age of Reinterpretation," *American Historical Review* 66 [1966]: 7).

7. Niebuhr, *Irony*, pp. 4, 13. See also p. 41.

8. D. W. Brogan, "The Illusion of American Omnipotence," *Harper's* 205 (December 1952): 21, 23. Richard Hofstadter, "Goldwater and Pseudo-Conservative Politics," in *The Paranoid Style in American Politics* (New York: Vintage, 1967), pp. 133, 135, 136.

9. Niebuhr, *Irony*, p. 7.

10. Ibid., pp. 48, 53, 56, 57, 29.

11. The process whereby both success and failure have been used to affirm America's chosenness has been brilliantly traced by Sacvan Bercovitch in his "Horologi)cals to Chronometricals: The Rhetoric of the Jeremiad," *Literary Monographs* 3 (Madison: University of Wisconsin Press, 1970), pp. 1-125. More recently Bercovitch has shown how this conviction of chosenness is embedded in the sense of identity that Americans derived from Puritanism. *The Puritan Origins of the American Self* (New Haven and London: Yale University Press, 1975).

12. Page Smith, "Anxiety and Despair in American History," *William and Mary Quarterly*, 3d ser., 26 (1969): 417, 423, 421, 419. Much of the new social history is devoted to uncovering the past working and familial lives of ordinary American women and men. Some of the studies point toward an ironic relationship between aspirations and realities in those lives.

13. David Potter, *People of Plenty* (Chicago: University of Chicago Press, 1954), pp. 60, 105-6.

14. Michael Kammen has presented a rich account of American history as charactertized by

paradox, polarity, biformity, tensions, contradictions, and other dualisms that are conducive to ironic behavior. See his conclusion for some suggestions as to how paradox in American history has led to "ironic contrasts between noble purposes and sordid results." *People of Paradox* (New York: Alfred A. Knopf, 1972), p. 290.

15. David Levin, *History as Romantic Art* (Stanford, Calif.: Stanford University Press, 1959), pp. 28, 30, 31¢, 45.

16. Ibid., pp. 103, 104. The last quotation is taken by Levin from Francis Parkman, *The Jesuits in North America in the Seventeenth Century* (Boston: Little, Brown and Company, 1884), p. 90.

17. Parkman, *The Jesuits in North America,* pp. 447, 443. See also Levin, *History as Romantic Art,* p. 139 and, for a different point of view on "Parkman's tough, ironic, masculine ideal," Lewis, *The American Adam,* pp. 165-73.

18. Donald Emerson's biography, *Richard Hildreth* (Baltimore, Md.: Johns Hopkins University Press, 1946) does not contain much discussion of Hildreth's *History* though it does provide evidence of his critical approach to the study of the past. Arthur Schlesinger, Jr., describes Hildreth's unusual combination of liberal principles and conservative policies. "The Problem of Richard Hildreth," *New England Quarterly* 13 (1940): 223-45. I am considering Hildreth after Parkman because, although he wrote earlier, his approach to history had more in common with some historians of the later nineteenth century. See David D. Van Tassel, *Recording America's Past* (Chicago: University of Chicago Press, 1960), p. 140.

19. Richard Hildreth, *The History of the United States of America from the Discovery of the Continent to the Organization of Government under the Federal Constitution* (New York: Harper Brothers, 1849), 1: 167, 238, 491, 594-95. Hildreth also uses an ironic tone in discussing such matters as Henry VIII's motives in breaking with Rome, ibid., 1: p. 153, the right to grant titles that was included in some colonial charters, ibid., 1: 173, the combination of asceticism and "money-making" in Puritanism, ibid., 1: 193, and the persecution of dissenters by the Puritans who themselves had been persecuted for dissent in England, ibid., 1: 154, 155, 242-44.

20. Richard Hildreth, *History of the United States of America from the Adoption of the Federal Constitution to the Sixteenth Congress* (New York: Harper and Brothers, 1852), 3: 313, 314, 315, 316, 319.

21. Ibid., 3: 567.

22. My comments largely follow Henry Rule's "Irony in the Works of Henry Adams," Ph.D. diss., University of Colorado, 1960. I am indebted to Rule for kindly lending me a copy of his interesting dissertation. Also of use on Adams's irony is J. C. Levenson, *The Mind and Art of Henry Adams* (Cambridge, Mass.: Houghton Mifflin, 1957). For a discussion of a particular, hostile use or irony by Adams, see Rule, "Henry Adams' Attack on Two Heroes of the Old South," *American Quarterly* 14 (1962): 174-84. For a view of Adams as trapped in his own ironies see Ralph Maud, "Henry Adams: Irony and Impasse," *Essays in Criticism* 7 (1958): 281-392. Rule offers a brief summary of the critical controversies surrounding Adams's irony in works published prior to 1960. "Irony in the Works of Henry Adams," pp. 1-9.

23. Rule, "Irony in the Works of Henry Adams," pp. 70-100, 101-48, 192, 216, 230, 260. Among Adams's later works Rule finds little irony in *Mont-Saint-Michel and Chartres,* except for Adams's treatment of St. Thomas, but Melvin Lyon finds irony in the basic structure of the book. *Symbol and Idea in Henry Adams* (Lincoln: University of Nebraska Press, 1970), pp. 82, 95, 112.

24. (New York: Charles Scribner's Sons, 1891); hereafter cited as *The History.*

25. Rule, "Irony in the Works of Henry Adams," pp. 155-59.

26. Adams, *The History,* 4: 454-55, 454.

27. Rule, "Irony in the Works of Henry Adams," p. 187.

28. This account of the dilemma of human responsibility in Adams's irony is rephrased in Niebuhrian terms from ibid., pp. 167-90. For other comments on irony in Adams's *The*

*History* see William H. Jordy, *Henry Adams* (New Haven, Conn.: Yale University Press, 1952), pp. 111, 120, and Levenson, *The Mind and Art of Henry Adams*, pp. 150, 151, 166, 170, and, for a recent interpretation of that irony that differs from the one offered here, Peter Shaw, "The War of 1812 Could Not Take Place: Henry Adams' History," *Yale Review* 62 (1973): 544-56.

29. Rule discusses various possible sources of Adams's irony, including the ways in which it met deep needs of his personality. "Irony in the work of Henry Adams," pp. 37-48.

30. According to Henry May "in Charles Beard and his followers, irony is present but often involuntary. . . .There are a few glimpses in Turner of the ironies of the expanding frontier" ("Perry Miller's Parrington," *American Scholar* 25 [1966]: 570.

31. "Napoleon — After One Hundred Years," *The Nation* 4 (May 1921): 646. This unsigned article is attributed to Becker by Burleigh Taylor Wilkins, *Carl Becker* (Cambridge, Mass.: MIT Press and Harvard University Press, 1961), p. 108 n.

32. Ibid., p. xi. See also Richard Hofstadter, *The Progressive Historians* (New York: Alfred A. Knopf, 1968), p. xi.

33. Wilkins, *Carl Becker, p. 228.* For references to Becker's "skeptical irony," his "Socratic irony," and other comments on his use of irony see Cushing Stout, *The Pragmatic Revolt in American History* (Ithaca, N.Y.: Cornell University Press, 1966), pp. 4, 50, 30, 32. For some comments on how Becker's "ironic humor" led to his being misinterpreted see Charlotte Watkins Smith, *Carl Becker: On History and the Climate of Opinion* (Ithaca, N.Y.: Cornell University Press, 1956), pp. 84-86.

Becker's thinking about history was affected by his efforts to come to terms with the ideas of that earlier ironist, Henry Adams. See particularly Becker's "The Education of Henry Adams" and "Henry Adams Once More," in *Everyman His Own Historian* (New York: Appleton-Century-Crofts, 1935), pp. 143-61 and 162-86, hereafter cited as *Everyman*. David Noble discusses the effect of Adams's vision of history on Becker, *Historians Against History* (Minneapolis: University of Minnesota Press, 1965), pp. 92-97. Of Niebuhr's attitude toward Becker, Wilkins writes: "Niebuhr welcomed Becker's social pragmatism and his apparent moral pessimism — probably because he regarded them as the secular equivalent of his Christian ideas about Original Sin. Most of all, he loved Becker's irony at the expense of the 'naive' and overly optimistic rationalists and democrats of the eighteenth and nineteenth centuries" (Wilkins, *Carl Becker,* p. 164). Niebuhr himself refers to Becker's "gentle cynicism" in "The Role of Reason," review of Becker, *New Liberties for Old, The Nation,* November 1, 1941, p. 431. See also Reinhold Niebuhr, "The Problem Stated," review of Becker, *Modern Democracy, The Nation,* April 12, 1941, p. 441.

34. David W. Noble, "Carl Becker: Science, Relativism and the Dilemma of Diderot," *Ethics* 67 (1957): 237, 233.

35. Carl Becker, *The Heavenly City of the Eighteenth Century Philosophers* (New Haven, Conn.: Yale University Press, 1932), p. 69 and "The Dilemma of Diderot," in *Everyman,* p. 280.

36. Becker, *Everyman*, pp. 47-80. A similar irony can be seen in Becker's account of how two eighteenth-century New Yorkers, men of similar backgrounds and close friends, moved in opposite directions in response to the Revolutionary crises. "John Jay and Peter Van Schaack," in ibid., pp. 234-93.

37. Becker, "The Spirit of '76," in *Everyman,* pp. 52, 57, 59, 59-62.

38. Ibid., pp. 65, 66, 68.

39. Ibid., p. 71.

40. Ibid., pp. 74, 75.

41. Ibid., 76.

42. Ibid., p. 77.

43. Strout presents an interesting account of irony in the development of Becker's social and political attitudes in response to changing circumstances, making it clear that Becker had the

humility and self-insight to recognize the irony. *The Pragmatic Revolt*, pp. 128-31. For an account of Becker's intellectual pilgrimage that can be read as a journey into irony and beyond see Noble, *Historians Against History*, pp. 76-97, 139-50.

44. Becker, "The Dilemma of Liberals in Our Time," in *Detachment and the Writing of History* (Ithaca, N.Y.: Cornell University Press, 1953), pp. 201-1. For similar comments on the contradictions between some of the consequences of the rise of science and what science had been expected to do see "What Are Historical Facts?" in ibid., pp. 62-64.

In addition to his historical writings, irony can also be found in Becker's own development as a philosopher of history. Strout shows how both Charles Beard and Becker were involved in an ironic dilemma in their revolt against traditional assumptions about the nature of history. Becker set out to liberate our understanding of historical knowledge from the passive model of nineteenth-century science. He asserted the importance of the climate of opinion within which the historian worked in determining his questions and his answers. This emphasis led him to a relativism that made impossible in theory the kind of history Becker actually wrote because it denied our capacity to transcend imaginatively the perspective of the time in which we live, a perspective that may color our study of the past but determines it only if we assume that mind is as passive before the pressures of the contemporary environment as the positivists assumed it was before external facts. Becker was unable to give a theoretical account that would allow for his own historical work because he had not sufficiently emancipated himself from those very nineteenth-century assumptions that he wanted to overturn, particularly the view that the only model for "real" knowledge is that provided by the natural sciences. Although the consequences remain in the world of thought, Strout's analysis fits the Niebuhrian pattern in showing that Becker was led to conclusions that undermined his intentions because of flaws in his own argument. Strout's attitude is also that appropriate to humane irony insofar as he points out the value of the contribution made by Becker's philosophy of history while at the same time exposing its inadequacies. Strout, *The Pragmatic Revolt*, pp. iv, 2, 29-49, 61.

45. Vernon Louis Parrington, *The Beginnings of Critical Realism in America* in *Main Currents in American Thought* (New York: Harcourt, Brace and Co., 1930), pp. 12, 10. John Higham treats both Becker and Parrington as in part disillusioned Progressives. Higham et al., *History* (Englewood Cliffs, N.J.: Prentice-Hall, 1965), pp. 196, 197. On Parrington's changing views see also Hofstadter, *The Progressive Historians*, pp. 428, 249, and Wise on the "anomolies" in Parrington's progressive vision that pointed toward a more critical history, *American Historical Explanations* (Homewood, Ill.: Dorsey Press, 1973), pp. 249, 258, 266. On his basic polarized approach and the way in which it affected his methods of writing see Robert Skotheim, *American Intellectual Histories and Historians* (Princeton, N.J.: Princeton University Press, 1966), pp. 124-48. Arthur A. Ekirch, Jr., has forcefully pointed out the note of pessimism in Parrington, finding it present in his treatment of events as early as the Revolution. Ekrich's reading of Parrington is by implication in conflict with my ironic interpretation. See "Parrington and the Decline of American Liberalism," *American Quarterly* 3 (1951): 295-308 and *The Decline of American Liberalism* (New York: Atheneum, 1967), pp. 26, 27, 37, 58, 130, 148, 264-65. For a fuller analysis and documentation of my ironic view of Parrington see Richard Reinitz, "Vernon Louis Parrington as Historical Ironist," *Pacific Northwest Quarterly*, 68 (1977): 113-19.

46. *The Beginnings of Critical Realism in America*, pp. 17, 21, 20. Another ironic aspect of the Gilded Age to which Parrington was sensitive was the destruction of the wilderness and some of the natural resources upon which the growth of the period was based. Ibid., pp. 16, 17.

47. Ibid., pp. 23, 25, 26.

48. Ibid., p. 26.

49. The ironic flaw that Parrington saw in America — the abandonment of communal values

for a democratic-capitalistic individualism – is very similar to that which a number of recent historians seem to find.

50. David Noble shows how the Progressive historians, particularly Beard, failed to break with the older view of America as a specially blessed nation, ultimately innocent of the corruptions of history that marked the peoples of Europe. See *Historians Against History*, pp. 138-38, on Beard's continued commitment to the national covenant, and p. 117 on Parrington's. Noble sees Becker's later work as an exception to this. ibid., pp. 139-56. Wise argues that optimism about America and mankind was an essential element of the Progressive "paradigm." "Progressives were not *just* cheerful and happy. . .; They *had to be* yea-sayers, they felt, else men would stop moving forward and would slide back into a dark and dreary past." (*American Historical Explanations*, p. 214). Christopher Lasch describes how Progressive history turned eventually into "a tiresome celebration of the American past" (Richard Hofstadter, "Forward," *The American Political Tradition*, rev. ed. [New York: Random House, 1973], p. viii.

51. This independence is frequently only relative. Although neither the imperial school's view of the Revolution nor the revisionist view of the Civil War can be reduced to progressive categories of economic conflict, they do share with Progressive history a more fundamental tendency that might be described in terms of a search for hidden realities in history and a willingness to discredit formerly revered American leaders. Edmund S. Morgan has pointed out how much the Progressive and imperial schools have in common in opposition to the Whig interpretation of the Revolution. "The American Revolution: Revisions in Need of Revising," *William and Mary Quarterly*, 3d ser., 14 (1957): 3-15.

52. Charles Andrews, *The Colonial Background of the American Revolution* (New Haven and London: Yale University Press, 1931), pp. 66, 126, 127, 156.

53. Thomas Pressly has illuminated the way in which the revisionists viewed the coming of the war both as unintentional and as the product of deliberate evil. See particularly his comments on the meaning of the term *needless* in their writings and his discussion of their treatment of the "extremists." *Americans Interpret Their Civil War* (New York: Collier Books, 1962), pp. 310, 314-318. For a more recent interpretation, written from a New Left point of view, which also finds the Civil War to have been unintentional and to have produced unsought consequences see John Rosenberg, "Toward a New Civil War Revisionism," *American Scholar*, 38 (1969): 250-72.

54. See n. 33 above.

55. Henry May refers to a "a permanent flaw in American nineteenth century thought: its inveterate optimism," *The End of American Innocence* (Chicago: Quadrangle Books, 1964), p. 397.

56. In a sense the earlier part of this process of disillusionment can be seen in ibid. Later and bitterer phases of it, involving the profound discrediting of the idea of progress itself and the recognition that increased modernization of society and politics could lead to moral deterioration, can be seen in Robert Skotheim, *Totalitarianism and American Social Thought* (New York: Holt, Rinehart and Winston, 1971). The Brogan, Van, Woodward, and Hofstadter essays cited earlier on the lack of the experience of limits in American history – a lack that can be regarded as conducive to ironic behavior – also describe our recent encounter with limits, an encounter that encourages an increased consciousness of that irony.

57. The process I have tried to describe in these brief paragraphs is obviously much more complex. Since the 1930s American historians have made two discoveries – or perhaps more accurately, rediscoveries – that I have telescoped into one since they had the common impact of sensitizing us to irony. First, they recaptured something of the Calvinist insight into the potential for evil in human nature in general and, more recently, they rediscovered injustice and poverty in the American present and other specific evils in our national past. The

discovery of one kind of evil underlay consensus, of the other, New Left history, movements that have been seen as in opposition to each other. While there is no dbout that there are significant political differences between the New Left and consensus historians, I would argue that the recovery of two different kinds of evil led many historians (but not all) in both groups toward a common ironic vision of the past. On the relation between consensus and New Left uses of historical irony see my "Niebuhrian Irony and Historical Interpretation," in Robert Canary and Henry Kozicki, *Literary Form and Historical Understanding* (Madison, Wis.: University of Wisconsin Press, 1978).

58. C. Vann Woodward, "The Irony of Southern History," in *The Burden of Southern History*, rev. ed. (Baton Rouge: Louisiana State University Press, 1968), pp. 209, 210. In 1968, in the light of intervening events, particularly the presidency of a Southerner, Lyndon Johnson, Woodward withdrew his suggestion that Southerners were "any the wiser for their historical experience, if it could be assumed that their fellow Americans have been the more misguided for theirs." (Subsequent events have underlined this point as we have witnessed the election of a candidate from the deep South who won in part by telling the American people how innocent they are of the corruption and evil of their government). Nonetheless, Woodward's general argument remains valid. The experience of defeat, if it could be internalized, is vital to contemporary American self-understanding. "A Second Look at the Theme of Irony," in ibid., p. 231.

# Chapter 4

1. Reinhold Niebuhr, *The Irony of American History* (New York: Charles Scribner's Sons, 1952), p. 153. Most of this book—the specific application of irony to American problems—consists of two series of lectures delivered by Niebuhr in 1949 and 1951. For publication in 1952 he added introductory and concluding chapters in which he presents his general ironic "framework." Ibid., p. vii. Some of the discrepancies discussed below between that framework itself and its application to America may in part be owing to these pecularities in the sequence in which the book was composed.

2. In a review of Niebuhr's *Faith and History,* Perry Miller describes how Niebuhr made insights into the human condition, derived from neoorthodox Christianity, accessible to modern intellectuals. Miller also suggests, as I do, that although these insights are derived from Christian theology in Niebuhr's work, they are finally independent of religious faith. "The Great Method," *The Nation* 169 (1949): 138-39. See chapter 5 below for an analysis of Hofstadter's critical irony.

3. See Niebuhr's *Moral Man and Immoral Society* (New York: Charles Scribner's Sons, 1934) for some expression of his critical attitude toward the United States and some aspects of American history in the midst of the depression, particularly pp. 98-108, 119-25, 131-36, 252-53, and 254-55. For a sympathetic account of the constant and changing elements in Niebuhr's account of the constant and changing elements in Niebuhr's thought and life up to Niebuhr's thought and life up to 1960 see June Bingham, *Courage to Change* (New York: Charles Scribner's Sons, 1961). Holtan P. Odegard outlines the changes in Niebuhr's political views, emphasizing the primacy and constancy of his neoorthodox theology. *Sin and Science* (Yellow Springs, Ohio: Antioch Press, 1956), pp. 6-7. Arthur Schlesinger, Jr., also traces the development of Niebuhr's political attitudes into the 1950s. "Reinhold Niebuhr's Role in American Political Thought and Life," in Charles Kegley and Robert Bretall, eds., *Reinhold Niebuhr* (New York: Macmillan, 1956), pp. 125-50. Robert E. Fitch shows how Niebuhr's concept of irony developed, culminating in *The Irony of American History.* "Reinhold Niebuhr's Philosophy of History," in ibid. pp. 291-332. In contrast to Fitch, Ronald H. Stone emphasizes the contrast between Niebuhr's reliance upon irony as a historical concept in the post-World War II period and his earlier philosophy of history. *Reinhold Niebuhr: Prophet to Politicians*

(Nashville, Tenn.: Abington Press, 1972), pp. 139-40. In general, Stone's periodization of Niebuhr's thought differs from that of most other commentators; he sees greater change in Niebuhr's theology along with the transformation of his political views. Ibid., pp. 50, 92, 129, 130. Gene Wise analyzes Niebuhr's *The Children of Light and the Children of Darkness* (1944) as an important step in the development of his ironic vision of America. *American Historical Explanations* (Homewood, Ill.: Dorsey Press, 1973), pp. 271-84. Paul Merkley places *The Irony of American History* firmly in the context of Niebuhr's more general theological and historical writings, emphasizing the dependence of his political judgements upon his religious faith. *Reinhold Niebuhr* (Montreal and London: McGill-Queen's University Press, 1975), pp. 213.22.

4. Niebuhr's failure to apply consistently his own ironic concept in *The Irony of American History* is explored from a somewhat different point of view in an unpublished paper that Wise has written with Barbara Scott. The authors also point to his Christianity as a source of this failure in that they show that Niebuhr confused the roles of "cultural analyst" and "moral prophet" in the stance he took in writing this book. "Making 'Irony' Operational: Nieburh's *Irony of American History* Revisited," p. 15. I am indebted to Wise for a copy of this unpublished paper that has aided my own analysis of Niebuhr's book.

5. Although my criticism here is from within Niebuhr's own theory and assumes no particular stance in regard to the historical controversy about the origins of the Cold War, perhaps it would be appropriate to indicate briefly where I stand on that issue. I agree with those who emphasize the incompleteness of our knowledge, because of our lack of access to Soviet archives, but nonetheless, on the basis of what we do know, I incline to the view that the Cold War was primarily the result of defensive misperceptions of each other on the part of both the United States and the Soviet Union. These misperceptions were in part based upon and compounded by pretensions on both sides to unique virtue and wisdom and by drives to become the dominant power. This view is one that could be derived from Niebuhr's ironic theory, and is very similar to the conception of the Cold War to which he came later in his life as his critical perceptions of America were again sharpened by events.

6. Niebuhr, *Irony*, p. 63.

7. Ibid., pp. 48, 49.

8. Ibid., p. 89.

9. Ibid., p. 33. See also p. 93.

10. Ibid., p. 31.

11. Ibid., p. 74.

12. Ibid., pp. 24, 28, 23.

13. Ibid., p. 2. See also pp. 38, 39.

14. Ibid., pp. 37, 38.

15. Ibid., pp. 42, 133.

16. Ibid., p. 133.

17. Ibid., p. 100, 101.

18. Ibid., p. 165. Gunnar Myrdal presented American race relations as a great contradiction of American values in terms that could be appropriate to irony. *An American Dilemma* (1944; reprint ed. New York: Harper and Row, 1962), particularly 1: lxix-lxxvi, 3-25, 31-32, and 2: 591, 1012, 1015, 1021-24. W. J. Cash analyzed Southern racial attitudes and behavior in terms of paradox and inner contradictions, terms that also suggest Niebuhrian irony. *The Mind of the South (New York: Alfred A. Knopf, 1941)*, particularly pp. 3-102. Even as sympathetic a commentator as Ronald Stone notes that Niebuhr is "guilty by omission of neglecting blacks in American history" (*Reinhold Niebuhr*, p. 145).

19. Niebuhr, *Irony*, pp. 74, 35, 36.

20. Robert Skotheim suggests how the concern with Stalinist totalitarianism tended to foster apologetic views of America in the post-World War II period. *Totalitarianism and American Social Thought* (New York: Holt, Rinehart and Winston, 1971), pp. 68-93.

21. Niebuhr, *Irony*, pp. 1, 22, 85, 127.

22. Ibid., pp. 15, 174, 173.

23. Ibid., pp. 143, 144.

24. Ibid., pp. 153, 169-70. See also p. 3 for a formulation of our irony as the result of the existence of the Soviets.

25. Ibid., pp. 80, 66, 67. Niebuhr sees many Western social scientists and psychologists as almost as demonic as communists in that they also ignore the limited, relative, and subjective character of all human understanding of history. Ibid., pp. 82-87. For a critique of Niebuhr's harsh treatment of social science in *The Irony of American History*, written from a point of view very different from mine, see Odegard, *Sin and Science*, particularly pp. 183-88.

26. Odegard recognizes the discrepancy between Niebuhr's ironic concept and his treatment of the Cold War, but his approach to it is directly opposed to mine. He assumes that Niebuhr means to apply his definition of irony to his use of the term in that context, that Niebuhr does hold the United States to some degree responsible for the conflict with the Soviet Union, and holds that such an idea is absurd. Ibid., pp. 181-82. Odegard's attitude in this regard, which can be understood as emanating from an even firmer hostility to communism than Niebuhr's, is rather surprising in the light of his general criticism of Niebuhr for unintentionally fostering conservatism. Ibid. pp. 175-76, 192-97.

27. Niebuhr, *Irony*, p. 115. See pt. 3 of the present chapter for Niebuhr's critical application of irony to American participation in the Vietnam war.

28. Ibid., pp. 150, 155.

29. Ibid., p. 88.

30. Ibid., p. 150.

32. Niebuhr, "Intellectual Autobiography," in Kegley and Bretall, eds., *Reinhold Niebuhr*, pp. 11, 12. In this same essay Niebuhr makes the exaggerated claim that "only the Biblical-Christian view sees that the evil in man is at the center of the self, and that it involves all his unique capacities of freedom which endow him with 'dignity' and make him, though a creature also a creator," (ibid.), while ignoring other approaches — for example, psychoanalysis — that offer similar visions of the human condition.

A number of commentators on irony disagree with Niebuhr's argument that the Christian view of man is fundamentally ironical; they suggest that irony and religion are basically incompatible. A remark of Douglas Muecke's about Kierkegaard might well be applied to Niebuhr. "Though he was himself a superb ironist and could employ a wide range of ironic strategies with great verve, subtlety, and originality. . .since he believed in God it followed that irony had to be subordinated to the ethical and religious" (Muecke, *The Compass of Irony* [London: Methuen, 1969], p. 246). Randolph Bourne treats a religious attitude as fundamentally opposed to an ironical one and uses it as a foil to contrast with the virtues of irony. "The Life of Irony," *Atlantic Montly* 111 (March 1913): 357-67. Stanley Hopper, a Christian writer, not an irreligious one like Bourne, also finds irony to be fundamentally at variance with Christianity. He calls it a "rationalistic profaning of the mysteries" ("Irony — The Pathos of the Middle," *Cross Currents* 12 (1962]: 39). Gabriel Vahanian, also writing from a basically Christian perspective, offers a view of the consequences of Christianity that, equated with Western culture, applies Niebuhrian irony to Niebuhr's own faith. He suggests that the very success of Christianity, with its consequent pride of "religiosity," is one of the factors that has produced some of those features of modern culture that Niebuhr finds pretentious and objectionable. It is in part Vahanian's ability to look at Christianity from a non-Western perspective that enables him to see this irony. *Wait Without Idols* (New York: George Braziller, 1964), pp. 33, 44, 4͡.

33. Niebuhr, *Irony*, pp. 128, 150.

34. Ibid., p. 113. As Niebuhr himself would have noted later, it must look rather peculiar to American Indians and Mexicans to describe the imperialism of the United States in the nineteenth century as only covert.

35. This ethnocentrism can be seen in some of Niebuhr's comments on the economic relations between the West and the Third World and on the politics of underdeveloped nations. Later in his life, perhaps as a result of the influence of the American Black Civil Rights movement with which he was deeply sympathetic, Niebuhr seems to have become more sensitive to what the Third World perspective could reveal about the West. See particularly "The Rising Tide of Color," *New Leader*, January 23, 1961, pp. 16-17.

36. Niebuhr, *Irony*, p. 57. See pt. 1 of this chapter.

37. A contrast with Louis Hartz in this connection is instructive. Niebuhr emphasizes the limitations of the Third World, suggesting among other things that its peoples may not be ready to learn about democracy from us. Hartz is concerned with what we can learn from contact with them, how our increased awareness of the rest of the world can make use conscious of the limitations in our own perspective. In this sense Hartz's use of irony is truer to Niebuhr's concept than is Niebuhr's own use of it. See chap. 5 of the present book.

38. Niebuhr, *Irony*, p. 155. Niebuhr does not, of course, say in so many words that Christians enjoy the same advantages of perspective as God, but he fails to distinguish between human limitations and divine vision in this context. In this he seems to be guilty of a Christian presumption that he himself warns against: "the devotee may simply identify his own judgments and purposes or those of his culture with the ultimate purpose and judgment." From Niebuhr's autobiographical remarks in Harold Fey, ed., *How My Mind Has Changed* (Cleveland and New York: World Publishing, 1961), p. 122.

39. Robert Fitch, in his sympathetic account of Niebuhr's philosophy of history, suggests that such anti-intellectualism, or rather Niebuhr's opposition to intellectuals, was characteristic and not unintended. He refers to Niebuhr's "lifelong polemic against them." "Reinhold Neibuhr's Philosophy of History" in Kegley and Bretall, eds., *Reinhold Niebuhr*, p. 309 n.

40. Douglas Muecke has inadvertently pointed out the immobile, ahistorical character of Niebuhr's book when he classifies its irony among the ironies of situations. "We are in. . .the . .situation of being both observers and victims when we see ourselves involved in the inescapable ironies of current history as so ably presented by Niebuhr in his *Irony of American History*" (*The Compass of Irony*, p. 114).

41. Even in his most uncritical period Niebuhr could recognize extreme statements of American virtue and uniqueness. This is evident in some of his comments in a generally favorable review he wrote of Daniel Boorstin's seminal *The Genius of American Politics*. Taking a comparative stance, Niebuhr observes, in contrast to Boorstin, that our lack of ideology may itself be an ideology. "America: Pragmatism, Not Dogmatism," *New Leader*, June 22, 1953, p. 15. This section traces the development of a more critical use of irony in some of Niebuhr's writings on specific aspects of American history and politics in the 1950s and 60s. It does not examine his more theoretical work of this period such as *The Self and the Dramas of History* (New York: Charles Scribner's Sons, 1955), *The Structure of Nations and Empires* (New York: Charles Scribner's Sons, 1959), and *Man's Nature and His Communities* (New York: Charles Scribner's Sons, 1965) although in fact an increased awareness of such American flaws as racism is evident in the latter.

42. Niebuhr, *A Nation So Conceived* (New York: Charles Scribner's Sons, 1963), pp. 11, 12, 10, 47.

43. Ibid., pp. 66, 67, 75, 69, 70, 77, 78, 114, 112, 118, 121.

44. Ibid., pp. 39, 42, 43. This ironic interpretation is very similar to William Taylor's in his *Cavalier and Yankee: The Old South and American National Character* (New York: George Braziller, 1961).

45. Niebuhr, *A Nation So Conceived*, p. 12.

46. Ibid., p. 132.

47. Ibid., pp. 148, 153.

48. See note 3 above.

49. Early steps in Niebuhr's movement away from a hard Cold War position can be seen in

two essays he published in 1961. His article in Fey, *How My Mind Has Changed*, revealed a slight softening in his anticommunism, although it also contained a strong attack on Karl Barth's Christian naturalism. Ibid., pp. 119, 125-28. A more significant change can be seen in another article in which Niebuhr says explicitly that "the foe is human and not demonic. He is informed by a creed with demonic pretensions" ("The Unintended Virtues of an Open Society," *Christianity and Crisis* 21 (1961): 137. While a similar point of view might be extrapolated from *The Irony of American History*, here communism becomes explicitly a part of the world of human beings, its evil relative and no longer absolute.

50. "The Mounting Racial Crisis," *Christianity and Crisis* 23 (1963): 121-22.

51. "The Negro Minority and Its Fate in a Self-Righteous Nation," *Social Action* 32, no. 21 (October 1968): 55, 58, 62.

52. Reinhold Niebuhr and Paul E. Sigmund, *The Democratic Experience* (New York: Frederick Praeger, 1969), pp. vi, 6, 7, 10, 12, 14.

53. Ronald Stone briefly discusses the development of Niebuhr's attitude toward American policy in Vietnam during the 1950s and early 1960s. He suggests, in contrast to my argument, that Niebuhr's criticism of that policy in the late 1960s was consistent with his earlier Cold War position, not only in the sense that both were informed by similar perceptions of irony and sin but also on a specifically political level. *Reinhold Niebuhr*, pp. 191-95.

54. "The Social Myths in the 'Cold War,' "*Journal of International Affairs* 21 (1967): 46, 47.

55. Ibid., pp. 50, 55.

56. "Vietnam: Study in Ironies," *New Republic*, June 24, 1967, p. 11.

57. Ibid.

58. Ibid., pp. 11, 12.

59. Ibid., p. 12.

60. "Toward New Intra-Christian Endeavors," *Christian Century* 86 (1969): 1662, 1663.

61. *Christianity and Crisis* 30 (1970): 70, 71, 72.

62. "Redeemer Natin to Super-Power," *New York Times*, December 4, 1970, p. 47.

63. Although I have argued that irony can be a radical historical tool and that Niebuhr recovered its critical power toward the end of his life, I do not mean to suggest that Niebuhr himself became a radical, certainly not a New Left one. For one thing, he was too much a Christian pessimist for the hope that kind of radicalism requires. Although he clearly was not one of them, Niebuhr was able to see the young radicals of the 1960s with a mixture of sympathy and criticism quite different from the jaundiced reaction of many liberals of his generation. He perceived the violence-prone young leftists of the late 1960s as caught in an ironic response to the immoral uses of power. "Thinking Aloud: Indicting Two Generations," *New Leader*, October 5, 1970, pp. 13, 14. Ronald Stone points out that Niebuhr's attitude toward peaceful protest was more unambiguously sympathetic. *Reinhold Niebuhr*, p. 244.

64. My view of the relationship between Niebuhr's concept of human nature and his changing political opinions differs sharply from Morton White's. White argues that although Niebuhr's political judgments in the 1950s were wise, they were not derived from his belief in original sin. White attacks that belief while at the same time accepting Niebuhr's politics. *Social Thought in America* (Boston: Beacon Press, 1957), p. 257.

65. It is possible to argue that in this Niebuhr was an ironic actor, not merely an observer of irony caught in a historical paradox, if one sees his earlier writing as influential enough to have contributed to the development of the background of the war in Vietnam, which Niebuhr abhorred. LaFeber came close to making this argument. He saw Niebuhr as very influential both in his own right and in the weight his early Cold War ideas had with such politically active intellectuals as George Kennan and Arthur Schlesinger, Jr. *America, Russia and the Cold War*, 2d ed. (New York: John Wiley, 1972), pp. 40, 54, 92. Because he perceived Niebuhr as having contributed substantially to the development of American Cold War policy, LaFeber was able to see the Vietnam War as an ironic fulfillment of some of Niebuhr's own ideas, and concluded the first edition of his book with a picture of Niebuhr as a repentant

ironic actor. Ibid., p. 259. In concluding the second edition of his book LaFeber also refers to Niebuhr but, recognizing the growing chnges in him, quotes Niebuhr himself on the ironic consequences of his earlier foreign-policy "realism." Ibid., pp. 300, 301.

66. Henry May, "A Meditation on an Unfashionable Book: *The Irony of American History* Revisited," *Christianity and Crisis* 27 (1968): 120. Although May is somewhat less critical of *The Irony of American History* than I, my treatment of the potential of the theoretical part of the book is similar to his.

For a discussion of the radical implicatins of Niebuhr's late work written from a very different point of view see Gabriel Fackre's comments on Niebuhr's contributions to "a theology of hope and politics of the future" (*The Promise of Reinhold Niebuhr* [Philadelphia and New York: J. B. Lippincott Co., 1970), p. 68).

# Chapter 5

1. A review by John Higham suggests by its tone the relative lack of professional response to *The Irony of American History*, *Mississippi Historical Review* 41 (1952): 357-58. Morton White judged the book harshly, but his very criticism suggests that he thought it generally, if not professionally, influential. "Of Moral Predicament," review of *The Irony of American History*, *New Republic*, May 5, 1952, p. 18. Arthur Schlesinger, Jr., whom Niebuhr clearly did influence, devoted a review largely to defending the book against its critics. His defense, however, is more on moral and political grounds than on historical ones. "Niebuhr and Some Critics," review of *The Irony of American History*, *Christianity and Society* 17 (1952): 25-27. On Niebuhr's influence on Schlesinger see Marcus Cunliffe, "Arthur M. Schlesinger, Jr." in Cunliffe and Robin Winks, eds., *Pastmasters* (New York: Harper and Row, 1969), p. 363.

2. Morton White, "Religion, Politics and the Higher Learning," *Confluence* 3 (1954): 404.

3. Perry Miller, "The Influence of Reinhold Niebuhr," review of *Pious and Secular America*, *The Reporter*, May 1, 19589, p. 40. Henry May suggests that although Miller was "at least an associate member of 'Atheists for Niebuhr' " his own "pervasive irony was perhaps confirmed, but it was certainly not begun by his exposure to Niebuhr" ("Perry Miller's Parrington," *American Scholar* 25 [1966]: 566, 568). In this review May shows how central irony was in this last, posthumous book of Miller's.

4. On the developoment and character of consensus history I have found the following particularly helpful: John Higham, "The Cult of 'The American Consensus,' " *Commentary* 27 (1959): 93-100; Higham "Beyond Consensus: The Historian as Moral Critic," in *Writing American History* (Bloomington and London: Indiana University Press, 1970), pp. 138-56; Dwight Hoover, "Some Comments on Recent United States Historiography," *American Quarterly* 17 (Summer 1965): 299-318; Richard Hofstadter, *The Progressive Historians* (New York: Alfred A. Knopf, 1968), pp. 437-66; and Robert Skotheim, *American Intellectual Histories and Historians* (Princeton, N.J.: Princeton University Press, 1966), pp. 173-288. For a recent account of the shift from Progressive to consensus history conceived of as a paradigm shift see Gene Wise, *American Historical Explanations* (Homewood, Ill.: Dorsey Press, 1973), pp. 223-95. Marian J. Morton's *The Terrors of Ideological Politics* (Cleveland, Ohio: Press of Case Western Reserve University, 1972) presents a hostile, radical critique of consensus history. Bernard Sternsher argues that much of the work of the major consensus generalizers has been confirmed by more recent research in history and political science. In his view, as in mine, the interpretations of Hartz and Hofstadter retain more validity than does Boorstin's work on politics. *Consensus, Conflict, and American Historians* (Bloomington and London: Indiana University Press, 1975).

5. Wise, *American Historical Explanations*, pp. 284-88.

6. In Higham's words: "As the progressive impulse subsided, scholarship was threatened

with moral complacency, parading often in the guise of neutrality" ("Beyond Consensus," p. 146).

7. Morton strongly emphasizes and criticizes the consensus historians' tendency to focus on human irrationality.

8. For a vigorous defense of the contributions of consensus history as well as a call to transcend it see Hofstadter, *The Progressive Historians*, pp. 437-66. While certainly not a defender of consensus history, Robin Brooks, in an argument that parallels mine here, has elucidated the critical aspects of the work of some of the leading scholars in the American studies movement of the postwar period in "The Radical Strain in American Studies," a paper read at the Annual Meeting of the Organization of American Historians, April 1970. I am indebted to Brooks for a copy of his interesting unpublished paper.

9. The maturation of American historical consciousness that I believe irony has fostered is to be understood as a relative maturity of an ongoing process, not a finished, ripened state that, once achieved, is to be maintained unchanging. I suggest later how subsequent developments in historical writing New Left History in particular may be understood as extending the process of maturation represented by the ironic side of consensus history.

10. The selection of these three particular historians to represent different aspects of the relationship between consensus history as a general interpretation of the American past and irony is of necessity somewhat arbitrary, but they clearly are among the most eminent and influential historical generalizers of their generation and there is precedent for treating these particular scholars as representative. For example, they are the three historians chosen to represent the consensus position in Skotheim's useful anthology, *The Historian and the Climate of Opinion* (Reading, Mass.: Addison-Wesley, 1969) and in Sternsher, *Consensus, Conflict, and American Historians*, and they are included in the five whom Morton examines.

11. I have found Stanley Elkins and Erik McKitrick, "Richard Hofstadter: A Progress," in *The Hofstadter Aegis* (New York: Alfred A. Knopf, 1974), pp. 300-367 useful in general on Hofstadter, but not particularly informative in regard to *The American Political Tradition* or his use of irony.

12. Hofstadter, *The Progressive Historians*, p. 466.

13. John Higham et al., *History* (Englewood Cliffs, N.J.: Prentice-Hall, 1965), p. 213 n. When *The American Political Tradition* was first published, Perry Miller saw the consensus interpretation as "a comprehensive thesis' running through it and recognized its originality and importance. "The New History," *The Nation*, October 16, 1948, p. 436.

14. Richard Hofstadter, *The American Political Tradition and the Men Who Made it* (New York: Vintage Books, 1958), p. viii; hereafter cited as *Political Tradition*. The title of this book can be read as a subtle comment on one of its major themes. Hofstadter argues that a major element in the American political tradition is the belief that the state should foster conditions under which men may rise socially and economically  in the vernacular, "make it." A number of the men he discusses as having made that tradition were also men who could be described as beneficiaries of that element in the tradition  men who "made it."

15. Ibid., p. xii. For some examples of particularly critical comments on American leaders see ibid., pp. 19, 77, 186, 209, 241.

16. Hofstadter, *The Progressive Historians*, p. 452 n.

17. Arthur Schlesinger, Jr., "Richard Hofstadter," in Cunliffe and Winks, *Pastmasters*, p. 289. Christopher Lasch, "On Richard Hofstadter," *New York Review of Books*, March 8, 1973, pp. 7-13.

18. Hofstadter, *Political Tradition*, p. viii.

19. Ibid., pp. 16-17, 179. Hofstadter's radical criticism of the mainstream can also be seen in his sympathetic treatment of the only consistent radical examined in the book, Wendell Phillips. Ibid., pp. 137-63.

20. Ibid., p. 185. For rhetorical or humorous ironic comments on the "religious psychology" of the abolitionists see ibid., p. 148; on Bryan's "socialism," ibid., p. 197; on Wilson as a

"pacifist," ibid., p. 260; and on Franklin Roosevelt's response to "the shadow of abundance" in New Deal agricultural policy, ibid., p. 333. Alfred Kazin has commented on Hofstadter's "lucid intellectual humor" and "his intellectual irony." "Richard Hofstadter, 1916-1970," *American Scholar* 40 (Summer 1971): 397, 399. That humor and irony may have owed something to the influence of Henry Adams. In *The American Political Tradition* there are thirteen references of one kind or another to Adams, more than to any other historian according to the index.

21. Ibid., p. 190.
22. Ibid., p. 59.
23. Ibid. pp. 59, 60.
24. Ibid., pp. 63, 64.
25. Ibid., p. 254.
26. Ibid., pp. 263, 265.
27. Ibid., pp. 267, 269.
28. Ibid., pp. 271, 272.
29. Ibid., pp. 273-75.
30. Ibid., pp. 279, 280.
31. Ibid., pp. 280, 281.
32. Ibid., p. 278. Although Hofstadter is very critical of the recent American statesmen he discusses, there are some passing Niebuhrian ironies in these chapters. See ibid., p. 223, for an account of how those businessmen who really disliked Theodore Roosevelt unintentionally gave him much help by making his pretense of reform plausible by their opposition to it, and ibid., pp. 291, 292, 305, for an ironic account of the unintended consequences of Hoover's international trade policies. For a penetrating ironic account of how World War I, which the Progressives turned into an idealistic crusade, produced a disillusionment that destroyed the moral energies on which Progressivism was based see Hofstadter, *The Age of Reform* (1955; reprint ed. New York: Vintage, 1960), pp. 272-82.
33. Hofstadter, *Political Tradition*, pp. viii, 16.
34. Ibid., p. 39.
35. Ibid., p. 57.
36. Ibid., pp. 103, 104, 106, 107. There is a striking similarity between Hofstadter's characterization of the ethos of the self-made man as "the legitimate inheritance of Jacksonian Democracy" and Parrington's reference to the consequences of that ethos in the Gilded Age as "the ripe fruit of Jacksonian levelling." Vernon Louis Parrington, *The Beginnings of Critical Realism in America*, in *Main Currents in American Thought* (New York: Harcourt, Brace and Co., 1930), p. 10. This irony is far more central to the core of Hofstadter's vision than it was to Parrington's, suggesting that irony was moving toward the center of American historical consciousness.
37. Hofstadter, *Political Tradition*, pp. 164, 165, 166, 167.
38. We may have here an indication of one reason why Hofstadter was able to "discover" the American consensus. As a critic of American capitalism who retained sympathy for the original impulse behind American democracy, his perspective on the American past revealed how that democracy had been compromised by the commitments of both major parties to the preservation and expansion of capitalism.
39. Ibid., pp. 93, 99. Hofstadter quotes the phrase about "the little engine" from Herndon.
40. Ibid., pp. 93, 95.
41. Ibid., p. 94.
42. Ibid., pp. 134, 135.
43. Ibid., pp. 135, 136.
44. *The Age of Reform* (1955) was affected by the Cold War atmosphere more than *The American Political Tradition*. There is irony in this book but less of it than in the earlier one, and its critical stance is muted. *The American Political Tradition* exhibits the tensions of a

man half inside and half outside the political culture about which he writes; the author of *The Age of Reform* had made his peace with America. That is not to say that he had lost all capacity for critical irony. Some of it is applied to the reform tradition that he examines in the 1955 book and in such later works as his introduction to Hofstadter and Michael Wallace, eds., *American Violence* (New York: Vintage, 1970) the irony and the criticism were quite general and very deep.

45. Schlesinger, "Richard Hofstadter," pp. 278. 294.

46. Hofstadter, *The Progressive Historians*, p. 466.

47. Ibid., p. 444.

48. Daniel J. Boorstin, *The Genius of American Politics* (Chicago: University of Chicago Press, 1953), pp. 9, 23, 132 hereafter cited as *Genius*. My analysis of Boorstin is devoted primarily to this book as the most general statement of his consensus interpretation in the same way that I have focused on *The American Political Tradition* as the most general statement of Hofstadter's view. J. R. Pole emphasizes the importance of *The Genius of American Politics* among Boorstin's works. "Daniel J. Boorstin," in Cunliffe and Winks, *Pastmasters*, p. 220. In two brilliant articles John P. Diggins has explored the philosophic implications of Boorstin's concept of givenness and revealed its weaknesses as an interpretation of American history. Diggins, "Consciousness and Ideology in American History: The Burden of Daniel J. Boorstin," *American Historical Review* 76 (1971): 99-118 and "The Perils of Naturalism: Some Reflections on Daniel J. Boorstin's Approach to American History," *American Quarterly* 23 (1971): 153-80.

49. Boorstin, *Genius*, pp. 66-98. See Diggins, "The Perils of Naturalism," pp. 163-65, for a comparison of Boorstin's view of the role of ideology in the Revolution with Bernard Bailyn's interpretation.

50. Boorstin, *Genius*, pp. 99-132.

51. Ibid., pp. 4, 180-84.

52. Ibid., pp. 173, 174.

53. Ibid., pp. 186, 187, 186. The critical nature of Hofstadter's history in comparison to Boorstin's can be seen in the former's ironic handling of this idea that America has been a nonideological model for Europe. Richard Hofstadter, *Anti-Intellectualism in American Life* (New York: Vintage, 1963), pp. 43, 44.

54. Boorstin, *Genius*, pp. 175, 179.

55. Ibid., pp. 133, 157, 162. Pole comments on the confusion in Boorstin's concept of givenness, asking: "Does Boorstin really believe that the encounter with the land gave Americans concrete values to live by, and does he himself proclaim these values, or is he only telling us that Americans were hallucinated into a kind of rapture?" ("Daniel J. Boorstin," pp. 223, 224).

56. Boorstin, *Genius*, pp. 169, 179, 187. Diggins discusses some of the ambiguities of Boorstin's own attitude toward the concept of givenness that he finds as characterizing American political thought. When it is exhibited by the New Left he finds it much less attractive than when he sees it in the thought of traditional writers. "Consciousness and Ideology in American History," pp. 117-18.

57. Boorstin's treatment of blacks under slavery in the second volume of *The Americans* cannot be subject to this criticism. He comments on some of the harsh and dehumanizing features of American slavery. *The American: The National Experience* (New York: Random House, 1965), pp. 190-191, 201-3; hereafter cited as *National Experience*.

58. Boorstin, *Genius*, p. 111. His sympathetic treatment of Nat Turner in *The National Experience* contrasts with his critical attitude toward the abolitonists. *National Experience*, pp. 183-85.

59. Boorstin, *The Americans: The Colonial Experience* (New York: Random House, 1958), p. 1 hereafter cited as *Colonial Experience*. In this book those colonists who adhered too

rigidly to their dreams, such as the Quakers, behave ironically but lie outside the American mainstream. See ibid., pp. 35-69.

60. Boorstin, *Genius,* pp. 37, 38.

61. Ibid., pp. 40, 52, 53.

62. Ibid., p. 53.

63. Ibid., pp. 38, 64, 65. The implicit reference to Puritan doctrine as "The Big Lie" suggests how extreme was Boorstin's distate for Puritanism in its original form. His account of Puritanism in *The Americans: The Colonial Experience* does not fit the ironic pattern so clearly as his treatment of it in *The Genius of American Politics,* but it can be glimpsed in the latter book as well. *Colonial Experience,* p. 35. The difference between his comments on the Puritans in this book and in *The Genius of American Politics* lies partly in his tendency here to play down the Utopian element in Puritan thinking from the beginning, to see Puritans as more consistently pragmatic to start. In this account, as in the one in *The Genius,* they lose whatever tendency they have toward Utopian aspirations – toward ironic action – as they become American. Diggins also notes how Boorstin's attempt to fit the Puritans into his pattern strains the concept of givenness and violates the Puritans' own sense of purpose. He also comments on how opposed Boorstin's interpretation of the Puritans is to Perry Miller's. "The Perils of Naturalism," pp. 155-62.

64. The implications of Boorstin's interpretation are directly contrary to those of some other historians who perceive the history of the New England Puritans ironically. Perry Miller, for example, also finds the Americanization of the New England settlers to have been the unintended consequence of some aspects of their own religion, but he does not equate being American with being nonironic. Rather, he conceives the Puritan legacy to America to be in part precisely those heightened expectations and illusions of uniqueness that induce ironic behavior. Miller's ironic account can be most clearly seen in *The New England Mind: From Colony to Province* (Boston: Beacon Press, 1953) and the title essay in *Errand Into the Wilderness* (New York: Harper and Row, 1956). Sacvan Bercovitch analyzes the persistence of Puritan rhetorical forms that foster ironic behavior in later America in "Horologicals to Chronometricals; The Rhetoric of the Jeremiad," *Literary Monographs* 3 (Madison: University of Wiconsin Press, 1970). For a clearly ironic interpretation of American Puritanism by a social historian see Kenneth Lockridge, *A New England Town* (New York: W. W. Norton, 1970).

65. Diggins, "Consciousness and Ideology in American History," p. 102.

66. Boorstin, Genius, p. 175.

67. Ibid., pp. 171, 172, 173.

68. Ibid., p. 161. Boorstin reveals his bias against recognizing the irony-producing proclivities of Americans in a passing comment he makes on the type of men most admired in America. "The character of our national heroes bears witness to our belief in 'givenness,' our preference for the man who seizes his God-given opportunities over him who pursues a great private vision" (ibid., p. 29). If we think of great private visions as grand political ideologies this comment makes sense, but it obscures the way in which the expectation of opportunity and the readiness to seize it are similar to great private visions in the sense of personal ambition. Both express the kind of heightened expectations that tend to lead men to act so as to contradict their own intentions.

69. Ibid., pp. 95, 169.

70. Morton has made this argument extensively in *The Terrors of Ideological Politics.*

72. I have focused almost exclusively on Boorstin's most general book because in it he expresses his basic interpretation of American history directly and explicitly. The wide-ranging volumes of *The Americans* are governed by the same overall point of view, but it appears less directly in their full and detailed examination of many varied aspects of our past. In a review Bernard Bailyn wrote: "*The Amerians: The Colonial Experience* is, in fact, a 400 page foot-

note to *The Genius of American Politics*" ("History and the Distrust of Knowledge," *New Republic*, December 15, 1958, p. 17). Occasionally in these books there are glimpses of irony, as in Boorstin's comment on "the suicide of the Virginia aristocracy" in the Revolution they served so well (*Colonial Experience*, p. 143) and in his account of the nineteenth-century South's self-destructive self-image as homogeneous "the most unreal, most powerful, most disastrous oversimplification in American history" (*National Experience*, p. 170). *The Americans: The Democratic Experience* (New York: Random House, 1974) is particularly rich in paradoxes and near ironies, as, for example, in Boorstin's treatment of the Kinsey Report: "The popularity of Kinsey's work was ironic and unpredicted. His life as a biologist had been devoted to proving the importance of 'individuals'. . . .But Kinsey's intentions were twisted by a public demand for simple norms" (ibid., p. 243). This example is characteristic of much of the book; the irony does not become Niebuhrian because there is no indication of moral responsibility, conscious or unconscious, on the part of the historical actor. If Boorstin's optimism about America has grown more muted in recent years, still he remains basically faithful to a sense of American mission. Three recent shorter works of Boorstin's are less apologetic than his earlier writings, but they remain basically true to that faith: *The Decline of Radicalism* (New York: Random House, 1969), *Democracy and Its Discontents* (New York: Random House, 1974), and *The Exploring Spirit* (New York: Random House, 1976). The first of these in particular does contain much criticism, but the main thing about contemporary America that Boorstin attacks is the prevalence of criticism itself. This book, like the other two, ends on a note of affirmation.

72. Louis Hartz, *The Liberal Tradition in America: An Interpretation of American Political Thought Since the Revolution* (New York: Harcourt, Brace and World, 1955), p. 78; hereafter cited as *Liberal Tradition*. Although I devote extensive attention only to one work each of Hofstadter and Boorstin in addition to *The Liberal Tradition*, I also examine the parts written by Hartz himself in *The Founding of New Societies: Studies in the History of the United States, Latin America, South Africa, Canada, and Australia* (New York: Harcourt, Brace and World, 1964), because in the later work Hartz expands and deepens an important ironic disucssion dimension of his earlier book.

73. Ibid., pp. 58, 60, 61. At least one commentator has found Hartz too critical. Marvin Meyers argues that American political thought has been "real and important" in contrast to Hartz's perception of it as illustory. "The Liberal Tradition in America: An Appraisal," *Comparative Studies in Society and History* 5 (1963): 267.

74. Hartz, *Liberal Tradition*, pp. 31, 32.

75. Ibid., p. 109.

76. Ibid., pp. 211, 219, 224.

77. Ibid., pp. 62, 136.

78. Among the historical development to which Hartz applies the term *irony* are the relationship between capitalism and democracy in the early national period, ibid., p. 89; Jefferson's fear of the "mob," ibid., p. 123; the lack of conservative tradition in America, ibid., p. 57; the differences between American and European bourgeois codes, ibid. p. 53; Orestes Brownson's disillusioned conversion from radicalism to Catholicism, ibid., p. 139; the antebellum debate concerning free versus slave labor, ibid., pp. 184, 193; the defeat of both Federalists and Southern extremists, ibid., p. 198; the socialist Daniel De Leon's agreement with Bryan and Theodore Roosevelt about the virtues of the American past, ibid., p. 245; the nationalism of the Spanish-American War anti-imperialists, ibid., p. 289; and "the irrational inward passion of 'Americanism' " as "the ironic end product of a Second World War originally fought against facism," p. 30.

79. Hartz, *Liberal Tradition*, pp. 86, 93, 112.

80. Ibid., pp. 118, 119.

81. Ibid., pp. 139, 140.

82. Ibid., pp. 204, 208, 216.

83. Ibid., pp. 13, 237-48.

84. Ibid., pp. 270, 277.

85. Ibid., pp. 307, 308.

86. Ibid., pp. 284, 285, 286.

87. Ibid., pp. 293, 286, 287.

88. Ibid., pp. 295, 296.

89. Ibid., pp. 304, 305, 306.

90. Ibid., p. 5.

91. Ibid., pp. 255, 287, 308.

92. I have used only Hartz's own contribution to this multi-authored study.

93. Hartz, *The Founding of New Societies*, pp. 60, 103, 60, 94.

94. Ibid., pp. 3, 4.

95. Ibid., pp. 20, 21, 22. Note how differently the Third World functions in Hartz's irony from the way it does in Niebuhr's. For Hartz our encounter with it can serve to open our eyes to our own limitations. For Niebuhr irony lies not in what the Third World can show us about ourselves but in the unjust accusations it makes against us.

96. Ibid., pp. 22, 23.

97. Ibid., pp. 7, 46, 119, 120.

98. Ibid., pp. 23, 121, 122.

99. Ibid., p. 69. Hartz argues that the recent direction of the development of American historical thought is toward the discovery or recovery of "cosmopolitanism, the prejudice of the eighteenth century" and a perspective appropriate to the perception of irony. "Comment," *Comparative Studies in Society and History* 5 (1963): 284. Hartz's hope for "comparative history. . .the intellectual expression of the new cosmopolitanism" is similar to the aspiration of ironic history to connect Ameica to the rest of the world, to "link us to humanity. .through the discovery of a common dilemma" ("American Historiography and Comparative Analysis: Further Reflections," *Comparative Studies in Society and History* 5 [1963]: 365, 377).

100. Hartz fits an ironic pattern. but not so closely as irony fits his comparative approach. His language tends to emphasize the causative role of abstract historical forces rather than human beings in history. The model of European conflict between ideological forces and related classes, which throws off fragments that then evolve according to an inner telos. tends strongly toward abstraction. Because of that abstraction one aspect of irony is not always clear in Hartz. He frequently reveals how actions in America lead to consequences that contradict the intention behind the original action. but it is less clear that the cause of the discrepancy lies in the actor himself.

I would argue that in Hartz's own terms this is a weakness in his approach. He comes closest to the ironic strategy in his conception of the curative role of historical consciousness. To know that we have fragment roots, that we are a fragment, can free us from continuing to act out of fragment limitations. To the extent that this is true it is logically necessary to assume that people are capable of acting with some degree of consciousness and effectiveness in history, that they are to some degree responsibile historical actors. Otherwise it makes no sense to assert that to know who we are can affect what we do.

One reason for this abstraction is Hartz's apparently conscious reliance upon a Hegelian framework. The book is shot through with references to Hegel and Hegelianism. Undoubtedly this interest in a Hegelian perspective is one of the things that enables Hartz to transcend the fragment, but one might suggest that, if he had used Marx instead of Hegel, his language would not have been so abstract and he might more clearly have recognized history as a product of human action. I am not arguing that Marxism is always free of this kind of abstraction, only that it more readily lends itself to such a freedom. As we have seen, both

Hegelianism and Marxism contain potentialities for historical irony, but in both human intention tends to be overwhelmed by abstract forces. The more voluntaristics versions of Marxism are relatively free of this. See chap. 3 above.

# Chapter 6

1. Irony is present in the work of the following consensus or post-Progressive historians, among others: Alexander and Juliette George, R. W. B. Lewis, Marvin Meyer, Perry Miller, David Noble, Charles Sanford, Henry Nash Smith, William R. Taylor, and John William Ward.

2. Sacvan Bercovitch has recently demonstrated how a sense of chosenness is integral to Americans' feeling of their own identity. *The Puritan Origins of the American Self* (New Haven and London: Yale University Press, 1975).

3. I have found Niebuhrian irony particularly evident in the work of Christopher Lasch, John Rosenberg, Stephen Thernstrom, and William A. Williams, among historians generally regarded as New Left. For documentations of Williams's use of irony, see my "Niebuhrian Irony and Historial Interpretation: The Relationship between Consensus and New Left History," in *The Writing of American History*, Robert H. Canary and Henry Kozicki, eds., Madison: The University of Wisconsin Press, 1978, pp. 93-128.

4. Among social historians I have found Niebuhrian irony in the work of Phillip Greven, Jr., Michael Katz, Kenneth Lockridge, William O'Neill, Darrett Rutman, Richard Sennett, and Sam Bass Warner. In addition to the categories already mentioned, it is also used by a number of historians of the South, particularly Steven A. Channing, Carl Degler, William Freehling, Winthrop Jordan, and C. Vann Woodward, by literary historians such as Bercovitch and Emory Elliott, and by a "new" intellectual historian like Thomas L. Haskell.

# Works Cited

## Books

Adams, Henry. *History of the United States of America During the Administrations of Thomas Jefferson and James Madison.* 9 vols. New York: Charles Scribner's Sons, 1891-98.

Andrews, Charles. *The Colonial Background of the American Revolution: Four Essays in American Colonial History.* New Haven and London: Yale University Press, 1931.

Arendt, Hannah. *Eichmann in Jerusalem: A Report on the Banality of Evil.* Rev. and enl. ed. New York: Viking Press, 1964.

— — —. *The Origins of Totalitarianism.* New York: Meridian Books, 1959.

Becker, Carl. *Detachment and the Writings of History: Essays and Letters of Carl L. Becker.* Ithaca, N.Y.: Cornell University Press, 1953.

— — —. *Everyman His Own Historian: Essays on History and Politics.* New York: Appleton-Century-Crofts, 1935.

— — —. *The Heavenly City of the Eighteen Century Philosophers.* New Haven, Conn.: Yale University Press, 1932

Benson, Lee. *The Concept of Jacksonian Democracy: New York as a Test Case.* New York: Atheneum, 1964.

Bercovitch, Sacvan. *The Puritan Origins of the American Self.* New Haven and London: Yale University Press, 1975.

Billington, James. *The Icon and the Axe: An Interpretive History of Russian Culture.* New York: Vintage Books, 1966.

Bingham, June. *Courage to Change: An Introduction to the Life and Thoughts of Reinhold Niebuhr.* New York: Charles Scribner's Sons, 1961.

Boorstin, Daniel J. *The Americans: The Colonial Experience.* New York: Random House, 1958.

———. *The Americans: The Democratic Experience*. New York: Random House, 1974.

———. *The Americans: The National Experience*. New York: Random House, 1965.

———. *The Decline of Radicalism: Reflections on America Today*. New York: Random House, 1969.

———. *Democrary and Its Discontents: Reflections on Everyday America*. New York: Random House, 1974.

———.The Exploring Spirit: America and the World, Then and Now New York: Random House, 1976.

———. *The Genius of American Politics*. Chicago: University of Chicago Press, 1953.

Booth, Wayne. *A Rhetoric of Irony*. Chicago and London: University of Chicago Press, 1974.

Braudy, Leo. *Narrative Form in History and Fiction: Hume, Fielding and Gibbon*. Princeton, N.J.: Princeton University Press, 1970.

Bruyn, Severyn T. *The Human Perspective in Sociology: The Methodology of Participant Observation*. Englewood Cliffs, N.J.: Prentice-Hall, 1966.

Burke, Kenneth. *A Grammar of Motives*. New York: Prentice-Hall, 1945.

Burke, Peter, ed. *Economy and Society in Early Modern Europe: Essays from Annales*. New York: Harper and Row, 1972.

Cash, W.J. *The Mind of the South*. New York: Alfred A. Knopf, 1941.

Corrigan, Robert W. *Tradegy: Vision and Form*. San Francisco, Calif.: Chandler Publishing Co., 1965.

Cunliffe, Marcus, and Winks, Robin. *Pastmasters: Some Essays on American Historians*. New York: Harper and Row, 1969.

Deutscher, Isaac. *Ironies of History: Essays on Contemporary Communism*. London: Oxford University Press, 1966.

Dyson, A.F. *The Crazy Frabric: Essays in Irony*. New York: St. Martin's Press, 1965.

Ekirch, Arthur A., Jr. *The Decline of American Liberalism*. New York: Atheneum, 1967.

Emerson, Donald. *Richard Hildreth*. Baltimore, Md.: Johns Hopkins University Press, 1946.

Engels, Friedrich. *Ludwig Feuerbach and the Outcome of Classical German Philosophy*. New York: International Publishers, [1934].

Erikson, Erik. *Young Man Luther: A Study in Psychoanalysis and History*. New York: W.W. Norton, 1962.

Fackre, Gabriel. *The Promise of Reinhold Niebuhr*. Philadelphia and New York: J. B. Lippincott Co., 1970.

Ferro, Marc, ed. *Social Historians in Contemporary France: Essays from Annales.* New York: Harper and Row, 1972.

Fey, Harold, ed. *How My Mind Has Changed.* Cleveland and New York: World Publishing, 1961.

Finley, John H., Jr. *Thucydides.* Ann Arbor, Mich.: University of Michigan Press, 1963.

Fletcher, Angus, ed. *The Literature of Fact: Selected Papers from the English Institute.* New York: Columbia University Press, 1976.

Frye, Northrup. *Anatomy of Criticism: Four Essays.* Princeton, N.J.: Princeton University Press, 1957.

Fussell, Paul. *The Great War and Modern Memory.* New York and London: Oxford University Press, 1975.

Gay, Peter. *Style in History.* New York: Basic Books, 1974.

Gibbon, Edward. *The Decline and Fall of the Roman Empire.* New York: Random House, The Modern Library, 1932.

Goodheart, Eugene. *Culture and the Radical Conscience.* Cambridge, Mass.: Harvard University Press, 1973.

Haller, William. *Liberty and Reformation in the Puritan Revolution.* New York and London: Columbia University Press, 1955.

– – – . *The Rise of Puritanism: Or, The Way to the New Jerusalem as Set Forth in Pulpt and Press from Thomas Cartwright to John Lilburne and John Milton, 1570-1643,* (1938). Reprint. New York: Harper Row, 1957.

Hartz, Louis. *The Liberal Tradition in America: An Interpretation of of American Political Thought Since the Revolution.* New York: Harcourt, Brace and World, 1955.

– – – . et al. *The Founding of New Societies: Studies in the History of the United States, Latin America, South Africa, Canada, and Australia.* New York: Harcourt, Brace and World, 1964.

Hegel, Georg Wilhelm Friedrich. *The Logic of Hegel.* Translated by William Wallace. London: Oxford University Press, 1963.

– – – . *The Philosophy of History.* Translated by J. Sibree. New York: Dover Publications, 1956.

Heller, Eric. *Thomas Mann: The Ironic German.* Cleveland and New York: World Publishing, 1961.

Herr, Richard. *Tocqueville and the Old Regime.* Princeton, N.J.: Princeton University Press, 1962.

Higham, John. *Writing American History: Essays on Modern Scholarship.* Bloomington and London: Indiana University Press, 1970.

– – – . et al. *History: The Development of Historical Studies in the United States.* Englewood Cliffs, N.J.: Prentice-Hall, 1965.

Hildreth, Richard. *History of the United States of America, From the Adoption of the Federal Constitution to the Sixteenth Congress.* 3 vols. New York: Harper and Brothers, 1851-52.

— — —. *The History of the United States of America From the Discovery of the Continent to the Organization of Government Under the Federal Constitution.* 13 vols. New York: Harper and Brothers, 1849.

Hofstadter, Richard. *The Age of Reform: From Bryan to F.D.R.* New York: Vintage, 1960.

— — —. *The American Political Tradition and the Men Who Made It.* New York: Vintage, 1958.

— — —. *Anti-Intellectualism in American Life.* New York: Vintage, 1963.

— — —. *The Paronoid Style in American Politics, and Other Essays.* New York: Vintage, 1967.

— — —. *The Progressive Historians: Turner, Beard, Parrington.* New York: Alfred A. Knopf, 1968.

Hofstadter, Richard, and Wallace, Michael, eds. *American Violence: A Documentary History.* New York: Vintage 1970.

Jordan, Winthrop. *White over Black. American Attitudes Toward the Negro, 1550-1812.* Chapel Hill, N.C.: University of North Carolina Press for the Institute of Early American History, 1968.

Jordy, William H. *Henry Adams: Scientific Historian.* New Haven, Conn.: Yale University Press. 1952.

Kammen, Michael. *People of Paradox: An Inquiry Concerning the Origins of American Civilization.* New York: Alfred A. Knopf, 1972.

Kaufmann, Walter. *Hegel: Reinterpretation, Texts, and Commentary.* Garden City, N.Y.: Doubleday, 1965.

Kegley, Charles, and Bretall, Robert, eds. *Reinhold Niebuhr: His Religious, Social and Political Thought.* New York: Macmillan, 1956.

Kierkegaard, Soren. *The Concept of Irony with Constant Reference to Socrates.* 1841. Translated by Lee M. Capel. Bloomington and London: Indiana University Press, 1965.

Knox, Norman. *The Word Irony in Its Context, 1500-1750.* Durham, N.C.: Duke University Press, 1961.

LaFeber, Walter. *America, Russia and the Cold War.* 2d ed. New York: John Wiley, 1972.

Levenson, J.C. *The Mind and Art of Henry Adams.* Cambridge, Mass.: Houghton Mifflin, 1957.

Levin, David. *History as Romantic Art: Bancroft, Prescott, Motley, and Parkman.* Stanford, Calif.: Stanford University Press, 1959.

— — —. *In Defense of Historical Literature: Essays on American History, Autobiography, Drama and Fiction.* New York: Hill and Wang, 1967.

Lewis, R.W.B. *The American Adam: Innocence, Tragedy and Tradition in the Nineteenth Century.* Chicago: University of Chicago Press, 1955.

Lifton, Robert J. *History and Human Survival: Essays on the Young and Old, Survivors and the Dead, Peace and War, and on Contemporary Psychohistory* New York: Random House, 1970.

Lockridge, Kenneth. *A New England Town: The First Hundred Years.* New York: W.W. Norton, 1970.

Lyon, Melvin, *Symbol and Idea in Henry Adams.* Lincoln, Neb.: University of Nebraska Press, 1970.

Marx, Karl. *The Eighteenth Brumaire of Louis Napoleon.* New York: International Publishers, 1935.

Marx, Karl, and Engels, Frederick. *Basic Writings on Politics and Philosophy.* Edited by Lewis S. Feuer. Garden City, N.Y.: Anchor Books, 1959.

Marx, Karl, and Engels, Fredrich. *Correspondence, 1846-1895.* Translated by Dona Torr. New York: International Publishers, 1935.

May, Henry. *The End of American Innocence: A Study in the First Years of Our Time, 1912-1917.* Chicago: Quadrangle Books, 1964.

Mazlish, Bruce, ed. *Psychoanalysis and History.* Englewood Cliffs, N.J.: Prentice-Hall, 1963.

Merkley, Paul. *Reinhold Niebuhr: A Political Account.* Montreal and London: McGill-Queen's University Press, 1975.

Merton, Robert. *Science, Technology and Society in Seventeenth Century England.* New York: Howard Fertig, 1970.

— — —. *Social Theory and Social Structure.* Enl. ed. New York: Free Press, 1968.

Matza, David, *Becoming Deviant.* Englewood Cliffs, N.J.: Prentice-Hall, 1969.

Miller, Perry. *Errand Into the Wilderness.* New York. Harper and Row, 1956.

— — —. *The New England Mind: From Colony to Province.* Boston: Beacon Press, 1953.

Morton, Marian J. *The Terrors of Ideological Politics: Liberal Historians in a Conservative Mood.* Cleveland, Ohio: Press of Case Western Reserve University, 1972.

Muecke, Douglas. *The Compass of Irony.* London: Methuen, 1969.

Myrdal, Gunnar. *An American Dilemma.* 2 vols. 1944. Reprint. New York: Harper and Row, 1962.

Niebuhr, Reinhold. *The Irony of American History.* New York: Charles Scribner's Sons, 1952.

— — —. *Man's Nature and His Communities: Essays on the Dynamics and Enigmas of Man's personal and Social Existence.* New York: Charles Scribner's Sons, 1965.

— — —. *Moral Man and Immoral Society.* New York: Charles Scribner's Sons, 1934.

— — —. *The Self and the Dramas of History.* New York: Charles Scribner's Sons, 1955.

— — —. *The Structure of Nations and Empires: A Study of the Recurring Patterns and Problems of the Political Order in Relation to the Unique Problems of the Nuclear Age.* New York: Charles Scribner's Sons, 1959.

Niebuhr, Reinhold, and Heimert, Alan. *A Nation So Conceived: Reflections on the History of America From Its Early Vision to Its Present Power.* New York: Charles Scribner's Sons, 1963.

Niebuhr, Reinhold, and Sigmund, Paul E. *The Democratic Experience: Past and Prospects.* New York: Praeger, 1969.

Nietzsche, Frederick. *The Use and Abuse of History.* Translated by Adrian Collins. New York: Liberal Arts Press, 1957.

Noble, David. *Historians Against History: The Frontier Thesis and the National Covenant in American Historical Writing Since 1830.* Minneapolis, Minn.: University of Minnesota Press, 1965.

Odegard, Holtan P. *Sin and Science: Reinhold Niebuhr as Political Theologian.* Yellow Springs, Ohio: Antioch Press, 1956.

Parkman, Francis. *The Jesuits in North America in the Seventeenth Century.* Boston: Little, Brown and Company, 1884.

Parrington, Vernon Louis. *Main Currents in American Thought.* 2 vols. New York: Harcourt, Brace and Co., 1930.

Potter, David. *People of Plenty.* Chicago: University of Chicago Press, 1954.

Pressly, Thomas. *Americans Interpret Their Civil War.* New York: Collier Books, 1962.

Rosenberg, Harold. *The Tradition of the New.* New York: Horizon Press, 1959.

Rude, George, *The Crowd in the French Revolution.* Oxford: Oxford University Press, 1959.

Sarte, Jean-Paul. *Search For a Method.* Translated by Hazel E. Barnes. New York: Random House, 1963.

Schneider, Louis, ed. *The Scottish Moralists on Human Nature and Society.* Chicago and London: University of Chicago Press, 1967.

— — —. *The Sociological Way of Looking at the World.* New York: McGraw-Hill, 1975.

Schneider, Louis, and Bonjean, Charles M., eds. *The Idea of Culture in the Social Sciences.* Cambridge: At the University Press, 1973.

Sedgewick, G.G. *Of Irony, Especially in Drama*. Toronto: University of Toronto Press, 1948.

Shinn, Roger, L. *The Search For Identity: Essays on the American Character*. New York: Harper and Row, 1964.

Skotheim, Robert A. *American Intellectual History and Historians*. Princeton, N.J.: Princeton University Press, 1966.

———, ed. *The Historian and the Climate of Opinion*. Reading, Mass.: Addison-Wesley, 1969.

———. *Totalitarianism and American Social Thought*. New York: Holt, Rinehart and Winston, 1971.

Smith, Adam. *An Inquiry into the Nature and Causes of the Wealth of Nations*. New York: Random House, The Modern Library, 1937.

Smith, Charotte Watkins. *Carl Becker: On History and the Climate of Opinion*. Ithaca, N.Y.: Cornell University Press, 1956.

States, Bert O. *Irony and Drama: A Poetics*. Ithaca, N.Y.: Cornell University Press, 1971.

Sternsher, Bernard. *Consensus, Conflict and American History*. Bloomington and London: Indiana University Press, 1975.

Stone, Ronald F. *Reinhold Niebuhr: Prophet to Politicians*. Nashville, Tenn.: Abington Press, 1972.

Strout, Cushing. *The Pragmatic Revolt in American History: Carl Becker and Charles Beard*. Ithaca, N.Y.: Cornell University Press, 1966.

Struever, Nancy, *The Language of History in the Renaissance: Rhetoric and Historical Consciousness in Florentine Humanism*. Princeton, N.J.: Princeton University Press, 1970.

Taylor, William. *Cavallier and Yankee: The Old South and American National Character*. New York: George Braziller, 1961.

Thernstrom, Stephen. *Poverty and Progress: Social Mobility in a Nineteenth Century City*. Cambridge, Mass.: Harvard University Press, 1964.

Thomson, J. A. K. *Irony: An Historical Introduction*. London: George Allen and Unwin, 1926.

Thucydides. *History of the Peloponnesian War*. Translated by Rex Warner. Harmondsworth, Middlesex: Penquin Books, 1954.

Tocqueville, Alexis de. *The Old Regime and the French Revolution*. Translated by Stuart Gilbert. Garden City, N.Y.: Doubleday Anchor, 1955.

Vahanian, Gabriel. *Wait Without Idols*. New York: George Braziller, 1964.

Van Tassel, David D. *Recording America's Past: An Interpretation of the Development of Historical Studies in America, 1607-1884*.

Chicago: University of Chicago Press, 1960.

*Walzer, Michael*. The Revolution of the Saints: A Study in the Origin of Radical Politics. New York: Atheneum, 1975.

Weber, Max. *The Protestant Ethic and the Spirit of Capitalism.* Translated by Talcott Parsons. New York: Charles Scribner's Sons, 1958.

Wheeler, Bennett John. *The Nemesis of Power: The German Army in Politics, 1918-1945.* 2d ed. London: Macmillan, 1964.

White, Hayden, *Metahistory: The Historical Imagination in Nineteenth Century Europe.* Baltimore and London: Johns Hopkins University Press, 1973.

White, Morton. *Social Thought in America: The Revolt Against Formalism.* Boston: Beacon Press, 1957.

Wilkins, Burleigh Taylor. *Carl Becker: A Biographical Study in American Intellectual History.* Cambridge, Mass.: MIT Press and Harvard University Press, 1961.

Wise, Gene. *American Historical Explanations: A Strategy For Grounded Inquiry.* Homewood, Ill.: Dorsey Press, 1973.

Woodward, C. Vann. *The Burden of Southern History.* Rev. ed. Baton Rouge, La.: Louisianna State University Press, 1968.

# Articles and Reviews

Bailyn, Bernard. "History and the Distrust of Knowledge." Review of *The Americans: The Colonial Experience* by Daniel J. Boorstin. *New Republic,* December 15, 1958, pp. 17-18.

Becker, Carl. "Napolon—After One Hundred Years." *The Nation,* May 4, 1921, p. 646.

Bercovitch, Sacvan. "Horologicals to Chronometricals: The Rhetoric of the Jeremiad." *Literary Monographs* 3, Madison, Wis.: University of Wisconsin Press, 1970. pp. 1-125.

Berman, Marshall. "All That Is Solid Melts into Air:' Marx, Modernism, and Modernization," *Dissent* (1978): 54:73.

Billington, James. "Six Views of the Russian Revolution." *World Politics* 18 (1966): 452-73.

Bourne, Randolph. "The Life of Irony." *Atlantic Monthly* 111 (1913):357-67.

Brogan, D.W. "The Illusion of American Omnipotence." *Harper's* 205 (December 1952): 21-28.

Diggins, John P. "Consciousness and Ideology in American History: The Burden of Daniel J. Boorstin." *American Historical Review* 76 (1971):99-118.

―――. "The Perils of Naturalism: Some Reflections on Daniel J. Boorstin's Approach to American History." *American Quarterly* 23(1971):153-80.

Ekirch, Arthur A., Jr. "Parrington and the Decline of American Liberalism." *American Quarterly* 3 (1951): 295-308.

Elkins, Stanley and McKitrick, Erik. "Richard Hofstadter: A Progress." In *The Hofstadter Aegis,* edited by Stanley Elkins and Erik McKitrick. New York: Alfred A. Knopf, 1974.

Elliot, J.H. "Mediterranean Mysteries." Review of *The Mediterranean and the Mediterranean World in the Age of Phillip II,* vol. I, by Fernand Braudel. *New York Review of Books*, May 3, 1973, pp. 25-28.

Fussell, Paul. "The New Irony and the Augustans." *Encounter* 34 (June 1970): 68-75.

Hartz, Louis. "American Historiography and Comparative Analysis: Further Reflections." *Comparative Studies in Society and History* 5 (1963):365-77.

―――. "Comment." *Comparative Studies in Society and History.* 5 (1963):279-84.

Higham, John, "The Cult of 'The American Consensus.' " *Commentary* 27 (1959): 93-100.

―――.Review of *The Irony of American History* by Reinhold Niebuhr. *Mississippi Valley Historical Review* 41 (1952):357-58.

Hollinger, David. A. "T.S. Kuhn's Theory of Science and Its Implications For History." *American Historical Review* 78 (1973): 370-93.

Hoover, Dwight. "Some Comments on Recent United States Historiography." *American Quarterly* 17 (1965):299-318.

Hopper, Stanley. "Irony—The Pathos of the Middle." *Cross Currents* 12 (1962):31-40.

Kazin, Alfred. "Richard Hofstadter, 1916-1970." *American Scholar* 40 (1971):397-401.

Lasch, Christopher. "On Richard Hofstadter." *New York Review of Books,* March 8, 1973, pp. 7-13.

―――."Forward." In *The American Political Tradition* by Richard Hofstadter. Rev. ed. New York: Random House, 1973. pp. vii-xxiv.

Loewenberg, Peter. "The Psychohistorical Origins of the Nazi Youth Cohort." *American Historical Review* 76 (1971):1457-1502.

deMann, Paul, "The Rhetoric of Temporality." In *Interpretation: Theory and Practice.* Edited by Charles S. Singleton. Baltimore, Md.: Johns Hopkins University Press, 1969. pp. 173-209.

Maud, Ralph. "Henry Adams: Irony and Impasse." *Essays in Criticism* 7 (1958: 281-392).

May, Henry. "A Meditation on an Unfashionable Book: *The Irony of American History* Revisited." *Christianity and Crisis* 27 (1968):120-22.

— — —."Perry Miller's Parrington." Review of *The Life of the Mind in America* by Perry Miller. *American Scholar* 25 (1966): 562-70.

Merton, Robert. "The Unanticipated Consequences of Purposive Social Action." *American Sociological Review* 1 (1939):894-904.

Meyers, Marvin, "Louis Hartz: The Liberal Tradition in America: An Appraisal" *Comparative Studies in Society and History* 5 (1963):261-68.

Miller, Perry. "The Great Method." Review of *Faith and History* by Reinhold Niebuhr. *The Nation* 169 (1949):138-39.

— — —."The Influence of Reinhold Niebuhr, Review of *Pious and Secular America* by Reinhold Niebuhr. *The Reporter,* May 1, 1958, pp. 39-40.

Mink, Louis. "History and Fiction as Modes of Comprehension." *New Literary History* 1 (1970):541-58.

Morgan, Edmunds, "The American Revolution: Revisions in Need of Revising." *William and Mary Quarterly*, 3d ser., 14 (1957): 3-15.

Niebuhr, Reinhold. "America: Pragmatism, Not Dogmatism." Review of *The Genius of American Politics* by Daniel Boorstin. *New Leader*, June 22, 1953, p. 15.

— — —."The Mounting Racial Crisis." *Christianity and Crisis* 23 (1963):121-22.

— — —. "The Negro Minority and Its Fate in a Self-Righteous Nation." *Social Action* 35 no. 2 (October 1968):53-64.

— — —. "The Presidency and the Irony of American History." *Christianity and Crisis* 30 (1970):70-72.

— — —. "The Problem Stated." Review of *Modern Democracy* by Carl Becker. *The Nation*, April 12, 1941, pp. 441.

— — —. "Redeemer Nation to Super-Power." *New York Times,* December 4, 1970, p. 47.

— — —. "The Rising Tide of Color." *New Leader*, January 23, 1961, pp. 16-17.

— — —. "The Role of Reason." Review of *New Liberties for Old by* Carl Becker. *The Nation*, November 1, 1941, pp. 430-31.

— — —. "The Social Myths of the Cold War." *Journal of International Affairs* 21 (1967):40-56.

— — —. "Thinking Aloud: Indicting Two Generations." *New Leader*, October 5, 1970, pp. 13-14.

— — —. "Toward New Intra-Christian Endeavors." *Christian Century* 86 (1969): 1662-67.

— — —. "The Unintended Virtues of an Open Society." *Christianity and Crisis* 21 (1961): 132-38.

— — —. "Vietnam: Study in Ironies." *New Republic*, June 24, 1967, pp. 11-12.

Noble, David W. "Carl Becker: Science, Relativism and the Dilemma of Diderot." *Ethics* 67 (1957):233-48.

Reinitz, Richard. "Nieburhian Irony and Historical Interpretation: The Relationship between Consensus and New Left History." *The Writing of History*, Robert H. Canary and Henry Kozicki, eds., Madison: The University of Wisconsin Press, 1978, pp. 93-128.

— — —. "The Use of Irony by Historians and Vice-Versa." CLIO 6 (1977): 275-88.

— — —. "Vernon Louis Parrington as Historical Ironist." *Pacific Northwest Quarterly* 68 (1977):113-19.

Rosenberg, John. "Toward A New Civil War Revisionism." *American Scholar* 38 (1969): 250-72.

Rule, Henry. "Henry Adams' Attack on Two Heroes of the Old South." *American Quarterly* 14 (1962): 174-84.

Schlesinger, Arthur, Jr. "Niebuhr and Some Critics." Review of *The Irony of American History* by Reinhold Niebuhr. *Christianity and Society* 17 (1952): 25-27.

— — —. "The Problem of Richard Hildreth." *New England Quarterly* 13 (1940):223-45.

Schmokel, Wolfe W. Review of *Deutsche Koloniaherrschaft in Afrika* by Karin Hausen, *Koloniale Entwicklung und Ansbentung* by Rainer Tetzlaff, and *Deutsch-Ostafrika 1900-1914*, by Detleff Bald. *American Historical Review* 77 (1972): 558-59.

Schneider, Louis, "Dialectic in Sociology." *American Sociological Review* 36 (1971): 667-78.

Shaw, Peter, "The War of 1812 Could Not Take Place: Henry Adams' History." *Yale Review* 62 (1973): 544-56.

Skotheim, Robert A. "The Writing of American Histories of Ideas: Two Traditions in the XXth Century." *Journal of the History of Ideas* 25 (1964): 257-78.

Smith, Page. "Anxiety and Despair in American History." *William and Mary Quarterly* 3d ser., 26 (1969): 416-24.

Solt, Leo F. "Puritanism, Capitalism, Decocracy and the New Science." *American Historical Review* 73 (1967): 18-29.

Walcott, Charles Child. "Irony: Vision or Retreat." *Pacific Spectator* 10 (1956): 354-56.

Ward, John William "Violence, Anarchy and Alexander Berkman." Review of *Prison Memoirs* by Alexander Berkman. *New York Review of Books*, November 5, 1970, pp. 25-30.

Welter, Rush, "The History of Ideas in America: An Essay in Redefinition." *Journal of American History* 51 (1965): 599-614.

White, Hayden. "The Burden of History." *History and Theory* 5 (1966): 112-34.

―――. "Interpretation in History." *New Literary History* 4 (1973): 281-314.

White Morton. "Of Moral Predicaments." Review of *The Irony of American History* by Reinhold Niebuhr. *New Republic*, May 5; 1952. pp. 18-19.

―――. "Religion, Politics, and the Higher Learning." *Confluence* 3 (1954): 402-12.

Wise, Gene, "Implicit Irony in Perry Miller's *New England Mind.*" *Journal of the History of Ideas* 29 (1968): 579-600.

Woodward, C. Vann. "The Age of Reinterpretation." *American Historical Review* 66 (1960): 1-19.

## Unpublished Material

Brooks, Robin, "The Radical Strain in American Studies." Unpublished paper.

Rule, Henry. "Irony in the Works of Henry Adams." Ph.D. dissertation, University of Colorado, 1960.

Wise, Gene, with Scott, Barbara. "Making Irony Operational Niebuhr's *Irony of American History* Revisited." Unpublished paper.

# Index

223